Writing
History
in Film

Writing History in Film

William Guynn

Routledge
Taylor & Francis Group
New York   London

Routledge is an imprint of the
Taylor & Francis Group, an informa business

Published in 2006 by
Routledge
Taylor & Francis Group
270 Madison Avenue
New York, NY 10016

Published in Great Britain by
Routledge
Taylor & Francis Group
2 Park Square
Milton Park, Abingdon
Oxon OX14 4RN

Printed in the United States of America on acid-free paper
10 9 8 7 6 5 4 3 2 1

International Standard Book Number-10: 0-415-97924-2 (Softcover)
International Standard Book Number-13: 978-0-415-97924-5 (Softcover)
Library of Congress Card Number 2005037151

Library of Congress Cataloging-in-Publication Data

Guynn, William.
  Writing history in film / William Guynn.
    p. cm.
  Includes bibliographical references and index.
  ISBN 0-415-97923-4 (hardback : alk. paper) -- ISBN 0-415-97924-2 (pbk. : alk. paper) 1. Motion pictures and history. 2. Historical films--History and criticism. I. Title.

PN1995.2.G89 2006
791.43'658--dc22   2005037151

Taylor & Francis Group
is the Academic Division of Informa plc.

**Visit the Taylor & Francis Web site at
http://www.taylorandfrancis.com**

**and the Routledge Web site at
http://www.routledge-ny.com**

For Stefanie

CONTENTS

INTRODUCTION

Facing the Skepticism of Historians

It is a risky business to write seriously about the historical film. The social sciences in general have shown a profoundly skeptical attitude toward the cinema. Anthropology, for example, long resisted using film technology as a tool of research, despite what would seem the obvious potential for visual observation the medium provides. When ethnographers hesitatingly adopted film as one technique of observation, notably through the practice elaborated by Margaret Mead and Gregory Bateson in their work in Bali, they were concerned to control the use of film through properly ethnographic guidelines. For Mead, this meant a strategy of observation grounded in the "holistic" vision provided by long takes from one observational position and by the all-encompassing long shot. "Fragmentation"—the effects of film editing in the mid to late 1930s that Mead associated with fiction—was to be avoided, as was the calculated mise en scène of documentary films of the period. Moreover, Mead argued that film as an instrument of observation belonged to the stage of work that preceded conceptualization and that film data should ultimately be examined, sorted, and reduced to written analysis.

For most anthropologists (and most historians), only writing provides the kind of distance and discipline that a scientific approach requires. The screening of an ethnographic film, particularly for a larger public, is at best vulgarization and has no justifiable scientific purpose. Producing such a film involved editing—and therefore distorting—documentary evidence, and there was no lack of examples of the exploitative use of edited ethnographic footage in film programs of the period to appeal to public taste for the exotic. Even more recent ethnographic filmmakers have been taken to task for distorting the authenticity of footage in the interest of constructing an articulated plot with dramatic interest. The film *Dead Birds* became notorious for the montage of "imaginary" battle scenes using footage taken in different locations and at different times.[1] Moreover, ethnographers have been apprehensive about the conditions of the darkened movie theater, so redolent of the imaginary and conducive to projection in the psychoanalytic sense, and this "conservative" position is scarcely out of date. Some anthropologists continue to argue that filmed documentation should not be projected at all but examined on an editing table so the footage can be stopped, rewound, and analyzed, often frame by frame.

If such skepticism is still current in a field that eventually made film one of its principal instruments of observation, then the distrust historians show toward the film medium comes as no surprise. Indeed, this skepticism is certainly justified by the genre of the historical film from its beginnings in film's "primitive" era to its development in the context of the Hollywood studio system, but also in many other cultural traditions, notably European and Asian. Such genre films have little pretense to authenticity. They are masquerades that disguise the trends and preoccupations of the day through "historical" mise en scène and reproduce the melodramatic plot structures of the fiction film in the guise of historic necessity. The bare frame of historical events and characters quickly dissolves into the drama of the fictional protagonist and general anachronism. *Costume drama* is the term of disparagement often used by historians to evoke such films' shallow and opportunistic treatment of the historical past. The historians' approach to these admittedly unworthy objects consists in fleshing out the errors and abuses of historical representation: distortion of historical chronology in the interest of dramatic structure, simplification of complex events, falsification of the historical figure to comply with the demands of the star system, emphasis on the spectacular rather than the analytic, reduction of historical observation to the evocation of the picturesque, and so forth. Unfortunately, for inveterate skeptics, all historical films are fictions; there is no real distinction to be made between films that exploit historical materials in the interest of fictional pleasures and those that have more serious intentions.

In the following pages, I propose looking at the attitudes historians in Europe and the United States adopted toward history in film in the sometimes-heated debates that appeared in professional periodicals and books beginning in the 1970s in Europe and in the 1980s in the United

States. I start with the French historians and cultural critics, many of whom have articulated generally negative positions on the question.

French scholar François de la Brethèque is characteristic of the dismissive attitude shared by many historians. He argues, in a special issue of *CinémAction* devoted to history and film,[2] that the historical film follows the recipe of the historical novel, citing a caustic epigram by Jacques Cellard concerning this "historical mayonnaise": "While turning regularly, you pour a thin stream of history into the yolk of the novel: sometimes it takes, sometimes it doesn't."[3] In Brethèque's view, the relation between filmic depictions and the reality of the past is never "direct" because film always distorts truth. Filmic representations of history are heavily mediated by "the discursive, mental, ideological training" of the social grouping to which the "various 'auteurs' of a film belong."[4] Filmic representations are further alienated from their presumed referents by the "cultural models" that impose a predigested way of seeing the past. Certain historical films, for example, imitate the pictorial composition and the iconography of the period they seek to represent as if this imitation were a guarantee of fidelity and realism. In Brethèque's view, even when the film makes use of historical "objects," the status of such objects is transformed. Vestiges of past reality become mere representations: "From the spectator's point of view, once an object is filmed, it becomes only *represented* reality. ... It has lost its reality, has changed status, in order to enter the text as one of the elements of fictional discourse. It has become a sign in a signifying chain."[5] The filmmaker attempts, then, an impossible substitution: the discursive moment of the film's production takes the place of the moment of history, while this fictionalized discourse seeks cover in the alibi of the historical. The result of this substitution is inevitable anachronism. Anachronism surfaces whenever the discursive moment of mise en scène emerges from behind its historical cover; of course, the more knowledgeable the spectator, the more anachronisms he or she discovers. Under the practiced eye of a professional historian, the whole edifice crumbles.

For Brethèque, the "internal" codes of filmic representation—particularly, one assumes, codes of mise en scène—ultimately are more decisive in the production of a historical film than concerns for accuracy, and the advice of a film's historical consultants is often overridden. Moreover, historical films rarely restrict themselves to what is known. Rather, they attempt to "fill in the blanks" of history: historical narrative in film is permitted to say anything that cannot be contradicted: "You could almost say that, by definition, the historical film situates itself exactly at the spots where one cannot know what really took place."[6] There is, then, an alternation between the known events of history that serve to drive the plot and the private lives of individuals, the "holes" of history that the filmmaker fills up with undocumented dialogue, imagined events, and inauthentic descriptive detail. This alternation, Brethèque asserts, leads to two types of scenes: the grandiose tableaus that give a spectacular representation of collective events in long shot, within which the individual protagonists play a significant role, and the intimate scenes involving two or three characters taken in closer shots, designed to provide the spectator with the kind of psychological drama he seeks. The historical film negotiates then between the two modes of representation, linking the spectacle of history to the destiny of the fictional protagonists.

Other French theorists have adopted more nuanced but equally negative attitudes toward filmic representations of history. The roundtable discussion that included historians Michel de Certeau and Jean Chesnaux and the editors of *Ça cinéma* in a series devoted to history and film give us good examples of different theoretical positions on the question. Michel de Certeau speaks of the problematic relationship between historical discourse and the past. What defines the past is its inescapable difference; historians cannot reconstruct the past, recast it in a discursive structure—that is, impose meaning on it—without betraying the past's historical character. The historian's act should consist in recognizing the "otherness signified by the past" and restrict itself to noting the signs of difference—the traces of the past that escape the historian's meaning. Indeed, Certeau is skeptical about the whole enterprise of history conceived as a narrative construction that imposes the historian's order on trace signs of the past:

> What we first call history is nothing but a narrative. Everything begins with the shop window display of a *legend* that lays out 'curious' objects in the order in which they *must be read*. [This discursive ordering] imposes a preconceived meaning, in a tautological organization that speaks of nothing other than the present. When we receive this text, an operation has already been carried out eliminating otherness and its danger.[8]

Although Certeau does not comment directly on the film medium, one can easily draw the implications. Filmic representations of history depend, in the main, on narrative ordering and cannot help but project onto the trace signs of the past a structure that betrays the past's otherness. Moreover, the filmic signifier, with the richness of its reference to concrete realities, ultimately overwhelms by its phenomenological excess Certeau's negative ontology of the past.

In contrast to Certeau, historian Jean Chesnaux takes the position of the militant historian who believes that history should serve the struggles of the present. Instead of arguing that filmic representations give an illusion of presence, he takes the position that film, by the nature of its signifiers, is incapable of fulfilling its mission of linking contemporary spectators to the reality of the past. Chesnaux advances the hypothesis that the power of a historical text depends on its signifying material. A historical text spoken by a living voice—a radical speaker at a political rally who reads passages from revolutionaries like Saint-Just or Babeuf, for example—is capable of touching the spectator directly and establishing a meaningful contact with the historical past. The real presence of the speaker brings about a kind of revivification of the past because of the voice's power of presence. Images, on the other hand, even the filmic transcription of an authentic visual document, are always experienced at a remove and therefore tend to engage the viewer in a Romantic, external relationship to the past. Chesnaux analyzes this "paradox" in the following way:

> The oral transcription of written documents, the re-creation of this written document in oral form, allows for a closer contact than does the visual document.... I said a moment ago that there are two types of relationships with the past, a past that is outside ourselves, *passéiste*, nostalgic, and a past that is an integral part of our goals, our research, our struggles. It seems to me that the image produces much more this external effect. An image of the Commune is still very distant from us whereas a voice is a living being who speaks.[9]

In filmic representations, the voice and the image are both recorded and therefore removed from the present. Film would seem, by dint of its distancing signifiers, unsuitable for fulfilling Chesnaux's notion of the proper social function of history.

Cultural critic Jean Baudrillard makes a quite similar point from a different theoretical perspective in his article in the same series in *Ça cinéma* entitled "L'Histoire: un scénario rétro." Baudrillard contends that history in the contemporary era has been "neutralized" by the antihistorical forces of economic and political globalization and the transformation of the potentially active public into passive consumers of simulated experience. This is the great traumatic period, he argues, in which we see the "death agony" of discourses that seek to represent

the real through the power of reason and the emergence of an era characterized by simulation. In this epoch, history has withdrawn from the
field of real experience and retreats, in its diminished form, into the
cinema, where historical simulation replaces the vital relationship to
the referential past:

> Myth, chased out of the real by the violence of history, found
> refuge in the cinema.... Today, history itself invades cinema
> according to the same scenario: what is at stake in history is
> chased out of our lives by this kind of gigantic neutralization
> called peaceful coexistence on the world scale, and pacified
> monotony on the scale of daily life; and this history, exorcised
> by a sometimes slow and sometimes brutal deep-freeze society,
> celebrates its triumphant resurrection on the cinema screens,
> according to the same process that formerly gave new life [in
> film] to lost myths.[10]

In cinema, then, history empties out its significance and leaves us with
the cold artifice of representation.

For some historians, European and American, however, the cinema
is not entirely lost; indeed, it can be salvaged if we acknowledge that
historical film is the "most fictional of genres" and abandon the idea of
film as a vehicle for historical representation. According to this view,
although film cannot be an instrument for representing the past, it
can, passively, bear material witness to the historical period in which it
is produced, like any other sphere of the vast field of cultural production. This approach works on the distinction historians make between
voluntary and involuntary testimony, which Antoine Prost defines in
the following way:

> [Voluntary testimony] has been constituted to inform its pres-
> ent or future readers. Chronicles, memoirs, all "narrative"
> sources belong to this category, as do prefects' reports, mono-
> graphs by local teachers on their villages for the exposition of
> 1900, and everything in the press.... [Involuntary testimony]
> was not meant to inform us. Marc Bloch puts it nicely in speak-
> ing of "these signs that, without premeditation, the past drops
> onto the road." Private correspondence, a really intimate diary,
> business accounts, marriage certificates, declarations of inheri-
> tance, but also objects, images, golden beetles found in Myce-
> naean tombs, pottery shards thrown into a fourteenth century
> well, or the iron found in shell holes, more instructive about the

battle field at Verdun than the voluntary testimony (fabricated and falsified) about the bayonet trenches.[11]

From this perspective, films are like any other artifacts dropped on the road of history. They bear unconscious witness to their own period, as do private letters, diaries, and marriage certificates that were never intended to be read from the historian's perspective. They provide a body of data to be analyzed and interpreted in terms of the *mentality* of a period, or they can, unwittingly, speak about unacknowledged realities, for example, in societies subjected to public censorship.

Studies of film as involuntary witness to history are not really new, but they have rarely been the work of professional historians. One finds, for example, historical analyses of this type rather commonly in 1970s political film criticism—the *Cahiers du cinéma*'s much-discussed reading of John Ford's *Young Mr. Lincoln*, numerous articles in film journals such as *Jump Cut* or *Cinéaste*, Brechtian analyses of 1950s melodrama, feminist reappraisals of Hollywood films, and so forth. In fact, most historians have shown little interest in film, even as involuntary witness to the past. It is as if they shared a certain highbrow condescension toward film in general. Commercial films in particular could not reflect meaningfully on the period in which they were produced because they are escapist in nature and intended to allow spectators to evade, through imaginary representations, the serious problems of their age. The musicals and screwball comedies of the Depression era are often-cited examples. Because historians do not see a meaningful relationship between filmic representations and their contemporary context, they have had little to say about commercial film production.

However, this skeptical position has been challenged by French historian Marc Ferro, who developed one of the first positive approaches to film analysis to come from the ranks of professional historians. He began writing seriously on film in the early 1970s and is today perhaps the most influential French historian in the neglected field of history and film. Ferro's approach is well articulated and worth following in some detail.

Ferro's argument begins with a negative thesis. He shares the skeptical position that historical representation in film always distorts the real past: "It is easy to think that film is not suited to represent past reality and that at best its testimony is valuable only for the present; or that, aside from documents and newsreels, the reality it offers is no more real than the novel's."[12] He reduces, for example, historical vision in *Alexander Nevski* and *Andrei Rublev*, in the first case to the Soviet Union as its leaders would have it seen and in the second to the Soviet Union as dissent envisages it. For Ferro, then, it is not the past that is "at the controls" of historical representation in film; it is the present. Ferro carefully justifies his position. First, historical films tend to present information that appears significant (to the film-makers and their public) at the moment of production, while trained historians maintain a more objective perspective grounded in the critical methods of the discipline. Second, in fiction—and, for Ferro, all historical representation in film is by nature fictional—aesthetic and dramatic concerns dominate, while the historian is interested primarily in correct chronology and the logical character of causal sequence: "History, as it was lived, or as it took place, does not obey the laws of melodrama or of tragedy." Third, works of history change with critical distance and progress in historical methods. Works of art, like film, because they obey the aesthetic impulse, perpetuate themselves and become immutable.[13] It is impossible, Ferro argues, to analyze consecrated works in the cinema because they have status as "revelation." Worse, historical representation in film tends to fix images of events and historical characters in the imaginary of the public that historical discourse must then struggle to dislodge.[14]

Ferro's principal thesis is, however, quite positive. He argues that a film, like any other cultural product, can become a rich resource of information on the period in which it was made. In his key statement, "Film, a Counteranalysis of Society?" (1971), Ferro deplores the fact that historians have neglected film almost entirely, despite the revolutionary work of the historians of the *Annales*, who broadened the notion of historical documentation and opened history to archives of all sorts. As he observes, "[Film] does not enter the historian's mental universe."[15] Ferro explains the reasons for this neglect in the following manner: History has always been in the service of power—"the Prince, the state, a social class, the nation"; that is, history has always been a political discourse. What is disturbing to politicians about a discourse of images is that it does not "correspond to the assertions of rulers, to the schemas of theorists, to the analysis of the opposition"[16] because images lack the transparency of written language and are not serviceable instruments of power.

Historians' neglect of cinema therefore has to do with the disturbing uncertainties of filmic discourse: "the language of film appears unintelligible," "like that of dreams,"[17] Ferro tells us. Historians resist approaching film because history and film are based in different sign systems that refer to the world in radically different ways. For the historian, "what is not written, the image, has no identity. How

could historians refer to the image, or even quote it?"[18] The irratio-
nal and the ineffable quality of filmic discourse that Ferro describes
recalls what Roland Barthes terms the polysemic character of the
photographic image, the "floating chain of signifiers" that can be controlled only through the anchoring function of verbal language.[19] As
Ferro observes, that control is always only partial, and it is by means
of the uncontrollable image that truth inadvertently speaks to the historian. To use Ferro's psychoanalytic terminology, the filmmakers'
unconscious intentions are expressed latently, and films always say
more than their filmmakers intend: "The unexpected and the involuntary can also play a great role."[20]

Faced with the irrationality of images, Ferro proposes the historian
adopt a role akin to the psychoanalyst's in relation to the "unconscious"
of the filmic text, the text as it documents the social repressed of a historical moment. He speaks of *lapses* on the part of a "creator, an ideology,
or a society" that unwittingly say more than was consciously intended.
Because filmic discourse, through its innate ambiguity, resists the inter-
dictions of powers-that-be and the neat categories of rational discourse,
it becomes a privileged source for a "counteranalysis of society." As
Ferro argues, "There is material there—one which certainly does not
claim to constitute a beautiful, harmonious, and rational ensemble
as does History—which can help to refine or destroy History."[21] *Cinema and History* anthologizes many of Ferro's counteranalyses of the
"repressed" content of film: latent antisemitism in the characterization
of the Jew in Renoir's *Grande Illusion*; a latent critique of Stalinist jus-
tice in *Tchapaev*, a film that seeks to extol the "democratic centralism"
of the party; or the "hidden" messages of documentaries that Ferro
exposes and analyzes in his television series, *Parallel Histories*.

There are limitations and inconsistencies in Ferro's theory. While
it is true that films retain something of primary process in the Freudian sense, they are complex discursive objects and therefore imbued
with secondary process. However, Ferro demonstrates little interest in
a film's consciously constructed meaning and tends to underestimate
the determining weight of cinematic "language" in the construction
of a film's messages at all levels. He seems unaware that the language
of film has its own "unconscious" that requires historical analysis and
generally fails to consider the specificity of the film medium and how
the filmmaker appropriates and transforms cinematic codes. His work
on the "anti-Semitic" dissolves in *Jüd suss*,[22] an analysis at the level of
the signifier, is quite exceptional in this regard.

The situation is not, in general, more positive among American
historians. However, there is a significant minority who take a more

sanguine view of the historical film and its social role and even advance the idea that the audiovisual media may offer legitimate "parallel" forms of historical narration. Much of the impetus for the reconsideration of the history film comes from Robert A. Rosenstone, an intellectual crusader who has acted as a polemicist within his profession, known for its entrenched attitudes toward film and other discourses of the "imaginary." In the December 1988 issue of *The American Historical Review*, Rosenstone organized a debate on the question, "History in Images/History in Words: Reflections on the Possibility of Really Putting History onto Film." The title addresses the critical issue of different modes of representation, a topic I take up at greater length in Chapter Two. Rosenstone's provocative introductory essay is, to my knowledge, the first attempt by an American historian (perhaps any historian) to construct a positive theoretical position from which to consider the legitimacy of the historical film.

Rosenstone's argument begins with the malaise historians feel when encountering cinematic history, the visualization of the past they find profoundly disturbing: "Inevitably, something happens on the way from the page to the screen that changes the meaning of the past as it is understood by those of us who work in words."[23] Rosenstone speaks from his own experience as the author of two histories that were made into films and his role as historical consultant to their production: *Reds*, the Hollywood epic on the life of American revolutionary John Reed, and *The Good Fight*, a documentary on the American volunteers of the Abraham Lincoln Brigade, who fought for the Republicans in the Spanish Civil War. Both films have their strengths, Rosenstone tells us—they render "authentic historical details," humanize the past by bringing out the personal as well as historical dimensions of the characters, and establish the vital connection between exemplary actions in the past and the needs of the present-day "body politic."[24] However, both films fail to satisfy historians' "demands for truth and verifiability." In the case of *Reds*, the filmmaker (Warren Beatty) indulges in "overt fiction" by altering historical facts for dramatic purposes; in *The Good Fight*, the oral testimony of the American combatants on which the film is based is never questioned, despite what we know about the unreliability of memory, open to constant revision. Worse, both films compress "the past to a closed world by telling a single, linear story with, essentially, a single interpretation."[25] Historical films typically give us an "unstoppable" sequence of narrative assertions that do not allow the spectator to pause for historical reflection. Gone is the complexity of historical events that historians strive to render; gone also is the critical apparatus of history that places the historian's narrative in the context of other historical accounts and substantiates it by reference to factual evidence.

Rosenstone's argument then changes gears. If he acknowledges the ambivalence he shares with other historians toward cinematic history, he also asks them to stand outside their discipline and take a critical look at their own practice. Historians' negative attitudes toward film are founded on what Rosenstone identifies as two problematic assumptions, which he articulates in a later article: "first, that the current practice of written history is the only possible way of understanding the relationship of past to present; and, second, that written history mirrors 'reality.'"[26] Because they are trained in a mode of discourse in which all data (even visual) are represented verbally and interpretation is the exclusive province of written language, historians tend to resist considering the validity of other forms of expression. Both the written word and the filmic image, Rosenstone argues, have distinct powers of representation. Film has the capacity to "directly render the look and feel of all sorts of historical particulars and situations," whereas written history has enormous powers of abstraction that enable it to present data in condensed form and to generalize about the historical past. Moreover, all historical representation, whether written or filmic, is constructed discourse, shaped by "conventions of genre and language," that "imbues [history] with meaning."[27] Should historians, asks Rosenstone, set aside the *parti pris* of language that leads them to see difference as defect? Is it possible to conceive of audiovisual history as a parallel and equally valid mode of historical representation? In the introduction to *Visions of the Past*, Rosenstone asserts that film has its own specificity, and its own legitimacy, as a discourse: "Film changes the rules of the historical game, insisting on its own sort of truths, truths which arise from a visual and aural realm that is difficult to capture adequately in words."[28]

However, historical truth is not to be found in every film that uses history. To defend historical film, Rosenstone argues, the filmmaker must struggle against the conventions that structure the dramatic products of Hollywood "or its suburbs in London, Paris, Calcutta, Tokyo"[29] and that work on the spectator's emotions and his anticipation of closure. It is Rosenstone's intuition that experimental films—semiologists would say films that rework the cinematic codes of representation—are more apt to be authentically historical: they upset conventions in order to construct a "language" capable of depicting social realities. Such films belong to several currents of historical filmmaking. In the radical practice of Western filmmakers, Rosenstone privileges films in the "presentational" mode or those that use Brechtian distancing devices such as deliberate anachronism. Despite postmodernism's theoretical commitment to destroying History, Rosenstone asserts the value of postmodern films that challenge old modes of reference and open up potential new ways of talking about the past. In non-Western practices, he points to the models offered by Third Cinema: the oral tradition of the African griot with its different narrative strategies and different modes of addressing its public or the commitment that Latin American cinemas demonstrate not only to social history from below, but also to formal innovation.

If Rosenstone is a motive force, it is important to acknowledge the work of many other American historians who have contributed to a new theory of the historical film, among them Hayden White and Natalie Zemon Davis, whose work informs discussions in the following chapters. However, most American historians, even those convinced of the importance of doing historical analysis of the audiovisual media, remain largely skeptical about film as an instrument of historical representation. Among the essays that follow Rosenstone's introduction to "History in Images/History in Words," David Herlihy's "Am I a Camera?" represents this conservative tendency. Herlihy argues from the position that a basic phenomenology of the cinematographic image governs absolutely what can and cannot be expressed in the film medium. The image's strength is its phenomenological richness, which creates the illusion of presence, and in the historical film the illusion of the presence of the past. Film thus puts the viewer in the false position of seeming to observe history directly and consequently encourages the viewer's lack of critical consciousness. The imagistic is, by nature, alien to the intellectual. There can be no analytic discourse in images because "doubt is not visual"; all historical criticism supposes a "retreat from the visual to the verbal." Moreover, given the phenomenology of the image, the only conceivable historical discourse in film would be a faithful imitation of the historical scene in all its detail. Historical representation would therefore require "thick descriptions" for which there is rarely a sufficient basis in the historical record. Any recourse in film to symbolic representations breaks from film's natural mode and constitutes an admission by the filmmaker that historical reality cannot be depicted in cinematographic terms. Finally, because of its illusion of presence, film speaks to the spectator inescapably in the present tense; even the flashback and flash-forward are incapable of maintaining their temporal markers and only succeed in "convert[ing] past or future into the present." Film is horizontal because "it scans the horizon" of an event; history is vertical because it links past and present. Thus, film represents events but cannot refer to the "abiding structures" that shaped them: "The visual only see skins and surfaces, not what lies beneath them or soars above them."[30]

In the same set of essays, John E. O'Connor is considerably more positive and argues for the relevance to the discipline of the historical study of film and television. He contends, moreover, that historians have a responsibility toward their students to train them "to be more thoughtful viewers of historical films and television."[31] Beyond the usual questions historians ask about historical film—whether its representations reveal the depth of the research required of historical writing, whether fiction intrudes to reshape or distort historical characters or the sequence of events, whether filmic representations correspond to what it is possible to know about past realities—O'Connor asks other probing questions that show his sensitivity to filmic modes of representation. His interrogative mode contrasts with Herlihy's certitudes:

> What elements of historical interpretation are presented, either overtly in the narrative or characterization or more subtly through *mise-en-scène* and visual language? How, if at all, does the film relate the past to the present (the period of the film's production)? How do the inherent limits of the medium restrict the ways that a story can be told or an issue addressed? What alternatives might have been considered?[32]

The logic of O'Connor's approach still assumes the primacy of written history that asks the audiovisual media to explain how they can construct equivalents to the descriptive and analytic statements of language. Yet, given the pervasive skepticism of historians, the very idea that film is capable of such feats is progressive indeed.

In his introduction to *Image as Artifact: The Historical Analysis of Film and Television*,[33] O'Connor takes his inquiry still further and proposes a structured method for film analysis that he conceives in two stages. The first stage involves the gathering of information about "the Content, Production, and Reception of a Moving Image Document"; the second proposes four "frameworks" of inquiry: film as a vehicle for historical representation; film as a material source for social and cultural history; documentary footage as source of historical evidence; and the history of the audiovisual media as industry and art. Compared to Marc Ferro's approach presented above, O'Connor's is more inclusive. Although two of the frameworks consider film and television as involuntary testimony, O'Connor's approach allows that a film may be analyzed as historical representation. Moreover, there is no reason, he argues, to privilege the documentary over the dramatic film, despite the traditional argument that documentary corresponds to "a standard closer to that of traditional historical scholarship."[34] Both genres are capable of thoughtful historical analysis as they are also capable of "mindless travesty and intentional misrepresentations."[35] Although O'Connor insists that filmmakers and their historical consultants "must seek out indirect evidence, to present things as they 'plausibly may have been,'" he does not believe that historical films should be judged solely on the accuracy of their mise en scène. He quotes historian/filmmaker Daniel Walkowitz on the making of his *Molders of Troy*, a study of the life of American ironworkers in the mid-nineteenth century (PBS, 1979):

> I am less concerned with the authenticity of the details of a scene—for example, whether the shoes are authentic—than with the pattern of a set of social relationships that exists in a period of time. Historians don't simply describe a moment in time. We usually write because there is a problem in the past that we want to understand and we want to find a strategy for getting people to look at it.[36]

For Walkowitz and O'Connor the (impossible) imitation of the past down to the finest detail is not the essential mission of filmic representations of history. They set aside the critique of anachronism, which underpins the positions of theoreticians like Marc Ferro, and refocus analysis on the representation of social relations.

The fourth framework that O'Connor proposes concerns the "History of the Moving Image as Industry and Art Form," that is, a sphere of inquiry that has been the province of the film historian. Indeed, historians who approach film tend to see themselves as latecomers, convinced of the importance of a historiographical approach to film history but apprehensive about their lack of training in film theory and analysis. As O'Connor makes clear, there is little communication between film historians and historians who study film. Although many historians recognize the necessity of understanding film "in its own terms," they balk at the heavy "theoretical apparatus of film studies," which constitutes an unbridgeable "chasm" between the two disciplines.[37]

I think we can read in O'Connor's remarks something more than incomprehension and frustration. Underlying the perception held by many historians that film studies is arcane and inaccessible to the uninitiated is the suspicion that the intellectual foundations and ultimate missions of the two disciplines are fundamentally at odds. Even if more recent developments in film history tend to emphasize the study of production systems, historical context, and actual audience reception, poststructuralism still casts a long shadow in the field. How can historians, whose object of inquiry is precisely the referential world—what really happened in the past—relate to Jacques Derrida's dictum that nothing exists outside of the text, that textual references lead only to other texts and never to demonstrable realities? How can they reconcile themselves to postmodern theory that disputes the very possibility of reconstructing a causality of events in an irremediably fragmented world?

In his perceptive article, "I'll see it when I believe it," Frank P. Tomasulo critiques poststructural approaches that engage in "intratextual narcissism" and seem to endorse "the unbridled play of polyvalent signifiers."[38] There is a real danger, Tomasulo argues, in questioning history's ability to speak about the reality of the past: "Although healthy epistemological skepticism about written accounts and interpretations of the past is an important corrective to dominant ideology, extreme nihilism toward history can undermine belief in even the most settled of historical facts, such as the existence of slavery or the Holocaust."[39] Robert Rosenstone is also clearly uneasy with a field that is preoccupied with "how the past means without caring about the thing which happened in the past that gives rise to meaning."[40] When language—written or cinematic—loses its referential function, history must abandon all pretense of constructing a discourse on the past.

Although the subject of this introductory chapter is about historians' skepticism on film—the attitude that dominates the profession, despite the work of historians such as Rosenstone and O'Connor—it is also important to acknowledge that film studies need to know more about the philosophy and methods of the historical discipline. One of the ambitions of this study is to promote a cross-disciplinary understanding of what constitutes historical representation in film.

My point of departure can be summed up by the following basic questions: Should we accept the skeptical majority's either/or proposition: either film is a passive cultural object dropped on the road of history that the historian picks up, subjects to verbal analysis, and integrates into a properly historical discourse; or film is the fictionalized account of historical events and therefore incapable of establishing a meaningful relationship between its discourse of images and sounds and the reality of the past? Are skeptical historians correct in flattening distinctions between different sorts of historical films so that the work of a Rossellini or an Eisenstein occupies the same anachronistic turf as historical spectacles like those of Cecil B. De Mille? Or can we argue that historical films are capable of providing valid historical representations and therefore play a legitimate role in managing the collective memory of social groups? Before presenting the broad lines of my argument for the legitimacy of the historical film, I would like briefly to sketch the historical context on which the current orthodoxy of historical discourse rests.

It is only recently that historians formed themselves into a profession and established the criteria that define them as professionals. Before the late nineteenth century, history was a form of narrative practiced by "amateurs," some of no account, others subsequently recognized as historians of genius. Historical narratives constituted, in the "prescientific" era, an unregulated form of discourse. In the seventeenth century, there was no significant separation between writer and reader, the reader being a "lesser writer" who could also dabble in the art. History was a genre which anyone could practice; indeed, as Lionel Gossman observes, history was a literary genre that had its place in eighteenth century manuals of rhetoric. In *Between History and Literature,* Gossman argues that the breach between literature and history was produced by the parallel but oppositional developments in the two spheres of practice in the course of the nineteenth century. In literature, the Romantic movement sought to retreat from the real into a world governed by the poetic and mystical authority of the visionary artist. History, on the other hand, began an interrogation on the reality of the past and refocused its discourse on questions of epistemology: how does the historian know about the world of the past? The decisive break, however, comes at the moment of institutionalization of the historian's profession that brought about "the break up of the republic of letters," that "free mingling of shared experiences and aspirations of historians, novelists, poets, philosophers, scientists, statesmen."[41]

In the 1860s, the example of German advances in scientific historiography, the *Historische Zeitschrift,* brought a new intellectual rigor. European historians, inspired by the German model, began to adopt new principles of methodology that separated them from the weak "literary" tradition of the past. The fruit of this "scientific" revolution, history by the 1880s made its appearance as an autonomous field of study in European universities. From that moment, the profession was institutionalized within the university as an exclusive body of scholars. Historians were defined as university professors and researchers, unified by shared norms of practice. These professional practitioners established the criteria for good historical research, determining what methodologies were authorized and what types of subjects were appropriate to study. Moreover, historians became linked by professional organizations and scholarly journals, which reviewed, regulated, and disseminated their work.[42] For the first time, not only was historical writing based in the sinecure of the university, but also the historians' reading public was significantly narrowed: their work was addressed principally to their peers, who served as professional consumer/critics of scholarly work. Although historians continued to write for the general public, particularly on matters of "public memory" or, later, "patrimony," they had to share this sphere with the unregulated work of nonprofessional historians.

Understandably, professional historians saw the need for taking defensive measures against those outside the profession by calling into question the legitimacy of other modes of writing that claimed, in the long tradition of historical narrative, to give representations of the past. The cinema, which emerged as a narrative medium at the very moment of consolidation of the historical profession, produced and continued to produce a great number of historical films that showed little concern for accuracy but had enormous impact on a broad public. It is not surprising, then, that film should have taken its place, in the eyes of historians, as the most debased mode of representation. The cinema had and has no norms of practice in the domain of nonfiction, except in those cases for which film is subsumed within a scientific practice, as in ethnographic or didactic films. It has no system of regulation to ensure that historical representations are based on a critical examination of facts or that the chronology of events is respected. Despite the discourse of critics and reviewers, commercial film continues to be regulated by profit and by the pleasure of the spectators, who establish their control at the box office. Obviously, considerations of historical accuracy take a back seat to the demands of the marketplace.

Beyond the question of truth and verifiability, there is the, often-unacknowledged, problem of language. The entire process of historical investigation—from the initial question the researcher asks to the finished narrative—takes place in writing and is governed by the powers of written language. Most professional historians use written language almost exclusively, reducing nonverbal data to written form or making limited use of illustrations, visual documents that are well integrated into the verbal text. In historical narratives, writing exercises its capacity for abstraction that allows it to establish time relationships, depict historical groups and collective events, and avoid the pitfall of the kind of detailed representation that often cannot be justified by what is known about the past. By contrast, cinema is a medium of the image and, after the silent era, of image and sound, in which written language typically plays a marginal role. By dint of the phenomenal richness of the photographic image, filmic representation is analogical and concrete and depicts very specific fragments of space and time. Resistant to generalities, the cinematographic image is endowed with a strong impression of reality, an impression of presence that seems to fly in the face of modern theories of historical representation.

At the beginning of this study, I feel the need to make clear the burden one assumes in suggesting, as I do in the succeeding chapters, that film is not only a resource for historical documentation but it is also capable of meaningful historical representations. The burden is particularly weighty because the only way to confront the historians' skepticism is to show that film can be authentically historical according to the notion of historicity established by the historians themselves. An impossible task if one is not free to reopen and retheorize questions that most historians have either not addressed or considered definitively closed.

To begin, I will point out, with Robert Rosenstone, a basic shortcoming in historians' approach to historical discourse: they consistently fail to raise the question of their own discursive practice. Work on the rhetoric of historical representation is not part of the literature of the discipline. Although historians engage in techniques of representation—they are, whether they acknowledge it or not, narrators of events—they have little to say about them. It is as if they were bound by the now-discredited idea of an objective discourse in which historians do their best to become instruments of the past: their work consists in simply exposing to view an alignment of events whose ordering originates in the past as much as do the facts they cite. Historian Henri-Irénée Marrou, among others, has elegantly refuted this philosophical positivism:

> In order to put...their position [the position of positivist historians] into a formula, we would propose, keeping to the same symbols they use above:

$$h = P + p$$

> For them, history is made up of the Past, objectively recorded, plus, *alas*, an inevitable intervention by the present of the historian, something like the personal equation of the astronomic observer, or the ophthalmologist's astigmatism, that is, a parasitic given, a quantity that one must struggle to render as little as possible, until it becomes negligible and tends toward zero.[43]

Unfortunately, as Marrou goes on to say, despite the critique of positivism on which modern historiography presumably rests, most historians continue to affirm implicitly in their concrete practice this discredited conception they would never voice in philosophical terms.

Facts are the raw material of history. "Facts are therefore, in the historian's discourse, the hard element, the one that resists contention."[44] Historiographical theorists acknowledge nonetheless that it is the historians who produce facts by selecting a trajectory across the "event-worthy" fields of the past. While respecting historical chronology, they arrange facts in a narrative order of their making that imposes on more or less inchoate material a causal order—a meaning—that is the end result of all historical research. In terms of narration, there is no specific kind of historical ordering; history employs the same narrative structures that literary critics discern in prose fiction. As French historian Paul Veyne puts it, historiography is a specific type of writing that is different from other literary work but responds to the same narrative impulse that characterizes written and oral storytelling of all sorts. Once the splendid isolation of historic discourse is breached, it is possible to examine the relationship between historical discourse, including the constraints of truth that characterize it, and other narrative discourses that lay claim to historical representation.

I believe it has been too easy to agree with skeptical historians' position that film is so dominated by the present that it cannot offer any meaningful representation of the past. Is a discourse of images guilty of the original sin of its signifier? Does film as a medium evoke too easily nineteenth-century theories of the "resurrection" of the historical body in "flesh and blood" that contemporary history repudiates? If, as semiologists have argued, film is a language capable of saying anything, why does historical representation belong to the realm of the unsayable? Is film incapable of giving voice to the historical critique that underpins contemporary conceptions of historical discourse? Is all cinema so dominated by production systems and box office that filmmakers find it impossible to create alternative cultural spaces? Is all historical representation in film a betrayal of the past that historians must struggle to eliminate from the public imagination?

My answer to all these questions is no. There are, I contend, films that set out to give an account of historical events; they do not lure the spectator into an imaginary world of spectacle but exonerate a debt to the past (to use Paul Ricoeur's notion). Films can also serve to create meaningful links between the past and the lived present of their audiences. Indeed, the historian's most urgent task is to fulfill this collective need to experience the historical. As Eric Hobsbawn observes, "We cannot help learning from [the past], for that is what *experience* means."[45] Reconstructing the past is a broad cultural enterprise that cannot be confined to the closed circle of an academic discourse. Cinema, as I argue, has a legitimate role to play in that enterprise.

The aim of this study is not only to defend the historical film but also to construct a framework within which to judge approaches to historical representation in film. By adopting a multidisciplinary perspective on the many issues such a study entails, I hope to reopen questions that seem to have been definitively closed. What interests me is the possibility of a dialogue between disciplines on that eclectic object called the historical film. In the interest of such an exchange, I turn to four disciplines: philosophy of history, narratology, semiology of cinema, and rhetoric, each of which has its own object and its specific methods and strengths.

Philosophy of history examines the great epistemological break between historical discourse and the discourse of fiction and describes the retrospective act of comprehension that characterizes historical representation.

After its long neglect of the nonfictional discourses, *narratology* has begun to reassess the theoretical basis for differentiating between two broad genres: the discourses of the imaginary and pragmatic discourses that act on the world of real experience. Literary theory also analyzes strategies of representation to determine whether nonfiction has its own specific narrative practice.

The *semiology of cinema* offers an instrument for describing the difference between written and audiovisual narratives and determining whether the film medium, which easily expresses concrete space and time, is capable of rendering the more abstract realities of historical representation.

Rhetoric identifies the processes of figuration, the *standing for* (Paul Ricoeur) that describes the relationship between historical narrative and the reality of the past to which it refers. It offers a set of tropes—metaphor, metonymy, synecdoche, irony—that serve to give rhetorical form to the representation of historical events (Hayden White).

In the following five chapters I call on these disciplines to address broad theoretical issues concerning the philosophical commitments historians make to the past and to the public they address and the basic structures of meaning and techniques of representation they deploy. These discussions frame the fundamental question of this study: how can film function as a form of interpretation and representation of the historical past?

Chapter One, "Historiography: Stories of a Particular Kind," takes up the question of the nature of historical narratives. Is history different from fiction because of its presumed objectivity and the ethical constraints the reality of the past imposes on a discourse of truth? What is the role of the imagination in historical writing? Is the sense of time in history different from that in fiction? Can history be distinguished from fiction on the basis of the position of the author or the reader? How does the notion of the historical trace help define what historical narrative is?

Chapter Two, "Signifying History: What Are Factual Narratives?" begins by assessing what narrative theory has contributed to charting the territory of nonfiction. How do we distinguish pragmatic discourses from discourses of the imaginary? Does nonfiction engage in the mimetic activity of representation in the same way as fiction? How can nonfiction be described as a practice? Does film, which as an expressive medium excels at representing concrete space and time, have the capacity for representing the more abstract narratives that history constructs? If so, then what kinds of strategies do filmmakers adopt?

Chapter Three, "The Historical Character," raises the issue of whether it is possible to represent historical characters in film. I approach the question from the perspectives of two disciplines. Narrative theory asks whether characters are psychological entities, akin to living people, or whether they emerge as semantic effects through the process of reading a text or viewing a film. Historiography describes historical characters as collective subjects that exist by dint of their participatory belonging to social groups. How can these theoretical perspectives be applied to historical characters in film?

Chapter Four, "Refiguring History in Film," raises the question of the relationship between historical narrative and the reality of the past to which it refers. Paul Ricoeur, through an analysis of three models of historical representation, concludes that the relationship is analogical in character: historiography is a mimetic activity that constructs a discourse that does not resurrect but stands for historical events. Hayden White proposes a rhetorical notion of analogy: historical representation is a poetic operation that draws on the major rhetorical figures—metaphor, metonymy, synecdoche, and irony—to prefigure the historical field to be represented. Can we detect in historical films this rhetorical work of figuration?

Chapter Five, "Film: A Place of Memory," addresses the following question: what is the role of film in managing public memory? The discussion begins with the problematic notion of collective memory: what have philosophers and social scientists said about the social group's capacity to remember? Historian Pierre Nora argues that, in the contemporary world, the public demands "hallucinatory recreations of the past" in places of memory, cultural spaces of all kinds to which memory clings. Is film one such place of memory, where the public recovers the psychological dimension of history?

Since my point of departure is theoretical, I do not present an analysis of a large corpus of historical films. I have chosen instead to include in most chapters discussions of specific films that I call _case studies_. My intention is not to give complete analyses of these complex texts. Rather, I look at how each film develops a strategy of historical representation that responds to the theoretical concerns of the chapter in question. As the following list shows, I have selected films from different periods of film history and from quite different cultural traditions. Three are historical documentaries; the remaining four are films that employ the presumably fictional techniques of mise en scène.

Roberto Rossellini's *The Rise to Power of Louis XIV* (1966)
Jean Renoir's *La Marseillaise* (1938)
Mikhail Kalatozov's *I Am Cuba* (1964)
Esther Schub's *The Fall of the Romanov Dynasty* (1927)
Theo Angelopoulos's *Traveling Players* (1974–1975)
Ken Burns's *The Civil War* (1990)
Rithy Panh's *S21: The Khmer Rouge Killing Machine* (2003)

1

HISTORIOGRAPHY

Stories of a Particular Kind

What distinguishes history from the other social sciences is its concern with human societies as they develop through time. To construct the temporal dimension essential to historical representation, the passage of time needs to be measured. Indeed, Claude Lévi-Strauss asserts that without dates history would cease to exist: "Dates may not be the whole of history, nor what is most interesting about it, but they are its *sine qua non*, for history's entire originality and distinctive nature lie in apprehending the relation between *before* and *after*, which would perforce dissolve if its terms could not, at least in principle, be dated."[1] Historical thought is, then, fundamentally diachronic, and even the slowest of histories of long duration (concerning seemingly permanent social, technological, or economic situations or even climatic conditions) never achieve a true synchronic analysis because their subject is, at its root, the study of social transformation over time.

What Paul Ricoeur calls the creative refiguration of time depends on such "instruments of thought" as the calendar. Calendar time, he argues in *Time and Narrative*, constitutes the "first bridge" that historians throw up between cosmic time and the lived time of the human individual. This *third time* is intermediary in scale: it does not attempt to embrace the universal, measured in the life and death of stars, for example, or restrict itself to the phenomenological perspective of time as experienced by the individual human mind. Historical time has a mixed character. On the one hand, calendar time creates for historical representation a system of measure, a frame of reference for historical action, calibrated in hours, days, months, years, centuries. On the other hand, historical time retains something of the character of psychological time because it represents "lived time," with its fluctuating moments of intensity and emptiness, of rapidity and slowness. This intermediary time "serves as a common marker for members of a group,"[2] a means for structuring the collective experience of the past in its objective and experiential dimensions.

Another feature of historical time is that it is always teleological; the question of the relationship between a beginning and an ending arises at the very moment that the historian asks the question that is central to a piece of research. As Antoine Prost puts it, "It is the question that constructs the historical object by carving an original slice out of the limitless universe of facts and possible documents."[3] This original slice not only sets up the chronological frame for the historical narrative, but also sets in motion the search for a chain of causality that will turn the *this-and-then-that* into the *this-because-of-that*. In his narration of events, the historian constructs the necessary connections between them and shows how they lead toward the culminating situation, the ending that is at the origin of the initial question, "How did we get to here?" In his *De la connaissance historique*, Henri-Irénée Marrou states the principle this way:

> History becomes intelligible only in so far as it shows it is capable of establishing, of detecting the relationships that link each stage of human development to its antecedents and its consequences: just as, statically, a historical situation, seized at moment *t*, always shows itself to be more or less structured, in the same way the unfolding of [historical] moments is not this discontinuous line of atoms of the real, isolated like beads of a rosary that the unfathomable will of God arbitrarily counts off (as Islamic theology likes to imagine it): the experience of history, which the conscientious researcher acquires from contact with documents, makes us discover that there are intelligible relationships between successive moments of time. Certainly, not everything is linked together: there are hiatuses in the

development of time as there are limits in static structures; but the historian's task is to discover these connections wherever they may exist.[4]

Constructing a causal development of events through time is the nature of historical understanding. To recount is to explain. In other words, historical narratives, like fictional narratives, have plots.

HISTORICAL OBJECTIVITY
AND THE HISTORIAN'S SUBJECTIVITY

Are there differences of nature between historical and fictional narration? Does the epistemological break between history as a discourse of truth and fiction as discourse of the imaginary impose distinct narrative forms? The question has been hotly debated in the wake of the rise of modern historical consciousness, which toward the end of the nineteenth century posited a difference of essence between history and the rest of literary production. History could no longer be considered a literary genre among others—it no longer belonged to literature at all—and the techniques of fictional representation could not continue to be tolerated in texts that had serious historical intentions. At issue was the scientific claim of history. If history chose as its object the study of the reality of the past, then its representations had to have an objective character; therefore, historians had to adopt the kind of critical detachment that imposes a distance, both temporal and personal, between themselves as psychological beings and the material they set out to analyze. History abandoned as Romantic excess the idea of an intimate bond between the historical text and its author. It repudiated the declarations of a Michelet, who, reflecting at the end of his career, observed that history is as much a work on the historian's internal life as it is the production of historical knowledge. Indeed, Michelet argued that the relationship between the creator and his creation is inverted in historiography because it is ultimately the progeny that gives birth to the procreator:

By penetrating deeper and deeper into the [historical] object, one grows to love it, and thereafter one regards it with increasing interest. The heart is moved at this second view, sees a thousand things that are invisible to the indifferent public. History and the historian are bound together in this look. For good? For evil? Something is operating here that has not been described and that we need to reveal: It's that history, as time progresses, makes the historian much more than history is made by him. My book created me. I was in fact its work. This son has made his father.... If we resemble each other, that's good. The traits he takes from me are in large measure those that I owed him and by which I am in his likeness.[5]

As part of a new reflection on their own practice, many historians since the twentieth century have acknowledged the role of subjectivity in the production of historic discourse. However, they have reformulated the idea of subjectivity in terms quite different from Michelet's. Every intellectual enterprise is based on a personal commitment and motivated by personal pleasures that sustain the researcher through the difficulties of his work. Historians cannot be pure analytic spirits. They are driven by their immediate context—intellectual, economic, social, political—and the individual concerns that move them to select one project over another. Each historian works from a specific position in relation to the historical object, a bias implicit in his "angle" of observation that carries with it the risk of ideological prejudice. One could add that, despite the most rigorous effort, the historian's text, like other writing, is not entirely the product of the conscious mind and is necessarily subject to forces of which the historian is by definition unaware. This is what Marrou terms, somewhat ironically, "this fearsome and devastating 'subjectivity'" that threatens to undermine the scientific claims of historical research. Indeed, it is only in taking their critical distance from the facts stored in historical archives of all sorts that historians are able to winnow the grain of history from the chaff of myth and ideology and pass judgment on the errors of their predecessors.

As a historian, Marrou draws on Augustine's *City of God* because, from his critical vantage point, he is able to distinguish the authentic representations of the Roman world the bishop of Hippo passes on to subsequent generations from the illuminations of the spiritual cleric. Historical practice that establishes truth through the techniques of documentation and analysis is not, by nature, different from practice in the "hard" sciences. He observes, for example, that there is broad agreement on how facts are identified and authenticated. However, whatever the rigors that historical method imposes, history, more than any other scientific discipline, runs the risk of losing its footing and slipping into the unscientific confusion of subject and object. It is precisely because the object of history is human action and its motivations that historians are prone to this slippage: "As knowledge of man by man, history is the capturing of the past through, and in, a human

thought that is living and committed, an indissoluble mixture of subject and object."[6] What the historian can do to subdue subjectivity is to
elucidate his own situation as a researcher and writer. As an integral
part of the historical method, the historian can record the workings
of his mind and emotions in a kind of Brechtian deconstruction of the
historical process.

> Scientific honesty seems to me to require that the historian,
> through an effort of self-awareness, define the orientation of his
> thought, specify its postulates (to the extent this is possible); that
> he show himself in action and make us observers of the genesis
> of his work; why and how he has chosen and demarcated his
> subject; what he was looking for and what he found there; that
> he describe his internal itinerary, for all historical research, if it
> is truly fruitful, implies a progress in the soul of its author: the
> encounter with the other.[7]

But the reality is, Marrou tells us, that few historians are inclined to
take such a critical approach to their own work; most act as if historical research were a rigorous method that can be applied in unproblematic fashion. Theoretical problems like subjectivity are put out of mind
and relegated to the domain of philosophy of history, whose abstractions remain disconnected from actual historical practice.

FICTIONAL STORIES AND HISTORICAL NARRATIVES

A second blind spot for historians is the narrative character of historic
discourse. Historians have generally resisted acknowledging that historical explanation takes place through the process of narration; they
work, rather, on the implicit assumption that history is a discourse sui
generis that scientific practice has separated from literary discourses.
This assumption would not remain unexamined. In an article published in 1967, Roland Barthes called into question the notion that history is a specific kind of discourse, basing his critique on the methods
of the emerging field of semiology. He argued that structural linguists
who apply linguistic methods to the analysis of discourses should not
concern themselves exclusively with universal discursive characteristics but should examine the accepted categories of discourse called
genres in order to determine whether or not there is a linguistic basis
for distinguishing between historical and fictional forms of narrative:

Is there in fact any specific difference between factual and imaginary narrative, any linguistic feature by which we may distinguish on the one hand the mode appropriate to the relation of historical events—a matter traditionally subject, in our culture, to the prescriptions of historical "science," to be judged only by the criteria of conformity to "what really happened" and by principles of "rational" exposition—and on the other hand the mode appropriate to the epic, novel or drama?[8]

Moreover, Barthes is critical of the notion of the fact, which presumably preexists the historian's act of narration as an autonomous element within the field of reference. Citing Nietzsche, he observes that a fact does not exist already formed; it is produced as a result of "introducing meaning," of integrating the "fact" as an element of human discourse about the past. Barthes is equally critical of the passive position historians claim to assume: it is as if they wrote under the dictate of past events, where facts are givens and discursive structures inhere in the material the historian is studying. The myth of the ascendancy of the referent obscures, Barthes argues, the properly linguistic character of historic narration. Why is it, he asks, that history is able to do away with the production of meaning that semiology discerns in every form of human communication? Such a conception would reduce the tripartite character of the sign to two terms: the signifier and the referent. Eliminating the signified, the language of historic discourse would directly express the real:

[T]he very idea that history can have a meaning (*signifié*) other than referential is rejected. The referent and its expression (*signifiant*) are seen as directly related; the function of discourse is confined to the mere expression of reality; and meaning, the fundamental term of imaginary structures, becomes superfluous.[9]

Paul Ricoeur also recognizes that historians tend to avoid the question of how meaning is produced in historical texts, a tendency rooted historically in epistemological concerns:

If this narrative continuity between story and history was little noticed in the past, it was because the problems posed by the epistemological break between fiction and history, or between myth and history, turned attention to the question of evidence, at the expense of the more fundamental question of what accounts for the interest of a work of history.[10]

By setting aside questions of representation, historians take a significant risk: they fail to examine critically the processes of signification that make historical representation possible.

There are, of course, historians who have questioned unspoken assumptions and have sought to dispel certain myths about history writing. In his iconoclastic *Writing History* (which Michel de Certeau suggests retitling *Decolonizing History*), Paul Veyne makes a frontal assault on a whole series of received ideas and makes the bald assertions that what historians do is tell stories, that telling stories is a universal mode of making sense of the world, and that historical narratives have a fundamental kinship, not only with fictional narratives, but also with the most mundane forms of storytelling in daily life. There is, he argues, no properly historical method, and no historian, if asked, could describe or define what it is. Historical explanation is not at all scientific but belongs to a more modest mode that Veyne calls *understanding*:

> Everybody knows that when he opens a history book, he understands it, as he understands a novel or what his neighbors are doing; put in other words, explaining, for a historian, means "to show the unfolding of the plot, to make it understood." Such is the historical explanation: entirely sublunary and not scientific at all; we will keep the name "comprehension" for it.[11]

Historical and scientific approaches are different, he argues, because the objects they study are different. Science deals with phenomena that are abstracted from natural or historical events, as if "cut to the measure" of scientific laws. To explain scientifically is to demonstrate that these phenomena operate according to unvarying principles. History, on the other hand, deals with the totality of shared human experience across time, in its infinite variations. Moreover, there is no properly historical object—anything can become a document for the historian, provided it is part of what really took place in the past—and objects cannot be isolated from the historic context in which they evolve. Therefore, Veyne argues, history has no method in the scientific sense: it cannot explain individual facts by reference to general laws. It has, rather, a critical apparatus that allows the historian to examine whether the meaning he attaches to an event by placing it in a chain of cause and effect is justifiable.

Although this analysis seems to reduce—some would say radically—the distance between narration in history and fiction, Veyne is careful to make the fundamental distinction. History is "Nothing but a True Narrative," as the first chapter of *Writing History* is entitled. Yet this apparently reductive "nothing but" turns out of course to be everything. History, like fiction, is "anecdotal," it "interests" the reader through telling a story. But the veracity that distinguishes history is essential: historical narrative recounts true events, and because they are true, the historian-narrator does not need to "captivate" the readership. The search for dynamism of plot or for aesthetic effect is not the historian's concern. Truth controls historical narration as verisimilitude controls the fictional.

Louis O. Mink, in his "Narrative Form as a Cognitive Instrument," arrives at much the same conclusion. Narrative in history, he argues, is unlike narrative in fiction because the historian constructs his story out of vestiges of the past. In elaborating a narrative, the historian is bound to follow the development of events according to the relationships of necessity he sees linking them together in sequence: "History-as-it-was-lived, that is, is an untold story. The historian's job is to discover that untold story, or part of it, and to retell it even though in abridged and edited form."[12] An "untold" story is, of course, not a story at all, and one cannot "retell" what has never been recounted. But Mink correctly points out that, in contrast to the relative freedom of imagination the novelist enjoys, the historian embraces ethical constraints: the story the historian tells is not an invention in the fictive sense but a representation of the past that adheres to the principle of fidelity.

It is significant that, in the first volume of *Time and Narrative*, Paul Ricoeur expresses his conviction that, despite twentieth century developments in historiography, including the idea of histories of long duration, history is indisputably narrative in its functioning: "If history were to break every connection to our *basic competence for following a story* and to the cognitive operations constitutive of our narrative understanding … , it would lose its distinctive place in the chorus of the social sciences: it would cease to be historical."[13] Historical narrative is not the outdated product of centuries of political history, a dramatic form of mise en scène that stages heroic events from the point of view of the ruling elite. Narrative is the essential structure of all historic discourse. For Ricoeur, the narrative character of history does not contradict the epistemological distinction between history and fiction; rather, it calls on the historiographer to study the development of historical narration in its links with the art of narrative in general:

My thesis is that history the most removed from the narrative form continues to be bound to our narrative understanding by a line of derivation that we can reconstruct step by step and degree by degree with an appropriate method. This method does not stem from the methodology of the historical sciences per se but from a second-order reflection upon the ultimate conditions of intelligibility of a discipline that, in virtue of its scientific ambition, tends to forget this line of derivation which continues nevertheless tacitly to preserve its specificity as a historical science.[14]

Ricoeur finds in W. B. Gallie's *Philosophy and the Historical Understanding* an argument that supports the derivative character of historical narrative. Whatever historical explanation may produce in terms of "content," it must be judged in relation to the narrative order on which it is based. Gallie posits that the reader's comprehension inheres in the *followability* of the story, whether the story belongs to a discourse of truth or the imaginary. Historical explanation can be more than the "pure" narration of events. In fact, the story may be interrupted by the historian who feels called on to fill in through his commentary what the causal sequence of events cannot tell on its own. The historian enables the reader to understand what might otherwise appear as a gratuitous or enigmatic connection between events. "Ideally," Gallie suggests, "a story should be self-explanatory," and indeed, certain historical narratives resemble realist fiction in that they require little intervention on the part of the narrator.

To follow a story is to understand actions, thoughts, and emotions as they move us toward a concluding moment, which is the end of their trajectory. Literary theorist Gérard Genette describes in functional terms this structure of narrative, common to history as well as fiction, that motivates events by moving backward from effect to cause:

> These *retrograde* determinations constitute precisely what we call the arbitrariness of narrative, that is, not really indetermination but determination of the means by the ends, and, to speak more crudely, *of the causes by the effects*. It is this paradoxical logic of fiction that requires that each element, each unit of the narrative be defined by its functional character ... and that we account for the first (in the chronology of the narrative) by the second, and so forth—from which it flows that the last is the one in command of all the others and that nothing commands.[15]

History is a narrative argument that begins with an ultimate effect and moves backward to the examination of causes.

Although many novelists in periods prior to modern realism have also been given to editorial explanations of character, situations, or events, discursive intervention on the part of the narrator is certainly more characteristic of "narratives of truth." Truth, as commentators since Aristotle have affirmed, is often "defective" in literary terms since it cannot consistently provide the "acceptable" succession of events that verisimilitude requires. The historian's commentary is not, therefore, an independent discourse; it is a functional supplement to the narrative that ensures the followability of the story. In Gallie's conception, then, narrative is the matrix of historical explanation and provides the structure of its discourse.

FOUR ESSENTIAL QUESTIONS ABOUT THE NATURE OF HISTORIC NARRATIVE

We have seen, following Barthes, Veyne, Ricoeur, and Gallie, that the discourse of history is fundamentally narrative, but that it operates under the constraints of historical truth. If history is, then, a narrative of a particular kind, how can its distinguishing features be described? What approaches have philosophers and historiographers adopted in their inquiries into the nature of historical representation? In the following pages, I examine several significant attempts to define historical narrative. The discussion is organized around what I see as four essential questions raised in the work of the following philosophers of history: Arthur Danto, Louis O. Mink, Paul Ricoeur, Henri-Irénée Marrou, and R. G. Collingwood.

Is There a Special Character to the Narrative Statement in History?

Arthur Danto was the first to address the question in *Analytic Philosophy of History* (1965). Danto argues that there is a fundamental difference between historical and other kinds of narrative, but the distinction he makes is not to be found in epistemology but in an analysis of the functioning of narrative statements. Danto examines what he sees as the complex temporal character of historical statements at the level of the sentence. The narration of an isolated action situated in a real past has no significance in and of itself; to have historical meaning, it must be linked in a causal chain to other actions that came after. Thus, the Ideal Chronicler—the direct observer of the action, placed at the best possible vantage point—may bear witness to events and situate them in a chronology. However, he is unable to understand the action historically because he lacks the critical distance that can exist only at some time in the future. From his retrospective vantage point, the historian is able to look back over the chronology of human actions and construct a sequence of events that obeys the laws of causality. Historical narratives can therefore be characterized as "the retrospective realignment of the Past."[16]

According to Danto's analysis, the minimal historical statement refers to two events, the first event positioned as the cause of the second. For example, the sentence, "The destruction of the European film industries during the Great War contributed to the hegemony of the American cinema," is a historical statement. The causal first event (destruction of the war) produces as effect the second event (the increasing dominance of the American cinema). This impact of the Great War on film might have been predicted by contemporary observers, but it was not a central intention of the historic actors to produce that outcome. It is only from the retrospective position of the historian that the meaning of events—their causal sequence—can be established. As Danto's analysis makes clear, there is a third temporal position implicated in historical narrative: the position occupied by the historian/narrator. In relation to the present moment of the historian's writing, historical events belong to the past, to the historical diegesis the historian constructs. The historian takes the position of an enunciating subject who is removed in time from the events he recounts and distanced again by the critical method he employs.

Danto's analysis raises certain problems. Is it possible to assert that only historical narration has this peculiar configuration of positions in time? Do other "discourses of truth" resemble history in this regard? What distinguishes history from autobiography? Both history and autobiography have a controlling consciousness, a narrator, who looks back over time past from the position of the present of enunciation. It is, for example, Rousseau in his fifties who narrates the events of his life in *The Confessions* beginning with his first childhood memories. We see the work of analysis in the way the older Rousseau examines his actions across the lapse in time: the young Rousseau is often unaware of the meaning of his actions or perceives his intentions in ways Rousseau the narrator corrects or reassesses. In book four, for example, Rousseau recounts how his still-adolescent hero abandons his benefactor, the composer M. Le Maître, and coldly rationalizes his conduct. From the critical distance of his maturity, Rousseau, still stinging from the shame of his action so many years before, judges the situation differently: "That was how I saw things then; today I see them differently. It is not immediately afterwards that a shabby action torments us; it is rather when, much later, we recall it; for its memory does not fade."[17] Moreover, in autobiographical texts, the events of a life are not simply linked together in a chronological order; they are placed in causal sequence so that the meaning of one event is determined by what comes after. Thus, the sixteen-year-old Rousseau who sees Mme. de Warens for the first time is dazzled by her beauty and an intuitive sense of the importance of the encounter, but it is the retrospective Rousseau who assesses the historical significance of their meeting: "At last I arrived; I saw Mme de Warens. This was the period of my life that decided my character; I cannot bring myself to pass over it lightly."[18] This arrival "at last" refers not only to the end of the hero's picaresque adventures since he found the gates of Geneva locked against him, but also to the retrospective judgment of Rousseau the narrator, who draws our attention to this event as a major key to the meaning of his life.

The configuration of temporal positions in autobiography is not then basically different from the configuration that Danto argues is one specificity of historical narration. Nor can autobiography be distinguished from history on the basis of reference to a real past since both forms claim to give accurate representation of past events. We apply, in fact, the same standard of truthfulness to the historian as to the autobiographer: both are held responsible for the veracity of their narratives. I would suggest that differences between autobiography and history can be made on two bases. The first is narratological and concerns the notion of narrative *voice*. According to the classification drawn by Gérard Genette, the historian takes up a narrative position that is *extradiegetic*—he is the "primary" narrator in the sense that there is no narrative voice that precedes his—and his position is *heterodiegetic* since he stands outside the events he narrates. The autobiographer, on the other hand, takes up a different position of narration. Like the historian, his position as primary narrator is extradiegetic, but unlike the historian, he does not stand outside the events he narrates. He is what Genette calls a homodiegetic narrator because the Narrating I and the Narrated I (Spitzer) are the "same" person, although separated by a difference in age that permits the narrator's critical or ironic perspective.

This narratological difference returns us to the second basis, epistemological differences, which are of two types. First, history presupposes a separation between the narrator and the narrated because the past in question is not accessible to the historian's memory. It is the inherently "interested" position of the narrator in autobiography that leads the reader to be more wary of the subjectivity of the autobiographer's representations and more skeptical of the accuracy of the account. How, indeed, can the autobiographer be expected to maintain objectivity since his narrative is by definition an apology of his own life?

The second difference has to do with the nature of the materials on which historian and autobiographer work. The historian works from traces—the vestiges of the human past that are necessarily separate from his consciousness. As R. G. Collingwood notes, one definition of historical consciousness is that it is intellectual, not perceptual: the historian narrates a past that he has not experienced. Although the autobiographer obviously relies on documentation of his life that comes in various forms (letters, diaries, newspaper accounts, interviews of witnesses, etc.), documents are in large part mnemonic devices. Autobiography depends by definition on the work of memory—the capacity of the individual mind to recall events from the past.

Can History Be Distinguished from Fiction from the Position of the Reader?

Louis O. Mink observes that, since the seventeenth century, philosophy has been dominated by problems of cognition and perception, and the basis of knowledge in the natural sciences. It has been concerned, that is, with the immediately perceptible world. From this perspective, the past had no standing in philosophical discourse because it was inaccessible to scientific examination. Only recently, Mink observes in 1970, have philosophers turned their attention to how it is possible to make meaningful statements about the historic past, which is by definition no longer perceptible.[19] Historians, for their part, have been preoccupied with the practice of inquiry into historic records and have shown little interest in developing a "theory of knowledge" applicable to historical discourse. Analytic philosophers, like Arthur Danto, have understood that history is not a science in the usual sense—it does not deal with scientific laws and predictability—and consequently does not apply the principles of deductive logic. History employs, rather, a set of "organizing schemes" that belong to the "art" of narrative.

Mink acknowledges that W. B. Gallie was the first to examine the logic of narrative as the organizing principle of historical discourse. Narrative allows us to *follow* what could not be predicted or logically inferred, and, no matter how rigorous the method is, Mink tells us, history produces knowledge by narrativizing the field of research: "But the researches of historians, however arduous and technical, only increase the amount and precision of knowledge of facts which remain contingent and discontinuous. It is by being assigned to stories that they become intelligible and increase understanding by going beyond

'What?' and 'When?' to "How?' and 'Why?'"[20] But Gallie's analysis, Mink argues, rests on the conception of a naïve reader who allows himself to be "pulled along" by the techniques of narrative toward an ending that, while acceptable (that is, motivated by all that precedes), contains an element of surprise. Mink disagrees with Gallie's central notion that historical narrative is based in the followability of a story. Reading a historical narrative does not consist in following the story; it consists in *having followed* it.

Mink's hypothesis, then, is that the reader adopts a specific position in relation to historical narrative that is different from the position he adopts in relation to fictional narrative. When reading a novel, the reader responds to the hermeneutics of narrative: he remains in a state of suspense, of anticipation because the sequence of fictional events is only partially foreseeable; he retains, as the reader of nonfiction does not, the impression of the contingency of events. The reader's "knowledge" is imperfect; he does not have access to the whole truth of the story that unfolds little by little and remains open to unexpected turns of events and unanticipated revelations (the *peripeteia* and *anagnorisis* described by Aristotle). In *S/Z*, Roland Barthes analyzes how this state of suspense and anticipation is ruled by the hermeneutic codes that structure the enigmas of classic narrative and create a special pleasure of reading that includes the anguish of the wait and the desire for resolution. The classic text is *reticent*, to use Barthes's term, and imposes delays and detours so that it is only at the culminating moment of truth that the reader can look back on the whole configuration of the story. Now armed with knowledge, he revisits the unfolding of the narrative in an act of comprehensive retrospection.

For Mink, the reader of historical narrative is never naïve and does not follow the unfolding of the plot in a state of suspense. The historian's readership—in the first instance, the public of his peers—knows the "truth" or at least that part of the truth that is known through already unearthed facts and already written histories. The destiny of Napoleon at Waterloo or of Union troops at the battle of Vicksburg is not subject to the manipulative technique of enigma and resolution. In Mink's formulation, the reader of history has *already followed* the story at the very moment that he becomes engaged in the act of reading:

> What I mean to suggest is that the difference between following a story and *having followed* a story is more than the incidental difference between present experience and past experience. Anticipation and retrospection are not simply different attitudes or vantage points which may be taken (or must be taken)

toward the same event or course of events.... My thesis is that the difference is crucial as well for cognition: at least in the case of human actions and changes, to know an event by retrospection is categorically, not incidentally, different from knowing it by prediction or anticipation. It cannot even, in any strict sense, be called the "same" event.[21]

For Mink, the meaning of having followed a story is this: the reader grasps "together in a single act ... the complicated relationship of parts which can be experienced only *seriatim*." Historical comprehension relies on the "configurational mode" in which we see the complex relationships between events held together in a synoptic, retrospective glance, a kind of human equivalent of God's knowledge of the world: "In the configurational comprehension of a story which one *has followed*, the end is connected with the promise of the beginning as well as the beginning with the promise of the end, and the necessity of the backward references cancels out, so to speak, the contingency of the forward references."[22]

As Ricoeur points out, the synoptic vision that Mink attributes to historical understanding does not completely cancel out the contingency the reader experiences in following the developing sequence of events. In his later study, "Narrative as a Cognitive Instrument,"[23] Mink emphasizes the inventive quality of historical narrative. Historical method can determine a fact or the relation between facts, but it cannot in the same way determine the "correct" relationships between events because there are no rules for constructing stories. The same event may belong to more than one story, and its significance will vary according to the narrative trajectory the historian has chosen. Mink concludes that we must "credit the imagination or the sensibility or the insight of the individual historian" for the construction of a narrative. If there are no rules for narratives, if the "same" events can be ordered in different causal sequences, then the reader's sense of contingency is still in play in the process of reading because the connection between cause and effect retains a certain openness. Indeed, good history offers the reader many surprises. Even in recounting the best-known historical events, the historian gives us new perspectives: a new point of vision, an unexpected link in the chain of causality, a new importance accorded to an aspect of an event, or even a whole new source of documentation that was previously relegated to the realm of the unmeaningful.

Narration of historical events inescapably brings about a "revival" of past reality because it requires the reader to experience the past through a representation whose credibility the historian has labored to achieve. However, it is Mink's work on historical narrative that establishes the retrospective and synoptic character of historical understanding that sets the boundaries of the reader's experience. The reader does not experience historical narrative as *presence*, as the literature of the imaginary exhorts him to do. The reader cannot place himself within the story because he sees the story as a reconstruction of what has already been. As Roland Barthes suggests in his study of the photographic image—that quintessential historical document—the sense of the photograph's *being-there* is overwhelmed by the sense of its *having-been-there*.

I think it is reasonable to conclude that the phenomenology of historical narrative places the reader in an ambivalent position. On the one hand, he does indeed follow the story, as Gallie insists, and historical narratives retain some of the experience of contingency that all narrative provides. On the other hand, the reader experiences historical events as belonging to the already past and is most often aware of the ending toward which the narrative is directed because, typically, the historian makes it clear in the first pages of his text. The historical narrative is therefore both contingent and determined, and the reader must add together the experience of the forward movement of the story and the retrospection he puts in play as he examines each step toward the resolution he knows in advance.

Can Historical Narrative Be Distinguished from Other Narrative Forms on the Basis of the Materials It Uses?

The historian seeks to know the past by means of documents, what the past has left behind as concrete testimony of its existence. Documents are not only the written record of human experience in the past; they are every kind of vestige the historian is able to utilize. Lucien Febvre tells us that history is made "with words. With signs. With landscapes and roof tiles. With the forms of fields and weeds. With eclipses of the moon and harnesses."[24] Although the historian has learned to make vestiges of all sorts speak, the record for most events, at least before the information age, is full of lacunae. Paul Veyne emphasizes the fragmentary character of documents in comparison to the whole of the lived past and describes history as "mutilated knowledge": "More exactly, we visit what is still visible of that city, the traces of it that remain; history is mutilated knowledge. A historian does not say what the Roman Empire was nor what the Resistance in France in 1944 was, but what it is still possible to know about it."[25] On the same theme, Marrou observes that history can know the past only indirectly and that this indirect knowledge imposes strict limits on what history is able to understand about the past: "We cannot attain the past directly, but only through the traces, intelligible for us, that it has left behind, *to the extent that* these traces have survived, that we have found them, and that we are capable of interpreting them."[26] The historian is reined in by the cruel fact of *partial* documentation, in the two senses of incomplete and biased. He may only narrate what he finds in the historic record and what he is able to extrapolate from the analysis of documents.

Paul Ricoeur examines the signifying properties of documents to which he gives the name of the *trace*. The trace is what remains of a passage and therefore refers to two moments in time. On the one hand, it marks the moment in the past to which the trace bears concrete witness: "a man, an animal passed this way." On the other hand, the trace is, like all signs, perceptible in the here-and-now; it is the mark that is the thing itself. The mark "invites" the historian to follow the trace back to the human activity that deposited it. This following-back is a trajectory that begins with the effect, the trace, and moves toward the identification of the cause. It is at the same time a tracing back that aims at identifying the correct signifying relationship between the passage and its vestige:

> In particular, it is because humans worked, and committed something to stone, or bone, or baked clay tablets, or papyrus, or paper, or recording tape, or a computer's memory, that their works outlive their working. People pass, their works remain. But they remain as things among other things. This "thing-like" character is important for our investigation. It introduces a relationship of cause to effect between the marking thing and the marked thing. So the trace combines a relation of significance, best discerned in the idea of a vestige, and a relation of causality, included in the thing-likedness of the mark. The trace is a sign-effect.[27]

Historical facts are thus produced by the historian through the application of the historical method to the traces left in human archives of all sorts. Once established, facts are presumed to have an objective existence and are not resubjected to critical analysis. They are the hard material of the discipline. "History," Marrou asserts, "is made with documents as the combustion engine functions on gasoline."[28] Historians cannot, he argues, give up the inviolability of facts without endangering the historical enterprise. However, the notion that history is able to separate facts from their ordering in discourse is nonetheless a mechanical one, as Marrou's "engine of history" already suggests.

It is, once again, Paul Veyne who problematizes the notion of the "atomic fact," an autonomous and already fashioned element that pre-exists the moment of discourse. While maintaining that facts have an objective existence, he argues that facts obtain their identity as they emerge from the "itinerary" the historian has chosen across the "event-worthy field." This itinerary is in fact a *plot*, and Veyne insists on the literary term long avoided by historians, who prefer to speak about "reconstruction." For Veyne, the narrative act is at the center of his-toric discourse: facts have meaning only within an ordered narrative sequence; emplotment produces the historical event from the unorga-nized mass of facts.

> Historians relate plots, which are like so many itineraries that they mark out at will through the very objective field of events (which is infinitely divisible and is not made up of eventworthy atoms); no historian describes the whole of this field, for an itin-erary cannot take every road…. In short, the eventworthy field does not comprise spots to be visited and that would be called events; an event is not a being, but an intersection of possible itineraries.[29]

Two historians can compare and evaluate the meaning of facts only if they have chosen to study the same historical question and cut across the field of events in exactly the same manner.

If, as one historian observed, history is a species of the genus story, then one can perhaps locate some of the specificity of historical narra-tive in the nature and form of the material it uses. The historical nar-rator, in contrast to the writer of fiction, must respect what he is able to know about the sequence of events he is recounting. He cannot fill in the lacunae of the historical record with imaginings that are justi-fied only by the fictional notion of verisimilitude. Thus, modern his-torians reject as ahistorical texts that include detailed representation of scenes—description in the novelistic sense—or extensive dialogue before the invention of recording devices. As Veyne argues, history is not mimetic, in the sense given to mimesis by Plato; that is, it is not direct representation in the manner of theater and other spectacles. It is narration, a telling that takes its distance from events and their phenomenological character. Therefore, historical narrative does not attempt to give the reader a sense of the presence of events, which is the vocation of fiction. The historian respects the limits and lacunae the historical record imposes, as he maintains a respectful distance from the narrated world it is his task to construct.

Can We Distinguish History from Fiction on the Basis of the Role of the Imagination?

The word *imagine* refers to the capacity of the human mind to create mental images of phenomena that are not available to perception. It is the psychic work of invention inherent in fantasy, and indeed, in the late Middle Ages imagination referred to an image evoked in dream. To imagine implies an internal process and a retreat from observation of the real. Because of the imagination's illusionary character, it is understandable that historians would hesitate to describe history as a work of the imagination. History is not the recounting of hypothetical worlds, historians often assert, but a recitation of factual developments to which historical analysis has given their proper order. However, philosophers of history have frequently spoken of the historical imagination and underscored the paradoxical importance of imaginary experience to the work of analysis of the real past. Paul Lacombe (1894) already made the categorical assertion: "I must say here a few words about a type of experience which is the only possible in history: imaginary experience."[30]

It is, of course, literally true that the only possible experience of the past is based on the historian's ability to evoke in his mind and in the mind of his readers tangible representations of those inaccessible worlds. However, Lacombe is referring here to an imaginary experience in history that operates under specific conditions and for specific purposes. The imaginative act consists in the historian placing himself back at the moment of the present of the historical actors he is studying and anticipating the unfolding of events as if they were still open to more than one possible course. He argues against the tendency of historians to consider history as fatalistic—the idea that events could not have happened any other way. In fact, it is the "real instability" of events that incites the historian to examine not only what happened, but also what might have happened. To weigh the influence of a factor on a historical event, the historian imagines its absence and reconstructs what *would have happened* in the resulting hypothetical situation. Raymond Aron proposes exactly this model of analysis for evaluating historical explanation. In his *Introduction to the Philosophy of History*, Aron describes the role of the imagination in counteracting the *"retrospective illusion of fatality"* and in reconstructing the role of causal factors:

Every historian, to explain what did happen, asks himself what might have happened. The theory merely puts into logical form the spontaneous practice of the *man in the street.* . . . If we are seeking the cause of a phenomenon we do not limit ourselves to adding up or bringing together the antecedents. We try our best to *weigh* the peculiar influence of each of them. In order to effect this discrimination we take one antecedent and think of it as having disappeared, or changed, and try to construct or imagine what would have happened under that hypothesis. If we must admit that the phenomenon under study would have been different in the absence of this antecedent (or in case it had been different), we shall conclude that it is *one* of the causes of the phenomenon-effect.[31]

The historian, unlike the writer of fiction, starts from a concrete set of historical circumstances and posits a hypothetical situation: "What if American forces had entered the war in 1939?" Beginning with this change in circumstances, the historian constructs a scenario of events that he imagines but that he subjects to rigorous analysis. He no longer benefits in the same way from the retrospective consciousness of historical narrative because he is "anticipating the future," projecting events toward an ultimate effect he does not know in advance. Philosophers of history are quite right to speak of the imagination because the process they describe is directly related to the conditions of the imaginary: I place myself in a situation that I acknowledge as false in order to produce a story that could never happen because it has already happened otherwise.

In the work of R. G. Collingwood, the historical imagination does not operate only at the level of hypothetical analysis of causality, it governs the whole elaboration of the historical narrative itself. For Collingwood the structure of narrative is the same for fiction and history. Both operate according to the principle of the a priori imagination: what the writer of fiction or history imagines takes on the quality of necessity; the narrator recounts a sequence of events that unfolds according to a compelling logic. The difference between history and fiction lies in the relative freedom or constraint the writer enjoys. The fictional imagination is restrained only by the dictates of verisimilitude. The writer is free to invent characters and events, but he needs to show that the behavior of characters and the sequence of events develop according to an internal logic that the reader accepts as credible. In other words, characters and events are wellmotivated and fit into a system of causality that is the essence of a well-crafted narrative.

The historical imagination, on the other hand, is constrained by its object: because his mission is to "imagine" the past, which really did exist but can no longer be perceived, the historian attempts to *reconstruct* a world that can be made to "live" only through recourse to the vestiges, the facts that have survived it.

While historical narration, like fiction, must produce a coherent logic that the reader perceives as necessary, it operates under other constraints. The narrator is responsible for the veracity of his argument, and his narrative logic must be consistent with the traces of the past. Although Collingwood does not acknowledge the distinction, necessity in works of fiction is not really the same as in works of history. In the first, it is only necessary to convince the reader of the *acceptability* of a sequence of events or a development of character: the writer avoids offending not only the reader's sense of the "possible," judged according to perceived norms of life experience, but also the conventions of fictional genres. While classic fiction gives the impression of a closed discourse, it is only because the writer's choices are no longer apparent, suppressed as it were by the realization of the text. In this sense, narrative sequence in good fiction only appears necessary, whereas in historical explanation narrative sequence makes a claim of necessity based on truth, for which there are no alternatives.

The a priori imagination is also at work as a supplement to perception: we can, as Collingwood says, *imagine* "the underside of this table, the inside of an unopened egg, the back of the moon" as necessarily existing if unavailable to perception: "We cannot but imagine what cannot but be there."[32] Of course, the historian does not apply his imagination to perceived phenomena but works rather on fragmentary materials of historical documentation. The a priori imagination permits the historian to fill in the voids of the record through a reasoning by necessity that is just as valid, Collingwood argues, as the imagination that operates as a supplement to perception. To cite Collingwood's simple example, the historian who knows from the historic record that Caesar was in Rome on one date and in Gaul on a later one is authorized to interpolate in his account the trip Caesar made between the two points. He may not, on the other hand, fill the journey with anecdotal material that he invents out of whole cloth. In history, at least, one cannot speak of what one cannot know. However, it is the task of the historian to deepen his knowledge of history and therefore increase his ability to *imagine* the historical world. Collingwood's theory of history is a theory of presence: the historian becomes so immersed in the past he is studying that the thoughts that underlie the development of events and situations in the past become revivified in his own mind. What the historian is able to recount goes well beyond the initial body of facts, even though these facts serve as the fixed anchors of his discourse, without which he would be cast adrift in the arbitrariness of fiction:

> The historian's picture of his subject, whether that subject be a sequence of events or a past state of things, thus appears as a web of imaginative construction stretched between certain fixed points provided by the statements of his authorities; and if these points are frequent enough and the threads spun from each to the next are constructed with due care, always by the *a priori* imagination and never by merely arbitrary fancy, the whole picture is constantly verified by appeal to these data, and runs little risk of losing touch with the reality which it represents.[33]

Although Collingwood clearly describes the constraints of the historic method, he grants enormous prerogatives to the imagination, which, first of all, allows the historian to imagine himself in the place of the historical actors he is studying and in the concrete circumstances that determine their lives. The historian works therefore on *representations* and not on real objects. Charles Seignobos (1901) already emphasizes the importance of the construction of images, which are the material of all historical analysis:

> In fact, in the social sciences, we operate, not on real objects, but on representations we make of these objects. We don't see the men, the animals, the houses we inventory, we do not see the institutions we describe. We are forced to *imagine* the men, the objects, the acts, the motives we are studying. It is these images that are the practical material of the social sciences; it is images that we analyze.[34]

The historical imagination is based then on images that are not memories of the events themselves, but representations that are made "in the image of our memories."[35] Without the capacity to visualize the succession of events in his imagination and by reference to the stock of remembered images he possesses, the historian would be unable to construct a historical analysis of events.

2

SIGNIFYING HISTORY

What Are Factual Narratives?

It is, I believe, evident that a discussion of fiction and nonfiction in film cannot be separated from the theoretical debates on the question in literature, linguistics, and philosophy, which have their historic roots in antiquity and have developed significantly in the course of the last century. Indeed, the most probing work on nonfiction film in recent years relies on theoretical perspectives that come from outside film studies. Even if nonfiction in film manifests itself in specific ways, particularly because film is an audiovisual, not a literary, discourse, the larger theoretical issues are the same. A review of the critical literature is particularly relevant to examining the nonfictional character of the historical film because historians and film historians have long hesitated to give it that status. Moreover, we are, I believe, at a critical juncture: the beginning of a reexamination of traditional notions of genre that have long held back the serious study of works of nonfiction. I begin the discussion with literary theorist Gérard Genette, who has been instrumental in stirring up debate on the question.

In 1991, Genette's *Fiction et diction* launched an appeal for the study of nonfictional genres so long neglected by literary theory. In this work, Genette makes the case that the discipline of narratology has been able to ignore factual narratives by restricting its field of investigation to the "literary," that is, the fictional genres, whether theatrical or novelistic. In so doing, it has effectively excluded from analysis the rich domain of nonfictional genres, on the basis of a difference of function. Nonfictional works are pragmatic, rather than aesthetic; they act on the reader/spectator with the intent to modify in some way his relationship to the world. The distinction goes back to Aristotle, who established the boundaries of the literary by his notions of *légein* and *poèsis*. As Genette argues, "Everything takes place therefore as if Aristotle had established a divide between two functions of language: its ordinary function (*légein*) to inform, interrogate, persuade, order, promise, etc., and its artistic function, which is to produce works (*poiein*). The first belongs to rhetoric—today we would say, rather, pragmatics—the second to poetics."[1] Moreover, *poèsis*, which designates *production of works,* is tied to the creative act of *mimèsis*, that is, the "*simulation* of imaginary actions and events."[2]

Literature is therefore defined by the creative act that separates the world of fiction from the world of practical experience; it is identified with the imaginative and the fictitious. The literary marks out its territory—the epic (or novelistic) and dramatic genres—and sets itself off from the whole field of pragmatic discourses. As Genette puts it, "To enter fiction is to leave the ordinary field of the exercise of language, marked by the concerns of truth or persuasion that command the rules of communication and the deontology of discourse."[3] Käte Hamburger, the most persuasive of the neo-Aristotelians, argues that the exclusion of factual discourses from the sphere of the literary can be justified on the basis of semiological differences between fictional and factual narratives. Factual discourses make use of a specific system of enunciation. They set in place a communicative relationship between the discursive partners: the "real" enunciating subject, the author of the text, speaks directly to the reader. The mimetic genres, by contrast, eschew the pragmatics of ordinary language and make use of "language as a material and instrument, like the painter with colors and the sculptor with stone."[4]

Thus, the bias of the Aristotelian and neo-Aristotelian classifications dismisses a vast field of literary production: all the works that belong to the class of discourses called nonfiction even if they possess undeniable aesthetic qualities. "Modern" aestheticism, in the domain of art history as in literary theory, tends to polarize works according to the criterion of utility. Roman Jakobson, for example, valorizes the literary object by giving it an aesthetic character in which the *poetic function* eradicates any pragmatic function.[5] The authentically poetic object is removed from the active sphere of the lived experience of the reader and refuses the entire referential dimension of language. Jakobson is very much in agreement with Panofsky, who cites Poussin on modern aesthetics in the visual arts: "La fin de l'art est la délectation."[6]

THEORIES OF FICTION, THEORIES OF NONFICTION

How is literary theory to deal with those vast domains of factual narratives: histories, biographies and autobiographies, travel narratives, ethnographies, and accounts of judicial proceedings, to cite obvious examples? Some theorists have responded by retaining the aesthetic criterion and annexing certain factual texts to the domain of the literary. Genette observes that this *conditionalist aesthetics*, since it is based on the *pleasure of the text* rather than on theoretical distinctions, makes the reader the arbiter of aesthetic value: "I consider as literary any text that produces in me an aesthetic satisfaction."[7] In the conditionalist perspective, poetics embraces the factual narrative on condition that the reader pay attention to the work's formal and stylistic features and turn a deaf ear to its communicative function. As Genette points out, the sense of beauty the reader finds in a factual narrative is related to the historic process of loss and gain between the utility of a factual narrative and its aesthetic value. The passage of time tends to lessen the urgency of a didactic or polemical communication, thus augmenting whatever literary qualities the text may possess: "The fact remains that, over the centuries, we see the field of conditional literariness ceaselessly extending itself because of the apparently constant, or perhaps accelerating, tendency to aesthetic salvaging ... which credits to art a great part of what the action of time takes away from the credits of truth or utility."[8]

But is it legitimate to designate aesthetics as the sole criterion of literariness? Should we allow the subjective assessment of even the most discerning reader to remove from the literary field all works it judges unworthy of consideration? Conditional aesthetics has had the advantage of breaking up the rigid generic categories that theory imposes on literature. But is it possible to substitute aesthetic judgment for properly theoretical distinctions? Genette does not think so, and to support his case he appeals to common sense: "The worst painting, the worst sonata, the worst sonnet remain painting, music, or poetry for the simple reason that they can not be anything else."[9]

To sum up Genette's analysis, the distinctions that have been drawn between legitimate and illegitimate genres have served to exclude factual discourse from the field of literary study: the pragmatic function obviates the aesthetic function. The conditionalist model, while reestablishing the legitimacy of individual nonfictional works, imposes subjective judgment as the sole criterion of art and neglects the significant feature, whether fictionality or poetics, that defines a literary work. In neither case does the factual narrative have the right to literary status by the specific character of its discourse. In reaction against these two exclusionist models, Genette abandons the aesthetic and mimetic criteria and proposes a simple inclusive model of literary genres. On the one hand, he retains two traditional classes of literary practice: fiction and poetry. On the other hand, he adds a third class of literary practice: the nonfictional discourses that he names *diction*. Finally, Genette takes aim at his own discipline, narratology, which has not been wise enough to recognize its failures of vision and has taken up an elitist position on factual narratives:

> Now, obviously, the two branches of narratology have, up till now, dedicated their almost exclusive attention to the behaviors and objects of fictional narrative alone; and it did so, not out of a simple empirical choice that would not prejudice in any way aspects that were momentarily and explicitly neglected, but rather by dint of an implicit privilege that hypostatizes fictional narrative into narrative *par excellence*, or into the model for all narratives.... At the stage we are at now, whatever may be the merits and defects of fictional narratology, it is doubtful that it can spare us from a specific study of factual narratives. It is certain in any case that narratology cannot indefinitely dispense with an investigation of the applicability of its results, and even its methods, to a domain that it has never really explored before annexing it silently, without study or justification.[10]

I think it is reasonable to retain certain aspects of the Aristotelian logic. Fiction and nonfiction can be distinguished by their differing functions. Nonfictional genres can be defined by their pragmatism and fiction by its creation of a space where the concerns of the world of real action are suspended in the interest of another kind of experience. It is less clear that fictional narratives can be differentiated from factual ones on the basis of a notion of mimesis that restricts imitation to the creation of imaginary events. The root of the word *fiction* in the Latin *fingere* suggests that fictional narratives are *shaped*, whereas nonfictional narratives are bound by the truth imperative that prohibits such structuring activity. However, as many contemporary theorists contend, it seems much more likely that the narration of imaginary and of real events have much in common. Indeed, Paul Ricoeur in *Time and Narrative* devotes considerable space to showing that historical narratives operate according to semiological principles similar to those that govern fictional narratives and that their difference, the moment of their "bifurcation," must be situated elsewhere.

It is important, however, not to rush to adopt one position or another. The theoretical debate on how to distinguish fiction from nonfiction has been probing and thought provoking, and the major issues are far from settled. In this chapter, I propose reviewing how literary theory has attempted to explain the difference between fictional and factual narratives, and my discussion focuses on a number of key texts: Käte Hamburger's *The Logic of Literature*; John Searle's "The Logical Status of Fictional Discourse"; Gérard Genette's *Fiction et diction*; Octave Mannoni's *Clefs pour l'imaginaire*; Jean-Marie Schaeffer's *Pourquoi la fiction?*; and Ann Rigney's *The Rhetoric of Historical Representation*.

Käte Hamburger bases her notion of fiction on an analysis of the use of grammatical tenses. The very condition of fiction assumes that the imagined time of fictional events is disconnected from the real time of the author's writing. Although literary critics of a certain persuasion go to great lengths to reestablish links between the lived experience of novelists and the world of their novels, fiction posits, as the condition of its discourse, its autonomy from such relationships. In the *discursive time* of nonfiction, on the other hand, the system of tenses is based on "the present or the present moment of the speaking subject."[11] The past or the future has meaning only in relation to the moment of enunciation, and for these tenses to belong to the order of the real, they must be emitted by a real subject, a speaker who assumes responsibility for the words he speaks.

Hamburger calls this subject the *I-Origo*, which she conceives as the originating point occupied by an *I* in the here-and-now of discourse. The *I-Origo* is less marked in historical narration since the historian is intent on recounting the past rather than present circumstances. However, the historian still takes up a position in time from which the past is constituted: "The possibility of the question as to the When of an occurrence proves the reality of the occurrence, and the question itself proves the presence of an *I-Origo*, be this implicit or explicit."[12] By the same logic, in a fictional narrative the preterit loses "its grammatical function of designating what has passed" because the narrator is not an *I-Origo*—is not the real author—and therefore the past has no discursive frame of reference. The narrator becomes, rather, an imaginary agent that is the product of the logic of fiction: "What is narrated is referred not to a real *I-Origo*, but to fictive I-Origines and is therefore fictive itself."[13]

Moreover, in a fictional text, dates or past tenses do not refer to actual moments in their pastness but to the plane of the "present" of narration that stands outside any real reference in time: "We can no longer pose the question as to When, not even when perchance a date is named, for instance: summer, 1890. With or without any date's being given, I learn from this, as a sentence occurring in a novel, not that Mr. X *was* on a trip, but that he *is* on a trip."[14] The reader does not acknowledge the preterit as a sign of pastness; it becomes something like the canvas that the observer ignores in studying the painting. The power of fiction consists in its ability to recount events that can be imagined as presently occurring. As Hamburger points out, fictive statements lose the validity of "logico-grammatical laws." Deictic or indexical signs (this/that, I/you, today/tomorrow) do not refer to the originating subject and the context of discourse but to the closed world of the fiction's diegesis. Adverbs of time, for example, can take on a paradoxical character in fictional texts, that is, seem to be in conflict with the pastness expressed by the tense of a verb: "*Today* he avoided the streets he had frequented only *yesterday*."

The distinctions Hamburger draws between fictional and pragmatic discourses are not all based on the relationship between the tenses and the enunciative act but also concern the position the narrator adopts in relation to the characters. In narrative, Hamburger argues, there are two kinds of action, which she distinguishes as "verbs of external action" and "verbs of internal action." Verbs of external action designate behavior that can be observed and are thus limited to the words, actions, and appearance of characters. Literary theory refers to this position of narration as external focalization. Behaviorist observation of character can be a feature of both fictional and factual narratives: the narrator's position obeys the same constraints of perspective whether the observations he makes are real or imagined. Verbs of internal action emanate from the consciousness of the individual character and represent mental and emotional states, the development of thought or intentions, or the internal activation of memory or fantasy. These verbs of inner action provide the reader with signs of a character's subjectivity through the power the narrator conventionally exercises in penetrating into the workings of another mind. The subject of verbs of inner action is in the third person: he or she thought, felt, imagined, or remembered.

Hamburger makes of this access to the character's inner world a defining feature of novelistic fiction: "Epic fiction [the novel] is the sole epistemological instance where the I-Originarity (or subjectivity) of a third person qua third person can be portrayed."[15] For Hamburger, "reality statements" are subject to the constraint of direct observation by the speaking subject (as opposed to the feigned observation of the fictional narrator). The historical character may be the subject of the narrative's action, but as readers we are not privy to his inner states of mind: he cannot be "portrayed in the subjectivity, in the I-Originarity of his inner, mental processes, of his 'existence.'"[16] Memory, for example, is an internal psychological process that binds together past and present experience: "For in personal memory vivid mental representation falls together with the feeling of the Then, of the Before, and when this image is reproduced from memory it in turn coincides with the temporal Now of the act of remembering and re-living."[17] Such subjective processes belong to the domain of fictional narrative alone since the historical observer has no access to the living mind of the character. Autobiography is the only nonfictional genre that authorizes the use of verbs of inner action since the narrator is the protagonist of his own story: only autobiographical texts—one could add all discourses that focus on the subjectivity of the speaking subject, including those of historical witnesses—can legitimately evoke nonobservable phenomena while remaining in the sphere of reality statements.

Another defining feature of fiction is that it creates an illusion of real existence, which Hamburger sees as the essence of Aristotle's mimèsis. The novel and theater are able to produce a semblance of life because the author of a fiction is freed from the constraints of the reality statement, based on documented observation, and empowered to represent life in all its perceptual detail. Such a semblance cannot be produced in historical narrative because what is past is, by definition, what can no longer be perceived. The historian does not narrate as if he could "see" the perceptual field of events; rather, he deciphers clues and interprets evidence. Any attempt to render actions as if they were present to the reader belongs to fiction. Thus, all detailed description of daily life and situations attached to presumably historical figures is fictional. Likewise, dialogues presented *in extenso* and the fluctuation between inner and outer speech of characters belong to fiction. Once the reader accepts the conceit of the invented character, every aspect of narrative is overtaken by fiction. In Hamburger's radical view, the fictional frame contaminates everything. Dated and verifiable historical information becomes part of the "play" of fiction in which reality statements are feigned like everything else. The laws of fiction "are so powerful that they can never be suspended or rendered ineffective 'in earnest,' but only 'in play,' and this means not at all. Non-reality, once it is constituted through the fictive persons, cannot admit reality into any area within its realm. That is, non-reality cannot assimilate a real I-Origo and thereby become its genuine field of experience."[18]

Hamburger's analysis is exceptionally rigorous, resolutely establishing lines of demarcation between fictional and factual narratives. The question remains: are these lines as absolute as Hamburger maintains? As we will see, other theorists are not so convinced.

John Searle examines the difference between discourses of fiction and nonfiction from another perspective. His approach consists in asking, what is the nature of the speech act that writers engage in when they make statements that are clearly intended to be understood as imaginary? How are these assertions different from those that are intended to have a direct impact on the reader's real experience?

Searle begins with the observation that fictional assertions resemble assertions in the world of ordinary language, that is, in the pragmatic situations of discourse. There is no way to distinguish on a semantic basis, for example, the statements a journalist makes in reporting events and situations from quite similar statements that occur in a piece of naturalistic fiction. Both include direct observations of the social world and descriptions of a recognizable physical environment. The difference lies, Searle argues, in the nature of the speech act involved in the two cases. In nonfiction, the author performs an *illocutionary act*: he is serious about the statements he makes and therefore commits himself to a serious relationship with the reader. Searle contends, in much the same vein as Hamburger, that real discourse is subject to the rules of pragmatics, which govern the use of language for the purpose of acting on one's interlocutor. To persuade his reader, the author "commits himself to the truth of the expressed proposition" and avers his ability to justify it through reasoned argument or evidence. Fictional statements, on the other hand, lack precisely this commitment to the truth of a statement and to the world of the reader. When a novelist asserts the existence of a character or represents a character's action, he does not vouch for the "reality" of the character or action, even if the character or action is based on a model known to the novelist through real experience. Fictional statements, Searle argues, are "pretended" assertions; they mimic the form of the assertion without meeting its conditions—the commitment to "truth" that the speaker assumes in addressing his interlocutor.

Pretense in fiction is not, however, "a form of deception"[19]; pretended assertions in fiction are not lies. Novelists do not attempt to fool the reader into taking the imaginary for the real. Rather, fiction offers what Searle calls a "nondeceptive pseudoperformance" that gives the reader representations clearly marked by the hypothetical act: the *as if* that suspends "the normal operation of rules relating illocution-ary acts and the world."[20] Searle invites us to conceive of rules of dis-course as "rules correlating words (or sentences) to the world. Think of them as vertical rules that establish connections between language and reality. Now what makes fiction possible, I suggest, is a set of extralin-guistic, nonsemantic conventions that break the connection between words and the world established by the rules mentioned earlier."[21] It is as if the author "goes through the motions" of making assertions while all the time knowing they are not true. He pretends to refer to a world that does not preexist his discourse but is the product of it.

By situating the defining moment of fiction in the nature of the speech act—outside questions of textual content or form—Searle avoids some of the pitfalls of Hamburger's position. He is able to acknowl-edge, for example, that there are factual representations that aim to restitute events in their full perceptual detail. Documentary film, for example, derives its power from the specificity with which it renders observed reality. Many journalistic stories are accounts of real situa-tions and events in their physical, social, and psychological detail. In literature, there are increasing numbers of factual narratives—on the model of Truman Capote's *In Cold Blood* or Norman Mailer's *Hang-man's Song*—that attempt to uncover the subjective side of factual events. Indeed, many contemporary theorists argue that history is not the simple narration of events but the discovery of intentions—the sub-jectivity without which historians cannot explain why social groups or individuals take the actions they do on the scene of history. For Searle, the basis of fiction is the contractual relationship between writer and reader, filmmaker and spectator, that sets the represented world apart from the world of experience.

Gérard Genette agrees with Searle that fiction and nonfiction can be distinguished on the basis of the author's relationship to his reader-ship, but his argument develops around the three narrative "actors": the author, the narrator, and the character. In fiction, the author is not the narrator (even if he presents himself as such), nor is he the character (even if he presents himself as such). In homodiegetic fiction, the author is not the narrator, but the narrator is one of the characters. In heterodi-egetic fiction, the author is not the narrator, and the narrator is not one of the characters. In factual narratives, on the other hand, the author and the narrator are one and the same. In autobiography, for example, Genette proposes the formula $A = N = C$, in which all three entities are assumed to be the same person who authors, narrates, and acts.

The formulation that Genette proposes for historical narration is the following: the author is the narrator, but the author/narrator is not the character (A = N ≠ C). The key to the distinction between fictional and factual discourses lies in Searle's notion of the responsibility or irresponsibility of the author in relation to his text. If the author is not the narrator, he takes his distance from his discourse and is not answerable for its truthfulness or seriousness. If the author is the narrator, he can be held accountable and may be judged in the legal sense (for example, cases of slander) or in the court of his peers (critical review of historical literature). Genette summarizes the relationship between author and narrator in fictional and factual discourses in the following terms:

> It seems to me that their rigorous identity (A = N), to the extent that it can be established, defines factual narrative—the discourse in which, to use Searle's terms, the author assumes full responsibility for the assertions of his narrative, and consequently grants no autonomy to any other narrator. Conversely, their dissociation (A doesn't equal N) defines fiction, that is, a type of narrative for which the author doesn't seriously assume responsibility for truthfulness.[22]

Genette argues therefore for the excision of N as a "useful category" in the description of factual discourses.

It is interesting to examine how this understanding of the fictional speech act finds its rather precise echo in the work of psychoanalyst Octave Mannoni in *Clefs pour l'imaginaire ou l'Autre Scène*. For Mannoni, the key to the imaginary—that is, access to the psychological state engendered by imaginary acts—is the splitting of belief that Freud designated as *Verleugnung*. Disavowal in the Freudian sense is not denial—the refusal to acknowledge real situations. It consists, rather, in a division of the ego into two separate and contradictory agents: one part of the ego retains its relationship with the real, while the other allows itself to indulge in imaginary representations. The statement of disavowal that Mannoni offers is one he heard repeatedly in his analytic practice: "Je sais bien, mais quand même" ("Of course I know, but all the same"). In his classic example, Mannoni attributes the "belief" of the young Hopi in the "reality" of the kachina to the desire to experience ritual as an illusion. *I know very well* that the kachina are my uncles and kinsmen, but *all the same* what emotions I feel in pretending they are not. The real aspect of the ego (*I know* ...) protects the imaginary aspect, which *all the same* takes its pleasure.[23]

In a brilliant essay on theatrical illusion, Mannoni analyzes the way in which the spectator's belief in theatrical representations is constructed by means of specific institutional defenses. Entering the theater (or the cinema or picking up a piece of fiction) is the equivalent of entering into a contractual situation. The spectator/reader is always aware that what he will experience is imaginary, that the theatrical sets, the actors, the dialogue are not real but "pretended": they only resemble real places, real agents of action, real interlocutory exchanges: "As long as the scene presents itself as a place other than what it really is, as long as the actor presents himself as someone else, a perspective of the imaginary will be created."[24] The disabused spectator engages in an act of collusion with the apparatus of spectacle that presupposes that he is well versed in the conventions without which spectacle could not exist. He identifies with the *magister ludi* of the theatrical game, the "great image maker" in film, the author in fiction, who set down the conditions and orchestrate the unfolding of the imaginary world. He embodies the ego's defense against the eruption of the imaginary into life. Meanwhile, the liberated half of the ego enjoys the pleasures of identification with characters and actions:

> When the curtain rises, it is the imaginary powers of the Ego that are at once liberated and organized—dominated—by the spectacle. It's hard to know how to put it, because metaphorically the word *scene* has become the term that designates the psychic location where the images exhibit themselves. One can say that the theatrical scene becomes the extension of the Ego with all its possibilities.[25]

Although Mannoni does not speak about nonfictional narratives, it is clear that the contractual situation that sets up the conditions of fictional "pretense" does not operate in nonfiction. Rather, the reader/spectator is given to understand that the persons and actions represented in discourse belong to the shared world of author and reader. I have argued elsewhere that in documentary film the contract of spectacle is nullified. The spectator is not protected against the incursion of the "real" into the situation of spectacle, and that he therefore adopts a "vigilant" stance in relation to the film.[26]

In *Pourquoi la fiction?* Jean-Marie Schaeffer also argues that the distinction between fiction and nonfiction is essentially pragmatic. It is not enough for the author to intend a work as fictional or factual; the reader/spectator must recognize the intention. The identifying signs of the fictional or the factual can be quite weak in the text itself: as Searle suggests, there is no narrative focalization or authorial style that distinguishes the factual from the fictional. The reader, whom Schaeffer characterizes as inclined to credulity, depends on markers that

Schaeffer calls *paratextual*. The simplest form of the paratextual mark of fictionality is the notation "a novel" that often follows the title of the work or the prenarrative titles of a film that acknowledge actors, set designers, and so forth. However, many subtler markers exist, for example, the place of a given text within the output of a noted novelist, historian, or filmmaker.

Schaeffer is particularly concerned with *cas-limites*, extreme cases of works in which the reader or spectator might confuse the imagined and the real. His position does not take account of markers that are in fact properly textual, in particular the conventions of genre that immediately assign a gothic romance (often nearly parodied by the image on the book's cover) or a science fiction film to the realm of fiction. It is indeed difficult to conceive of a work of serious nonfiction that would seem to adopt the conventions of genre that belong to popular fiction or film. That said, Schaeffer is quite correct in asserting, following Searle, that the attitude the reader adopts in relation to a work is based in the intersubjective agreement by means of which the writer makes his intention known and the reader acknowledges it. In fiction, Searle observes, the contract is negotiated through *shared dissimulation*: the writer and the reader agree to engage in representing a world as if it were real when they know it is not.

Schaeffer develops Searle's argument by contesting what he terms the semantic position. This position holds that the essential difference between fiction and nonfiction is a question of their reference or lack of reference to the real world: a factual discourse can be verified and is therefore referential; fictional representations are not open to verification and are therefore not referential. According to this position, fiction, in contrast to nonfiction, is characterized by propositions that only pretend to refer to an existing world, and because actors, objects, descriptions, and actions in fiction are only imagined, their denotation is illusory and vacant. Schaeffer disputes the centrality of the question of verifiability. He argues that the distinguishing feature of statements of fact (propositions we are asked to believe, *whether true or false*) is that they are based on the reality principle, lay claim to truth, and solicit action or reaction in pragmatic terms, whereas fictions are imaginative constructs that escape from the reality principle and therefore exist outside questions of truth and falsehood. Playful dissimulation relies on disengaging representation from cognitive and practical interaction with the world. Fictional representations do not call on us to act.

This does not mean, Schaeffer continues, that pragmatic and imaginative discourses have different modes of representation. On the contrary, he argues that both fiction and nonfiction use the same general "posture of representation": "All representation possesses a structure of reference in the logical meaning of the term, that is, it is 'about something,' it 'bears on something.'"[27] The nature of representation does not change according to whether the world it models is real or imaginary. Fiction, like nonfiction, has the same classes of referents: the environmental context, the action of characters, and their physical and mental states. Although fiction refers to situations, characters, and objects that do not have their counterparts in a specific, lived reality, these imagined elements cannot be represented as nonexistent because representation always posits representational content. Indeed, the very existence of fictional texts that imitate nonfictional genres demonstrates the extent to which it is impossible to establish distinct boundaries. Hildesheimer's *Marbot, Eine Biographie*, which Schaeffer analyzes at length—a "false" biography in which the paratextual markers of fiction are hidden in order to exploit the reader's credulity—or the "false" documentary film that withholds paratextual markers of fictionality until the final credits, are certainly extreme cases, but they do make the point that fiction and nonfiction cannot always be distinguished in terms of their representations.

We must therefore abandon the notion, concludes Schaeffer, that there are "two modalities of representation, one fictional, the other referential. There is only one: the referential mode."[28] Indeed, the internal organization of discourse varies relatively little according to whether what is represented is real or imagined; it varies dramatically according to the "vehicle of representation" the discourse puts in service: oral or written language, audiovisual "languages," and so on. Moreover, Schaeffer rejects Hamburger's basic notion that the novel is the only literary form that is authorized to give an account of the internal life of a character in the third person: "Factual narratives also have always put into use elements of internal focalization, and for the very general reason that, as soon as we interpret the behavior of an entity in an anthropomorphic perspective, we cannot but attribute to him mental states, and therefore 'see' him from the inside."[29]

The great strength of *Pourquoi la fiction?* is that it reexamines fiction (and by implication, nonfiction) in the light of theoretical work in several disciplines, notably philosophy, linguistics, biology, sociology, narratology, and aesthetics, and draws on a broad range of works from European and American perspectives. Through a process of analysis and evaluation, Schaeffer clears his way through the thorny controversies that have made the idea of mimesis problematic in the theoretical literature, with the clear intention of defending imitation as a central notion in narrative theory. It is useful to the study of historical narratives to retain Schaeffer's definitions. The type of imitation that concerns us is *mimesis as representation*, which Schaeffer defines as the "production of a mental or symbolic model based on an isomorphic relation to the reality to be known, therefore by virtue of a resemblance (direct or indirect) between the two."[30] With written or filmed narratives, we are dealing with symbolic models, as opposed to private mental representations such as fantasy or dream. These are representations in the public sphere, "publicly accessible, invented by man as means of representation."[31] Schaeffer refers here to the "semiotic apparatuses"—linguistic or audiovisual representations that can be shared by social groups, in our case written and cinematic narratives.

All forms of mimesis rely on resemblance: the representation imitates the thing to which it refers. However, the similarity is always relative because it is the result of "selective attention." In the act of representation, we "privilege" specific properties of the thing we are representing. This process of discrimination—including specific aspects while excluding others—is basic to human cognitive processes that structure the world in terms of similarities and differences. Moreover, Schaeffer insists on the active character of mimesis: representation constructs resemblances that "didn't exist in the world before the mimetic act and whose existence is caused by this act."[32] He calls each element of similarity a *mimème*. Each *mimème* is a cognitive tool that provides knowledge of the thing we are imitating; it constructs a model of the thing:

> Imitation is never a (passive) reflection of the imitated thing, but the construction of a model of this thing, a model based on a selective grid of similarities between the imitation and what it imitates.... We discover here ... a new example of the fact that the relationship between representation and reality is interactive: although the *mimème* is constrained by the properties of what is being imitated, it is only through its construction that we discover the properties of the object that constrain it.[33]

We find in Schaeffer one explanation for the tendency in the social sciences to shy away from associating the work of the historian with representation. Mimesis, Schaeffer argues, is a means to acquire knowledge, but philosophical rationalism has never legitimized it. Apprenticeship, for example, is relegated to the sphere of simple skill acquisition largely because it does not depend on rational thought. And yet the greater part of human learning depends on the social process of imitation, often divorced from rational examination. Imitation requires the learner to internalize knowledge through immersion, en bloc, without subjecting it to critical analysis. Indeed, the historian's work doubtless convinces the reader as much by the strength of its narrative coherence as by the signs of erudition or critical method. Immersion requires us to perform the act of mimetic modeling, and "it does this by leading us to adopt (to a certain point) the attitude (the mental, representational, perceptive or actantial disposition) that would be ours if we were really in the situation for which the *mimèmes* construct the semblance."[34] There are without doubt degrees of difference between immersion in a fictional, as opposed to a historical, model, and doubtless the differences have to do with the maintenance of a certain critical distance. However, Schaeffer tells us, the basic process of representation is the same. The author and the reader (or the filmmaker and the spectator) together construct a discursive world that is meaningful to the extent that it emulates the coherence of the world and allows them to immerse themselves in it.

What distinguishes fictional and nonfictional models is, Schaeffer argues, nonfiction's cognitive constraints. In historical narrative, for example, the mimetic-homological model, which Schaeffer ascribes to nonfiction, obeys the law of historical fact: "It must maintain local structural equivalencies." In other words, the elements of narrative representation—*mimèmes*—are bound in a relationship with the facts-in-the-world, a relation we would call motivated. When *mimèmes* construct a correspondence between discourse and the world, they do so within the constraints of the real, in the case of history, the constraint of what has really taken place. Fiction also offers mimetic models—an imitation of the world—but they are not bound by structural homology. Rather, fiction establishes a relationship of *analogy* with the world of lived experience, a relationship that is weaker and not defined by direct structural correspondence. In Schaeffer's words, "A fictional modeling is de facto always a modeling of the real world. Indeed, our representational competencies are those of the representation of the reality we are a part of, because they have been selected by this reality itself in a process of permanent interaction."[35] If nonfiction is bound by its truth function, fiction obeys the principle of its own internal coherence.

Schaeffer's analysis is crucial to understanding the work of representation that lies at the base of all narrative. He asserts the primacy, in chronological terms, of the act of representation. It comes *before* we consider whether a representation is a "truthful" account of events in the world of lived experience. Therefore, it is not possible, Schaeffer concludes, to posit one mode of representation for factual narratives and another, separate mode for fictional narratives: "Before the question of truth, and, a fortiori, the question of referential truth in the logical meaning of the term, comes into play, representation has already posited the object (to which it refers) *as* represented object. This structure is common to all representations."[36] Thus, the reader/spectator performs the same operations of representation that a text induces in him, whether the text is fictional or nonfictional.

THE PRACTICE OF NONFICTION

The theoretical positions proposed by Hamburger, Searle, Genette, Mannoni, and Schaeffer establish through philosophical argument the boundaries that define different types of discourses or literary genres. However, what happens when we put theory to the test through an examination of actual texts? Do we find that fiction and nonfiction sort themselves out according to the demarcations that theory proposes? Schaeffer's insistence on the textual similarities between works of fiction and nonfiction and the importance of paratextual markers as the primary means of differentiation suggests the potential ambiguity of texts. Searle contends, for his part, that certain fictional genres make "nonfictional commitments"; in naturalistic fiction, for example, the author may indeed represent real places or events that have as much "truth value" as observation in nonfictional genres. There is, Searle argues, a kind of contract between author and reader that creates "understandings about how far the horizontal conventions of fiction break the vertical connections of serious speech."[37]

Genette goes even further in raising doubts about the power of the fictional speech act to cast all utterances in the imaginary mode. As he observes, fictional discourses are not exclusively made up of statements that are confined to the world that fiction creates. The diegetic world is not an autonomous construct with its own internal rules; indeed, the fictional world and the real world are at many moments inextricably linked. A fictional narrator—who, we suspect, is at such moments much closer to the real author—is quite capable of seriously commenting on the extratextual world, even if his remarks serve the interest of the development of the fiction. Genette argues that the novelist can "introduce islets of nonfiction or uncertainty into the text of a fiction."[38]

The "serious" historical novel, I would argue, is a prime example of this admixture of fiction and nonfiction. Stendhal's *The Red and the Black* is dense with sometimes specific, sometimes veiled references to contemporary and historical realities, and many of these real references are not incidental "history effects" but become pivotal to the development of plot. Moreover, annotated editions of the work go to great lengths to clarify or reveal links between the world of fiction and historical and biographical realities. Similarly, a novel like Henry Roth's *From Bondage* creates uncertainty in the reader. Despite the paratextual statement, "This novel is certainly not an autobiography, nor should it be taken as such," the reader is confronted by unsettling parallels between the fictional characters it describes and events it recounts and aspects of the author's own life. Even in less "referential" works of fiction, statements of fact abound; although they belong to the narrated world of fiction, they still retain their verifiability: "It is the same with the countless statements of the historic or geographical type whose insertion in a fictional context and subordination to fictional ends don't necessarily deprive them of their truth value." Genette suggests that the "'discourse of fiction' is in fact a *patchwork*, or a more or less homogenized amalgam of dissimilar elements borrowed for the most part from reality." Indeed, Genette argues, there is never anything that is purely imaginary in fiction: "It is doubtless the same for fiction as discourse as for fiction as an entity, or as an image: the whole is more fictive than any of its parts."[39]

There is, Genette argues, a dearth of systematic analyses of nonfictional texts and a vast inquiry is needed to arrive at an understanding of the *practice* of nonfiction. One of the strengths of Genette's *Fiction et diction* is that it sets out to consider what might be the peculiarities, the specificities of factual texts on the basis of categories of narrative analysis he developed for fictional texts:

> I would like ... to examine the reasons factual and fictional narrative might have to behave differently in relation to the story they "recount," by dint of the fact that this story is in the one case (supposed to be) "truthful," and in the other fictive, that is, invented by the person who presently is telling it, or by some other from whom he inherits it.[40]

Genette places particular emphasis on four narrative categories he previously identified and described in *Narrative Discourse*: the order in which events are recounted; the speed with which events are told; the mode of narration; and the signs of the narrator's voice.

There is no reason to believe, Genette argues, that fiction and nonfiction can be distinguished in terms of narrative *order*. Indeed, nothing constrains the factual narrator to a simple linear chronology of events. Like the fictional narrator, he may make use of *analepses*, flashing back to moments in the past, or *prolepses*, flashing forward to moments in the future, with respect to the present time of the narrative. Indeed, historical narrative often needs to show relationships between different historical moments. It is a principle of method, as we saw, that the historian begins by describing a culminating event or situation and turns back in time to recount the actions and circumstances that led to the result. Or, in the process of describing a developing situation, it is quite common for the historian to flash forward to the situation's outcome, or the historian may move quickly from the intention of a social group or historical figure to the resulting realization or failure of the initiative. It is therefore not surprising that historical narratives move easily between moments in time. Indeed, historical narration makes, I would contend, more frequent use of analepses and prolepses than is characteristic of fiction. To take another example, autobiographical narratives retain all the flexibility of an authorial consciousness that "knows" the relationship between events and can negotiate meaningfully between moments in the past.

The *speed* of narrative can be described as the relationship between the duration of the events the narrator is recounting and the amount of time he takes in narrating them. The narrator gives more time and more detail to moments of greater importance and skips quickly across those he judges peripheral. Genette observes that varying speeds of narration are characteristic of factual as well as fictional narratives and operate for the same reasons. Important events, whether actual or imagined, are treated more slowly and in more detail and are hence more vivid than secondary incidents; they are set in relief by the text. However, is it possible for historical narratives to achieve the kind of vivid richness prevalent in fiction? Genette agrees with Hamburger that finely detailed scenes and extensive dialogue are characteristic of fictional narratives. Not that such scenes are impossible in nonfiction—particularly, one could argue in autobiography. However, in history the critique of method always raises the question, "How do you know?" As we have seen, the historian may only recount what he can know or infer.

The *mode* of a narrative has to do with the distance the narrator takes from the narrative information he is communicating. A narrative may be given in the mode of *telling*, in which the narrator's voice mediates the account of events and therefore takes a relatively more distant stance with respect to the action. In the mode of *showing*, the narrator allows the actors and actions to "speak for themselves," and events are represented in greater detail and duration. The narrator thus allows a more direct relationship between reader and narrative than is characteristic of a telling. The mode of a narrative can also vary according to how it is focalized: internal focalization, when the account is mediated by the subjectivity of a character, and external focalization, when the account is limited to observation of a character's behavior. Genette argues that all signs of internal subjectivity in factual narrative raise again the question, "How do you know?" It is possible to obtain direct introspective information in historical narratives only if the archives provide it in the form of diaries or other personal accounts. Factual narratives can in general be characterized by a narration that is relatively distant and externally focalized. In fiction, "the author *imagines* thoughts [of characters] as he pretends to report them: you only perceive for sure what you *invent*."[41] In principle, the historical narrator's imagination submits to limits: human thought in the internal, psychological sense can only be the result of a cautious analysis of information. In practice, however, the situation seems less pure. If historians avoid lengthy descriptions of the internal thought processes of historical actors—one of the defining features of the historical novel—they quite routinely attribute to individual and collective figures the language of human intentionality and even state of mind.

Voice in a narrative text concerns the narrating agency itself and "the traces it has left—or has presumably left—in the narrative discourse it has presumably produced."[42] The narrator cannot avoid situating the act of narration in time in relation to the events he recounts: he narrates actions that have already happened, that will happen in the future, or that are happening at the moment of the telling, or the narration is intercalated, that is, it shifts between narrative agents, as in the epistolary novel. The narrative voice is also characterized by *level*. The narrator may stand outside the diegetic world he recounts and therefore be termed extradiegetic. A narrator may be intradiegetic in that he inhabits the same diegetic world as the characters and actions he recounts. A secondary narrator may be homodiegetic in the sense that he is a character in the narrative he recounts and refers to himself in the first person, the "I" of Proust's *A la recherche du temps perdu*; or he may be heterodiegetic if he narrates a story in which he is not a character (Scheherazade in relation to the tales she weaves).

As Genette suggests, nothing prevents factual narratives from using the *ulterior narration* (the pastness of all historical accounts), *anterior narration* (all predictive scenarios based on an analysis of facts), *simultaneous narration* (ethnographic notes that detail the unfolding of a ceremony), and *intercalated narration* (as in exchanges of real letters). Factual narrators may also be either heterodiegetic or homodiegetic according to whether they participate or do not participate in the events they are recounting. However, factual narratives do not make "too massive" a use of different narrative levels. As Genette observes, "One has trouble imagining a historian or a writer of memoirs giving over to one of his 'characters' the task of recounting an important part of the narrative."[43]

As Genette observes, it is rare to find examples of the application of literary theory to nonfictional texts. Ann Rigney's *The Rhetoric of Historical Representation* is therefore quite exceptional as it undertakes the comparative analysis of three nineteenth-century histories of the French Revolution: Alphonse de Lamartine's *L'Histoire des Girondins*, Jules Michelet's *L'Histoire de la Révolution française,* and Louis Blanc's work of the same title. Rigney is concerned with the ways in which three historians, using the "same" historical material, write three very different histories of the revolution. What rhetorical procedures, she asks, make possible such radically different interpretations?

Rigney responds in the following terms. The meaning of an event and the intelligible relationship between events are not givens of historical data; rather, it is the act of narration, whether performed by contemporary witnesses or historians analyzing events retrospectively, that produces meaning and links a set of events in causal sequence. Moreover, events that actually took place necessarily undergo a transformation in which the mainly nonverbal reality is mediated by the verbal signs of language: "Events are invested with significance, are constituted as signifiers, in the very act of being referred to and represented in discourse."[44] This discourse is shaped by the narrative codes according to which the historian selects and configures historical actors, actions, and situations. It is useful, I think, to follow in some detail how Rigney applies narratological analysis to historical texts.

The Rhetoric of Historical Representation pre-dates the publication of *Fiction et diction*, but Rigney has already taken up Genette's call for exemplary analyses of works of nonfiction based on what literary theory has established about narrative practice. Indeed, she uses as her tools the categories of narrative that Genette proposes in *Narrative Discourse,* as outlined above. First, is the *order of representation.* Verbal narrative discourse is linear in the sense that it is unable to represent at the same time events occurring simultaneously in different locations, as complex historical events most frequently are. The historian cannot avoid constructing an order of events that is unfaithful to the chronological relationships set forth in documentary sources. By establishing a narrative order, the historian arranges events on the chain of discourse and in so doing imposes a "particular contextual relation" between them.[45] For example, the historian may choose to represent a "secondary" set of events only when they impinge on the narration of the primary set of events. Or, the historian may use a narrative flashback to fill the reader in on what was going on at the same time in another location relevant to the primary set of events. These choices result in structures of meaning. The historian chooses to foreground specific actions while relegating others to the background, focusing the reader's attention on what he takes to be the dominant sequence of actions.

In Rigney's example, Lamartine chooses to make the Tuileries the center of action for the insurrection of August 10, 1792, thus privileging the point of view of the royal family and inviting us to identify with the king and especially the queen, the central image of pathos and courage. This focalization of events contrasts with the version of the "same" events as Michelet recounts them: we are positioned narratively on the side of the Commune and experience the "hopes and fears of those about to engage in combat and the difficulties confronting the newly elected Commune." Only later does Michelet take us to the Tuileries to analyze the king's defenses. The narrator's authority to situate the reader in relation to the action is a powerful technique for producing meaning. The historian centers the action and thus creates a dominant narrative development; he articulates the dominant sequence of actions with other centers of activities, carefully timing the "cuts" between one actorial sphere and another. Differences of narrative focus impose different ideological perspectives.

A second important notion is the *degree of presence*. Relying on Genette's concept of narrative speed, Rigney points out that an event's importance can be judged according to the amount of textual space the historian gives to it in relation to other events in the same account. This is what Menachem Brinker calls the event's "signifying relief." Textual expansion is a technique of foregrounding. In scenic representations, narrative pace is slowed down in order to evoke an action in all its detail. The reader is invited to visualize the scene and to "revivify" it in his imagination. In nineteenth-century historical representation, Rigney shows, "'signification' and 'vividness' work closely together":

> Those instances where unique historical moments are scenically represented—where "the events themselves" appear to speak for themselves or where the reader is made an "eyewitness" to events—may be paradoxically the locus of the heaviest symbolic and rhetorical investment on the part of the historian.[46]

A similar kind of foregrounding can be found in the historian's use of *singulative* as opposed to *iterative* representations. A narrative event made up of similar, repeated actions—the example Rigney gives is the insurgents' slaughter of members of the Swiss Guard attempting to escape from the Tuileries—can be treated in radically different ways. Lamartine represents the event as a series of individual "blow-by-blow" accounts and thus underscores what he sees as the insurgents' blood-thirsty character. Michelet refers to the same events in sylleptic fashion; that is, he condenses the various "repetitions" into a relatively brief passage, a detachment that undercuts any sense of pathos.

Representation en creux is the name Rigney gives to strategies that defuse and neutralize the (unwelcome) significance of events that the historian cannot omit because the historical record or other historians have brought them to prominence. Those who would "rehabilitate" the Revolution, for example, must deal with the Terror by making it retreat into the "hollow" of history. One method for discovering what the relief of a text leaves in shadow is to analyze the text's unfolding, paying attention not to what is included, but to the elements of the historical *fabula* (story material) that have been excluded. Taking her cue from the work of Philippe Hamon, Rigney observes that narrative triage is at the center of the production of meaning: "to signify is to exclude." Very often, she points out, the events the historian foregrounds are "a reflection *a contrario*" of what he wants to cast in shadow. Michelet's emphasis on the fraternal and conciliatory character of the insurgents can be seen as the inverted image of the sometimes gratuitous violence of the insurgents' actions of August 10. Likewise, Lamartine's portrait of the "charismatic" Marie-Antoinette hides the indecision and weakness of Louis XVI.

The theoretical texts I have surveyed here address the problem of distinguishing fictional and nonfictional literary texts. Most rely on the fundamental distinction between the poetic or imaginative role of fiction and the pragmatic role of nonfiction. Hamburger's notion that "reality statements" are predicated on an identifiable speaking subject is universal in its application and therefore historical narration in film must, in ways that are specific to that medium, acknowledge the existence of this pragmatic entity. Real pastness can be established only in relation to the real presence of the discursive voice. Searle's work on speech acts—the relationship between word and world—confirms Hamburger's view. Genette formulates this relationship in terms of the equation: the author = the narrator, which eliminates the buffer between author and text and therefore between the author and his public. Mannoni conceptualizes the conditions of spectacle—and of fiction—on the basis of a contract that organizes the pleasure of the spectator by suspending the conditions of the real. Hamburger's assertion that the representation of the subjectivity of characters *from the inside* belongs to fiction alone is certainly far from absolute; as Schaeffer argues, any analysis of historical action is an attempt to understand the intellectual and emotional constitution and attitudes of the actors.

As we saw in Chapter One, historical narratives often speak of intentions, reactions, states of mind, and other features of mental activity. However, several theorists raise the question of semblance: to what extent are historical narratives authorized to give to their texts an impression of reality, replete with scenic tableaus and dialogue *in extenso*? Genette's work in *Fiction et diction* has the immense value of establishing that fictional and nonfictional texts do not call on different categories of narration. In Schaeffer's formulation, fictional and factual discourses have the same "posture of representation"; both are representations of the world of experience, and both engage therefore in mimetic activity. The difference between the factual and the fictional, Schaeffer argues, is that fiction is free of constraints other than its own internal coherence, whereas history is bound to produce a representation of events that is homological with events as they actually occurred in the historical past; the historian can only recount what it is possible to know about past occurrences.

However, as Genette and Rigney demonstrate, historians can and do play with the order of narrative. They take advantage of the relative speed of narration as an essential tool of emphasis, and they render certain events in relative richness of detail while relegating others to the shadows. Similarly, historical narration is characterized by a specific placement of narrative voice: the historian/narrator is always an extradiegetic narrator, by definition placed by time on the outside of the events he relates. Historical narration is also by definition ulterior: historical events exist as pastness in relation to the present of narration. Rigney gives us an exemplary analysis of great historical texts and elucidates the ways in which strategies of narration create meaning. Her comparative reading of several texts shows how the rhetoric of history consists in adopting a narrational perspective that distinguishes between primary and secondary narrative actions, what belongs to the foreground or background of historical events.

SIGNIFYING HISTORY IN FILM

This section addresses the question of how two very different signifying systems—written discourse and audiovisual discourse—approach the representation of history.

I have argued that literary theory has been crucial in understanding the nature of nonfictional narratives and provides useful tools for analyzing the historical film. However, to state the obvious, literary theory emerges from the study of written texts, and its application to filmic narratives must take account of the differences between the exclusively verbal nature of written narratives and the audiovisual nature of film. We are now raising the crucial question of the *vehicle* that conveys narrative and discursive information. How do the different mediums of expression—the written language of the historian, the audiovisual language of the filmmaker—shape the representation of historical events? Is written language the only legitimate vehicle for historical narration? Does cinema fail in its attempts at representing history because it is an inappropriate medium for such discourse? Or does the cinematic signifier impose differences of expression that can nonetheless produce legitimate forms of historical discourse?

In his well-known article, "Historiography and Historiophoty," Hayden White calls on historians to revise their approach to visual material. He observes that, in the age of photography and cinematography, sources of historical evidence are as often visual (or audiovisual) as they are verbal. Enclosed in a discipline of words, history has failed to recognize the specificity of the visual media and has attempted to master the image by reducing it to the status of illustration, a simple complement to written discourse. The use of visual evidence, White argues, requires historians to revise their methods of analysis and learn the "lexicon, grammar, and syntax" appropriate to visual media. Moreover, the image is not just another source of historical information; it can constitute "a discourse in its own right," with modes of representation that are fundamentally different from those of written language. White suggests that visual representations of history have their own genius, particularly in the realms of "landscape, scene, atmosphere, complex events such as wars, battles, crowds, and emotions." Such representations are not only more verisimilar, he contends, but also more accurate.

Other historians and film historians point to the disturbing impact film has on what historiography has traditionally conceived as legitimate modes of reference to the past. Robert Rosenstone speaks of film's "new ways of thinking about our past," which historians may find "unsettling because they escape the confines of words and provide elements—visual, aural, emotional, subconscious—that we don't know how to admit into our knowledge."[47] Marcia Landy describes the sense of history communicated through film as "fictive and eclectic," qualities that historians are bound to find disconcerting: "To acknowledge its fictiveness and its affectivity is to invoke a sense of history as construct, further, to extend the ways in which it functions in more heterogeneous ways than is often acknowledged in the question for an objective measure of the 'truth' of the events enacted."[48] In his article "Hitler: A Film from Germany," historian Rudy Koshar reflects on Syberberg's film as an example of how "cinema can array jarring, immediate, specific and compelling narratives." In spite of its apparently ahistorical perspective and antinarrative structure, Koshar suggests the film "moves us closer to the 'structure of feeling' that nurtured Nazism, gave it its popular resonance, and ensured its mass support."[49]

How can we begin to discuss the difference between filmic and written representations of history that seems to unnerve some historians and call for a radical rethinking of the discourse of history? As a first step in the inquiry that preoccupies the following chapters, I propose turning to the question of film language and to the semiology of cinema, which has closely studied the specific characteristics and capacities of the film medium.

As the work of Christian Metz has shown, the semantic power of the cinema is unlimited: there is no area of human experience about which film cannot speak. Indeed, the filmic signifier is unusually rich as it brings into play five matters of expression, to use Louis Hjelmslev's formulation. Film is made up of photographic images in movement that imitate observable phenomena in the world—an indexical system of signs that is often designated as the essential feature of film as discourse. But the cinematic image can also incorporate written language, in the form of intertitles (utterances that belong to the plane of narration and by means of which the narrator intervenes directly in the telling) and filmed written texts—letters, proclamations, newspaper headlines, scrolling texts on a computer screen, and the like— that belong to the plane of the narrated, to the diegetic world of the characters. The visual and graphic systems are complemented by the soundtrack, which accounts for three of the matters of expression: spoken language, which can take the form of the narrational voice-over or dialogue between characters; the noise track, which is a major source of information about the diegetic environment the film constructs; and the music track, which has great connotative power, both in the musical score (coming from the narrational plane) and in the diegetic music that emanates from the world of the characters. Moreover, the relationship between the visual and the auditory increases the complexity of cinematic discourses and their powers of representation. The relationship between sound and image plays on differences. The elements of speech, noise, and music may or may not be synchronous with the image, they may belong to the world of the diegesis or not, and they may come from different levels of narration. This extraordinary diversity of the filmic signifier makes it a rich instrument of communication, and because film includes verbal discourse, both written and oral, cinema is capable of using all the semantic resources of language.

In *Récit écrit, récit filmique*, Francis Vanoye offers a table of the differences between written and filmic narrative based on the distinctions formulated by Hjelmslev.[50] This table is helpful in rethinking what the specificity of signifying systems has to do with the character of a narrative discourse: in particular, the way the *how* of the signifier affects the *what* of the signified.

Categories	Written narrative	Filmic narrative
Substance of expression (or of the signifier)	Graphic traces blank spaces	Moving image, noise, musical sound, phonetic sound, graphic traces
Form of expression (or of the signifier)	Sentences, paragraphs, chapters, distribution of surfaces	Editing of images; counterpoints of image/ sound, image/music, image/speech; layout of forms and colors according to relationships of opposition or complementarity, play on the scale shots
Substance of content (or of the signified)	Real or imaginary events, emotions, ideas, drawn from the historical, legendary, mythic, social, human, and other substrata [common to written and filmic narrative]	
Form of content (or of the signified)	Structure of narration, emotions, ideas, themes [common to written and filmic narrative]	

Vanoye's table nicely juxtaposes the features of written and filmic systems of signs. First, we notice that written and filmic narratives are distinguished primarily by the substance of expression—the different tangible materials that serve as the base of the two systems. The signifier in written language is homogeneous—graphic traces that stand out from the white background of the page; the signifier in film is heterogeneous—that is, it makes use of several materials. If we tend to accept the moving photographic image as the defining feature of the system, we have to acknowledge the signifying functions of the soundtrack and the inclusion of the graphic traces of written language. In the case of written language, the graphic traces, as linguists have established, stand in an *unmotivated* relationship to the signifieds they support; the letters—and the voiced phonemes they represent—have no necessary relationship to the representations they evoke in the mind. As philosopher C. S. Peirce would have it, verbal language is of the order of the symbol, operates according to laws of interpretation, and is therefore, in Saussure's sense, linguistically arbitrary. André Martinet makes a similar distinction in talking about the double articulation of language: the choice of units of meaning (from a paradigm like *before, during, after*) operates at a level that is separate from the second articulation in which the user/speaker chooses distinctive units from the paradigm of phonemes (the choice of consonants distinguishes the phonemic sequence of *die* from *pie*).

When we consider the filmic signifier par excellence—the photographic image in movement—we have to agree with Christian Metz's careful semiological analysis. The filmic image has nothing that corresponds to the double articulation of language:

> There is nothing in the cinema that corresponds, even metaphorically, to the second articulation. This articulation is operative on the level of the signifier, but not on that of the significate [signified]: Phonemes and *a fortiori* "features" are distinctive units without proper signification. Their existence alone implies a great *distance* between "content" and "expression." In the cinema the distance is too short. The signifier is an image, the significate [signified] is what the image represents.[51]

In film, the relationship between signifier and signified (between the signifying material of patterns of light and dark, color, etc., and the representations they make) is *motivated*. The filmic image is an indexical system, to use Pierce's notion: there is a phenomenological relationship between the sign and the denoted object. The patterns of light and shadow that form the image of a horse are produced through the direct "contact" between the recording medium and the object. The filmic image, to use André Bazin's metaphor, signifies a bit in the manner of the skin the serpent sloughs off: it is no longer part of being but retains something of its living features.[52] Thus, in the production of the image, there is no process of symbolization, none of the arbitrary character of linguistic signs, and therefore very little of the kind of mediation that results from double articulation. The filmic image establishes a quite different set of relationships between the three aspects of the sign: the signifier (the matter), the signified (the mental representation), and the referent (the denoted object conceived as part of the real). The process of signification in film appears to conflate the signified and the referent. The spectator receives the image "from outside" and not through an internal mental operation in which the word evokes an image in the mind. Signification is then a process of recognition in which the spectator "reads" the distinctive visual traits of "objects" produced by the film in the richness of their phenomenological detail. Reading the signs of the manufactured image is then analogous to reading the visual landscape in life, and the spectator is unable to completely detach the image/index he is reading from the phenomenal reality it represents. Film's strong sense of presence is due not only to this richness of its signifier, but also to the spectator's impression that he is gaining access to a world of reference without the alienating mediation of language: the film does not signify "horse" but gives us "this horse" in all the concrete detail of its existence.

If we return to Vanoye's table, we notice that, on the level of the substance and form of the content, there is no difference indicated between written and filmic narratives. Both represent "real or imaginary events, emotions, ideas taken from the substratum of history, legend, etc." Both produce "structures of narration, feelings, ideas, themes." However, as Vanoye points out, the fusion of the planes of expression and content—the *how* and the *what*—produce meanings that are specific to the medium. The fact that film produces meaning through patterns of editing results in narrative sequences that are different in nature from narrative sequences recounted in written language. A film may adapt and narrate the content of a novel and therefore produce in film the "same" story; yet, even in the most routine or faithful adaptations, the film is obliged to subject the narrative material to the specificity of filmic expression. Thus, Vanoye insists, "the four elements of signification can only be considered together. The temporal structure of a narrative (form of the content) cannot be separated from its realization through the forms of the signifiers."[53]

Differences in the nature of the signifier in literary and cinematic narratives lead to the particular genius of each medium. Cinema gives us a convincing analogue of concrete space, mimics to perfection the flow of time within the single shot, and reproduces the movement of real phenomena in space. Given the concreteness of its expression, it is not surprising then that film has difficulty expressing abstract notions.

Literary texts, on the other hand, have immense powers of abstraction since language is the source of all intellection, but fall short of producing a persuasive imitation of real phenomena as they occur in space and in time. André Gaudreault expresses this difference in the following terms:

> The "all powerful" word ..., which can at once serve to discourse on the world and on itself, actually runs up against certain limits: it cannot render the least exact image of the world, which it intends, all the same, to stand for. And it is nonetheless this quasi-universal capability of standing for, which it owes to its faculty for abstraction, that constitutes all its strength. But this is also, paradoxically, all its weakness: this faculty for abstraction prevents it from rendering with exactitude certain realities, in terms of their spatial relationships, but also to a lesser degree in terms of their temporal relationships.[54]

By their form of expression, literary narratives are extraordinarily versatile. Homogeneously verbal, written texts can move with ease between moments of "objective" narration and others in which the narrator intervenes to editorialize about characters or events. They shift fluently between levels of narration: a secondary narrator imposes his perspective without the visual devices that classic cinema invented to express subjectivity. Written narration negotiates movements in narrated time with simple temporal markers; it is the master of the narrative's tempo, accelerating or slowing the depiction of events.

The form of expression in film is less pliable. The individual shot has, as we have seen, a kind of spatial and temporal integrity that resists abstraction. It preserves absolute spatial and temporal continuity and shows, rather than tells, the actions and the setting it represents. However, as the filmmaker edits shots into sequences, he acquires the narrational power that belongs to the author of written narrative. This paradox of a showing that is also a telling is evoked in one of Christian Metz's early essays:

> Béla Balàzs already demonstrated how film, the apparent twin brother of the theatrical play ... in reality comes closer to the novel because of the image-track, which an invisible narrator, very similar to the novelist and, like him, standing outside the events he recounts, unfolds before the eyes of the spectator in the same manner as the novel's narrative aligns sentences that move directly from the author to the reader.[55]

André Gaudreault analyzes the complex character of cinematic representation by showing that the film is constructed at two different stages of the process of production and that the "filmmaker" is in fact two "authorial" agents with different functions at the moment of mise en scène and at the moment of editing. In the first stage, the film calls on a *monstrateur* (an "exhibitor") responsible for "putting into the film can a multitude of micronarratives [shots] that, each and all, have ... a certain narrative autonomy."[56] One task of the *monstrateur* consists in preparing the material to be shot—actors, sets, lighting, costumes— that is, performing the function that is analogous to theatrical staging. The second function of the *monstrateur* is more properly filmic: the *mise en cadre*—the compositional and semantic function of framing the individual shot.

Once the images are "in the can," a second agent—the author as the narrator of the story's events—appears whose function it is to shape and organize the material of the shots into a coherent whole. As Gaudreault puts it, the filmmaker/editor must "work on the narrative substance in order to cancel out the autonomy of the shots and to inscribe in it the itinerary of a continuous reading."[57] This process constructs a continuity in space and time through the technical matching of shots, the creation of narrative sequences, and the relationships the film establishes between image and sound. The filmic narrator performs the function analogous to the author of written narratives: he organizes the materials into a chain of narrated events. (I would add that this division of filmmaking into two distinct phases is not a temporal reality. It is clear that the filmmaker, in setting up and framing the shot, is already preparing for the discursive moment when the shot will assume its place in the edited sequence and the story's unfolding.)

It is important to underscore the difference to which film's two-phase process gives rise. The filmic *monstrateur* works to put in place the elements of a scene, which he subsequently frames through positioning the camera. The resulting shots are defined by the concrete quality of space and time they imitate and by the strict perspective imposed by camera placement. It is also important to note that the historical development of film as a discourse—in particular, through the productive act of editing—has tended to impose certain limits on the capacity of the moving image to narrate. As Noel Burch points out, the cinema, in the so-called primitive period, was able to codify the relationship between succeeding shots in terms of their greater or lesser spatial proximity and their relationship in time. That is, the creation of a narrative "whole" from the pieces of the shots depends on the spectator's ability to "measure" the space and time of each succeeding shot in terms of its relative closeness or distance from the one that preceded it.

> Starting from the alternating shots in the work of Porter and the British film-makers, and the earliest contiguity matches (matches of direction and eyeline), this evolution, through the increasing ubiquity of the camera, was ultimately to succeed in establishing the conviction that all the successive separate shots on the screen referred to the same diegetic continuum. In other words, the time spans represented were linked together by relations of immediate succession, simultaneity, or a more distant anteriority or posteriority; the spaces pictured communicated directly or at one or more removes; and above all the whole [chain of shots] constituted a milieu into which the spectator might penetrate as an invisible, immaterial observer, yet one who not only saw but also "experienced" all that transpired there.[58]

Thus, the specificity of cinematic narration developed as film acquired the ability to produce continuity from successive, disparate shots without recourse to verbal language in the form of either a "lecturer" present during the screening or frequent and controlling intertitles. To refuse the intervention of language at this level—the placing of shots in sequence—is to accept the limits of representation that the filmic signifier imposes.

A similar analysis can be made of film's attempts to construct the equivalent of editorial commentary. Commentary that uses the medium of dialogue is perceived as cinematic, on condition that the verbal exchange is credible in the context of the diegetic world the film produces. Extradiegetic verbal commentary (voice-over or intertitles) has the "weakness" of signaling the intrusion of a narrating voice and calling into question the "self-sufficiency" of the discourse of images. "Cinematic metaphors"—like Eisenstein's comparison of Kerensky and a strutting mechanical peacock in his film *October*—have the "disadvantage" of creating a heterogeneous alternation of images: one is diegetic (Kerensky, who belongs to the narrated world of the October Revolution), the other extradiegetic (the peacock, which intrudes into the diegetic world on the sole "authority" of the authorial voice). The resulting sequence as a whole has an abstract character because the spectator is called on to realize in thought the comparison between the signifieds of the images: Kerensky is like a peacock and is therefore endowed with the connotation of strutting vanity ascribed to the peacock. Only the musical score, relegated to the perceptual background of the spectator's experience, retains a "cinematic" character because its intervention is essentially emotional rather than intellectual. Unless it becomes pointedly commentative—as in the ironic counterpoint between image and sound—music in classic cinema remains the "unnoticed" instrument of narrational manipulation.

We come then to the crux of the problem of cinematic representations of history. Given the qualities of the cinematic signifier and the kinds of stories film seems "destined" to tell, should we conclude that cinema as a signifying practice does not show an aptitude for narrating history? There are, I think, two aspects to the question. First, since actors and events in historical narratives are essentially collective in nature, is the filmic image, grounded in the specificity of a moment and a place, an unsuitable vehicle for representing such abstract entities and actions? Second, does film tend to preserve the autonomy of the diegetic world it creates and therefore suppress the kind of authorial intervention—the historian's voice—that is a hallmark of historical narration? If we answer yes to these questions, then we are led to ask a third: do representations of history in film demand a conscious reworking of the "natural" modes of cinematic narrative? I believe that writing history in film requires precisely this kind of reworking, as I attempt to show in the analyses of films in the succeeding chapters.

As I have argued, one major difference between fictional and historical narration comes from the way in which the two types of narrative "justify" a sequence of actions. In fiction, it is the principle of verisimilitude that rules over the believability of succeeding moments of action: the spectator accepts characters and actions as credible if they correspond to his perception of what is "normal" in "real" life or if they correspond to the sets of conventions that determine what can be expected in the more artificial world of genres. In historical narratives, motivation is predicated on historical truth. "Truth" is not reader centered in that historical narratives do not seek to construct historical events according to what the public is inclined to take as believable. It is, rather, author centered, in that the historian is expected to explain the reasons for events, especially when they do not correspond to what the public perceives as credible.

Many historical narratives, like many fictional narratives, are constructed as chronological sequences of events that imply at the same time the causal relationship between them. However, the historian is often called on to intervene because the causal link between events is not obvious to the ordinary reader and must be explicated by historical commentary. History cannot rely consistently on the reader's perception of what is "normal" in the world because the narratives it tells belong to the "strangeness" that Michel de Certeau sees as the essential character of the historical past. Moreover, there is the general (although not obligatory) expectation that historical discourse make reference to its apparatus of erudition. This implies frequent discursive interventions that interrupt the "reading in continuity" to cite archival sources or the work of other historians, either directly in the text or in the form of the footnotes. All such interventions are evidence of the historical text's ability to become discursive and comment on itself.

For the reasons suggested above, the filmic text does not "naturally" take up the discursive mode. When film speaks about what the images and sounds represent, it has to work at producing its commentary. Narratologists would say that these moments of exegesis are relatively "costly" because they demand a change in discursive mode—the narrator does not simply narrate; he explains what he is narrating. When a text speaks about itself, it necessarily evokes the situation in which it was produced, what linguists call the text's *enunciation*. It is important, I think, to consider the special modes of enunciation in film, as described by Christian Metz in *L'Enonciation impersonnelle ou le site du film*. For Metz, the linguistic model of enunciation is not wholly suitable to film because it is based on the structure of verbal communication: the dialogic exchange that sets up a subject of discourse and his discursive partner (I/you) and anchors itself in a discursive situation through deictic signs: *I* designates the person speaking, *you* his partner in discourse, *here* is the place in which the dialogue takes place, *yesterday* is the day before the moment of the enunciation.

As we have seen, in written historical narratives, the enunciator does not usually make a show of the communicative act. Historians use an impersonal language that avoids signs of their subjectivity: they rarely say "I" or specifically acknowledge the reader/addressee. Historical enunciation reveals itself in the text's ability to shift from narrative to discursive modes—the telling interspersed with the author's interpretation or commentary—and in the critical apparatus of historical analysis referenced in the text or in footnotes and bibliography. In film, the enunciator is even more impersonal. He does not say "I" (except in the voice-over identified with the film's author, and that very rarely); he does not address the spectator as his discursive partner and in fact avoids all such references; he offers little direct information on the context of his enunciation, the context of the film's production. The so-called nobody's shot—the shot that cannot be attributed to the point of view of a character or the perspective of the filmmaker—shows few palpable signs of the enunciative activity. And yet, enunciation in film is never hidden. As Metz argues, it is because the film addresses itself to our perception as projected images and sounds that we remain conscious of it as cinematic construction and never mistake it for the real. The universal mark of enunciation is the existence of the text itself, which is unable ever to eclipse itself behind the world of reference it invokes. To understand modes of enunciation in film, Metz suggests a broader, semiological definition of the term. Enunciation is a "reflexive construction," made possible by the ability of a text to double over on itself:

> It is not necessarily, nor always, 'I—HERE—NOW' [deictic marks of enunciation]; it is, in a general fashion, the ability of many utterances to fold over in places, to appear here and there as if in relief, to slough off a thin skin of themselves that bears the marks of indications of *another nature* (or of another level), concerning the production and not the product. ... Enunciation is the semiological act by means of which certain parts of a text talk to us about this text as an act.[59]

As Metz points out, the marks of enunciation in film may be more or less conspicuous. The authorial voice-over is the most obvious manifestation of the enunciative act, particularly because it acknowledges that the film is a piece of communication between the narrator and the public he addresses. Metz describes this kind of authorial intervention as *commentative* because it assumes its role so overtly. Other marks are *reflexive* in character and do not stand so obviously apart from the narrative world. They are therefore subtler and may be more or less perceptible to the spectator depending on how knowledgeable he is about the culture of film. The singularity of the way in which a shot is constructed, for example, is a palpable mark of enunciation but will certainly strike with more impact the spectator who is able to measure the distance between the exceptional shot and the "normal" one. Marks of enunciation become perceptible "against a background of norms and codes." Whereas in written discourse marks of enunciation appear in quite prescriptive ways, in film such marks can appear anywhere in the text and derive from any aspect of mise en scène, any effect of the stationary or moving camera or of framing, any relationship established through editing of image or sound.

Metz gives us a brief inventory of the kinds of marks of enunciation common in film, and it is, I think, valuable to cite them briefly here. There is first the construction of the shot, which becomes remarkable to the extent it plays with the codes that constitute its normative background. The use that Miklós Jancso makes in his historical films of wide-screen shots in which the flatness and depth of landscape dwarf the human figures is a quite extreme example of departure from "normative" shot construction.

Second, there are the *voix d'adresse* (modes of addressing the spectator), as in the voice-over mentioned here, but there is also the case of the direct address of the spectator by the actor, signaled by the look into the camera. As I will show in Chapter Four, Angelopoulos's historical film, *The Traveling Players*, includes striking examples of this transgressive communication between the characters of the diegetic world and the real world of the spectator. The musical score speaks directly to the spectator from the plane of enunciation. If the principle of the musical score is to be unobtrusive, any emphatic effect or ironic counterpoint between music and image becomes a palpable mark of enunciation. Written language, in the form of intertitles, scrolling text, or filmed documents, may also address the spectator in more or less frontal fashion and appear quite frequently in historical films concerned with providing the "historian's perspective" and with marshalling the evidence provided by documents.

Third, there are the effects achieved through *secondary screens*, which obey the principle of doubling that is at the source of reflexivity. In contrast to the modes of address, the frame within the frame is a "silent redoubling" because it simply includes within the same space the two "planes" that are at once conjoined and separate. In *The Traveling Players*, for example, in which theatrical performance is a constant theme, the cinematic frame is frequently doubled by the theatrical frame—at times, quite literally the proscenium arch—and the interplay between the real and theatrical worlds becomes one of the central enunciative strategies of the film.

Fourth, there are the effects due to the *diegetization of the apparatus*, that is, the foregrounding of "technical" effects that play a role in the construction of the diegesis. The heavily stylized use of light and shadow, the nonnormative use of lenses, protracted dissolves, filming through fabric or other diegetic filters, among other effects, shape the way we look at the world of the narrative while making it clear that this vision is the result of the discursive intervention of an enunciator. Eisenstein's *October* is full of such diegetization of the apparatus, for example, in the "overlapping" shots that slow the raising of the bridge separating the government offices and the workers' demonstration or the "reverse motion" in which the demolished statue of the tsar reassembles itself in the first sequence of the film. Metz also mentions the choice of the actor, whose presence and performance are highly visible, as I will discuss in the next section, devoted to the analysis of Rossellini's *The Rise to Power of Louis XIV*.

Fifth, there is the power of the film to "quote" from other texts and other media. The film-within-the-film is the most obvious manifestation: the inclusion of documentary footage in Tarkovsky's fiction film about the Russian front in World War II, *Ivan's Childhood*, for example. But films are quite as capable of citing all types of literary, visual, and audiovisual production, and such citations are frequent in historical films, such as the montage of visual and verbal documents that constitutes Ken Burn's *The Civil War* or Resnais's *Night and Fog*.

A few perceptive historians have come to very similar conclusions about the need in historical films to open up the closed narrative world that film excels at producing. Natalie Zemon Davis argues for a *reflexive* approach to historical filmmaking that calls into question the singular, linear, apparently self-sufficient cinematic narrative of historical events. "Film has," Davis asserts, "countless possibilities for showing more than one story at once and for indicating in a concise and arresting way the existence of other interpretations."[60] Reflexive strategies should aim to restore to historical film the kind of complexity that written history requires, and Davis enumerates numbers of cinematic techniques—what Metz calls marks of enunciation—that enable film to discourse about itself: "Some have simple Brechtian distancing functions; some evoke multiple tellings or controversy; some locate the film in relation to historical knowledge; some do all three at once."[61] Special effects that disrupt the "transparency" of the image, ironic effects achieved by juxtaposing musical score and action, the mirroring structure of the film-within-the-film, witnesses who comment on characters and action, footage of the filmmaker discussing his intentions, or the simple use of the credits to acknowledge historical sources are all strategies, argues Davis, that can serve to reestablish historical distance in the mind of the spectator, multiply perspectives on historical events, and reveal the process by which the historian/filmmaker uses historical knowledge to reconstruct historical events.

CASE STUDY: CONSTRUCTING THE KING'S BODY IN ROBERTO ROSSELLINI'S *THE RISE TO POWER OF LOUIS XIV* (1966)

How can we apply narrative theories of fiction and nonfiction to the historical film? In the following discussion of Roberto Rossellini's *The Rise to Power of Louis XIV*, I attempt such an application. The aim of the analysis is to understand where we should situate Rossellini's film. Is it essentially a work of fiction that dresses up in historical guise, a sophisticated version of the costume drama? Or is it possible to argue that the film belongs to the category of nonfictional discourses, in this case a discourse of historical representation?

I approach the film from three standpoints. First, does the film belong to the category of pragmatic discourses? Is it an act of persuasion? Does the director assume responsibility for the film's "truthfulness?" Second, what sort of mimesis does the film engage? Does it abide by the cognitive restraints that characterize nonfiction? What strategies of emplotment does it use? What is the relationship between the film's audiovisual representation and the written representation of the film's "sources"? Third, what is the impact of film as vehicle of expression on the historical material *The Rise to Power* seeks to communicate? Was the historical subject chosen because it is apt for cinematic representation? What techniques does the film adopt to thwart the sense of presence that characterizes fiction and the easy identification of the spectator with the characters?

The Question of Pragmatics

If we begin with the stated intentions that Rossellini communicated in detail, particularly in his often-cited interview with the *Cahiers du Cinéma*,[62] there is no doubt that *The Rise to Power of Louis XIV* was conceived as *diction* (to use Genette's term): a didactic film aimed at educating the mass public about a seminal historical event. Rossellini's notion that the cinema can deviate from its role as an instrument of pleasure and become a vehicle for the propagation of historical information in the mass media was revolutionary in the period. He adopted the form of the didactic narrative, rejected the constraints of commercial cinema, and worked in the institutional context of Italian television (the RAI). Part of his mission was to address the television public directly. Rossellini believed that he could participate in breaking the conventions of an oppressive "pseudoculture" that held the masses in its sway: "We need to spread among the masses the true essence of the great discoveries and of modern technology.... Doing this, we will help the large masses find themselves in the new world."[63]

Despite his educational aim, Rossellini argues that the maker of historical films should resist the urge to interpret historical materials or organize them pedagogically; rather, he should adopt the role of a simple instrument of transmission, a worker of the image: "I try to interfere the least possible with the image; my only interference consists in finding the point of view and saying what is essential, nothing more. That's why I insist most emphatically that I am not at all an artist; I am only a worker, and I love being a worker."[64] In taking such a position,

Rossellini glosses over the problem of the historian's subjectivity and denies the discursive character of historical representation. However, his conception of his role is not far from the (largely unspoken) one that underlies the practice of many contemporary historians: the willful subjugation of the vice of subjectivity in the interest of producing an unbiased historical account, a retelling that finds its story already nascent in the given of historical facts.

Equally significant is Rossellini's caveat concerning the pleasure-driven character of cinematic experience. He warns against the "danger" of the cinematic apparatus and the misuse of the image that reduces it to an instrument of seduction for the spectator. Moreover, he repudiates cinema's aesthetic quality, the pleasurable experience of beauty that detaches the spectator from the image as a meaningful representation of real experience and contradicts the film's pragmatic act of communication. Art, he argues, has lost its functionality. It is no longer interested in the historical meaning of events or in making this meaning accessible to a broad public. The historian/filmmaker must take on the role of the pragmatic communicator, and in the interest of preserving the image's powers of documentation, construct a strategy to prevent the spectator from seeking refuge in the imaginary:

> There is another really important problem: the image, in the dark of the movie theater is seductive, one can so easily take it for a dream that it becomes a refuge, an escape.... If one wants to make cinema into a means for communicating knowledge, all that must be forgotten ... I don't want to seduce, that is, destroy the image in order to keep only those aspects that can seduce. I want to remain as close as possible to things.[65]

Rossellini in fact ascribes to the image the power to directly communicate the real, even the historically real. He declares with fervor that the filmmaker should make use of the power of the image—the photographic image in movement—to render past reality in its *presence*, something to which verbal language can only aspire :

> Images, with their naked purity, directly demonstrative, can show us the road to take in order to orient ourselves with the greatest possible knowledge.... All of our intelligence, as we know, expresses itself thanks to the eyes. Language, this human conquest which has justly been made divine (it is said that God is the Word), is the ensemble of the phonetic images by means of which, not being able to fix and save the images, we have

catalogued all our observations, the great majority of which are visual. [Language] has allowed us to express our intelligence by discerning, classifying, and connecting. Today, finally, we have the images; we have television, we have the RAI.[66]

The views reflected in Rossellini's statement are certainly naïve. Historical reality cannot be directly observed and therefore cannot be directly represented in images. There is nothing transparent in historical mimesis. Indeed, I have argued, using narrative theory, that representation in history is a discursive act: the historian sets up a trajectory across the historical field, includes or excludes historical materials, foregrounds certain acts while relegating others to the background, and so forth. As I show, Rossellini's practice does not always correlate with his pronouncements, but the paratextual markers of his communicative intention are clear. Rossellini seeks to use cinematic "language" to reach and inform a broad public—the fundamental pragmatism of his discourse cannot be questioned.

Rossellini sets out through *The Rise to Power of Louis XIV* to establish a meaningful relationship between the present from which he is speaking and the historical world of past events. Therefore, his film meets certain criteria of nonfiction. Rossellini is both author and narrator of his film (A = N is Genette's definition of nonfiction); he speaks from the position of Hamburger's real *I-Origo*; he engages in a speech act for which he carries social responsibility. Rossellini submits the historical representations of his film to be judged on the basis of reason and evidence, as indeed they have been. François de la Bretèque, for example, observed that "in a film reputed to be more 'serious,'" Rossellini does not hesitate to give us an account of the Sun King's private "*faits et gestes*" and allows us to "read what he reads," a reference to the closing moment of the film in which Louis recites, in the privacy of his cabinet, a maxim from La Rochefoucault: "Ni le soleil ni la mort ne peuvent se regarder fixement" ("Neither the sun nor death can be looked at fixedly").[67] Certainly no such critique would be raised against a Hollywood historical spectacle precisely because we know, through conventions of the genre and the star system, that we are not supposed to take seriously any of its representations. As Schaeffer convincingly argues in *Pourquoi la fiction?* the essential difference between fiction and nonfiction is not the "truthfulness" of a work's representations but the work's claim that it operates according to the reality principle.

The Question of Mimesis

In Schaeffer's view, all narrative, fictional or nonfictional, assumes the same "posture of representation"; all narrative is based in imitation, that is, the resemblance between the discourse and the world for which it stands as a model. He insists on the active character of mimesis that constructs a representation that did not preexist discourse. Representation, by its nature, positions us as readers/spectators so that we relate to the discourse *as if* "we were really in the situations for which mimèmes [mimetic statements] construct the semblance."[68] If, as Schaeffer contends, there is only one referential mode for fiction and nonfiction, both involving semblance, should we not admit the possibility that filmic representation can be a vehicle for historical as well as fictional narrative? Is it possible to concede that the major differences in modes of representation have to do with the *vehicle* of narrative: in the case of written history, exclusively verbal representations, and in the case of film, audiovisual and verbal representations? Are we stuck with the notion that film's use of the image is a kind of original sin, a surfeit of the concrete, which can only produce an anachronistic revivification of the historical world?

As Schaeffer, Veyne, and others have argued, the major distinction between fiction and history resides in the cognitive constraints that nonfiction embraces: the historical narrative maintains "local structural equivalencies" between the model the discourse proposes and historical reality, knowable only through the traces it has left. Is it possible to construct "local structural equivalencies" if the historical film depends on the inventions of mise en scène? Doesn't R. G. Collingwood reason that one identifying feature of historical events is their unavailability to perception, the phenomenological absence that writing seems to respect? If one could argue for the authenticity of documentary footage of historical events, a kind of perception in the second degree, can the same be true of historical mise en scène in which every representation is artificially staged? Doesn't Rossellini belie his conception of "simply looking" at history by using mirrors to create the illusion of place (the Palais du Louvre replaced on the banks of the Seine near Meudon)? Indeed, in interviews Rossellini has described the painstaking work of representation involved in reconstructing an "image" of the past: the choice of written historical texts and the "archaeological" research on the period that makes visualization possible, the replication of social relations and behaviors, the selection of locations, the construction of costumes and accessories, and so forth. The verbal message takes on "substance" through the visualization of documented facts. This work of incarnation precedes the process of emplotment that gives narrative form to a sequence of visualized facts. Is Rossellini's incarnation of documents simply the kind of revivification that contemporary historians reject as antithetical to the pastness of the past, or can it be seen as responding to the "local structural equivalencies" that historic discourse imposes?

As Rigney argues, historical events take on meaning as the result of the historian's act of writing. The mainly nonverbal material of history is invested with significance through its transformation into written language. Is it possible to say that Rossellini's film is based in an analogous act of transformation in which the film's discourse stands as a constructed model for real historical experience? Does historical film, like written historical narratives, place factual events on the chain of discourse and impose "particular contextual relations between them?" Do the acts of mimesis and narrativization that Rossellini performs constitute structures of historical meaning? Let's examine the mimetic and narrative strategies that Rossellini adopts.

The Rise to Power of Louis XIV seems to be predicated on the model of political history in which the central protagonists are not collective entities or representative figures, but individuals whose actions have had a demonstrable influence over the lives and destinies of large social groups. In general in his historical films, Rossellini adopts what Peter Brunette calls the model of the great man "who is examined as a representative of his age, usually an age in which ... some profound change occurred in the history of human consciousness."[69] In *The Rise to Power*, Rossellini narrates Louis XIV's struggle for absolute dominion that resulted in the creation of the modern, centralized state. Louis pits himself against members of the court who hope to exploit the tradition of the king too distracted by pleasures of war or the hunt to exercise his legitimate power. As Rossellini portrays him, Louis XIV imposes himself, not only through political action, but also through a deliberate program of self-representation. Indeed, Rossellini shows how the iconography of the regime emerges from the construction of the closed, synthetic world of Versailles, the ritualized behavior and hierarchy of the court, and the adornment of the royal body that becomes both an instrument of subjugation and the emblematic expression of power.

Let's look closely at the process of emplotment. Rossellini makes specific narrative choices by deciding what he will foreground in the event-worthy field of Louis's rise to power and what he will cast into shadow through exclusion. He narrows the scope of historical events, giving us what appears to be a plot of court intrigue: Louis XIV defies the tradition of kings who rule in name only; he plots, with Colbert, the downfall of the surintendant Fouquet, who aspires to replace Mazarin as ruler in fact; and he takes political power into his own hands, constructing an apparatus of absolutism in which power is invested in the fetishized body of the king. In literary terms, *The Rise to Power of Louis XIV* can be described as an *action plot*, in which the central protagonist achieves in the course of events a significant change of situation (a structure common to the "heroic" plots of political history): the determined Louis, cognizant of his historical situation, imposes himself through a strategy of political action and manipulation. The film's narrative also corresponds to the *plot of character*, in which the protagonist undergoes a process of maturation that enables him to achieve this successful outcome: an already determined but untried Louis assumes the heritage of Mazarin, takes on his historic responsibilities, and fulfills the cardinal's political testament. Rossellini thus chooses to restrict the film's action to the closed world of the court over a circumscribed period of time, from the death of Mazarin in 1661 to the installation of the full court at Versailles in about 1678.

In the Rossellinian manner, *The Rise to Power* tends to dedramatize action and interpolates into the linear development of the plot moments of apparent "dead time." The film has nonetheless a clear causal structure. There is the inciting moment, the death of the king's regent, Mazarin, which poses the question of succession and power. Exposition occurs through conversations in which the characters comment on the background of the action: the dialogue between the dying Mazarin and his confessor evokes the period of the regency, the Queen Mother's monologue recounts the history of the distracted and dissipated French kings, Colbert instructs the king on the misdeeds of Fouquet. Louis's political move to assume control over the council initiates the rising action that leads to the arrest of Fouquet, a moment of tension and climax. The remainder of the film concerns itself with the political problem of imposing and perpetuating political power. Although this long section lacks the dramatic tension of the first (for reasons I discuss shortly), it develops as a causally constructed sequence of events that results in the narrative's goal, the embodiment in Louis of state power. Rossellini enjoys the advantage of the unity of action that comes from the stable configuration of characters, juxtaposing protagonists (Louis XIV, Colbert) and antagonists (Fouquet and those who support the surintendant's ascent to power). In the manner of fictional narratives, it is the characters' individual acts that constitute the plot, in contrast to the more complex shifting fields of actions and actors, characteristic of the history of social groups. Indeed, Rossellini has been criticized for this narrow focalization of his narrative because he excludes from discussion the broader social situation and the ramifications for the French people of Louis's "coup d'état."

Rossellini's circumscribed narrative has another advantage. By restricting the action to historical figures about whom a great deal is known, he is able to make use of the unusually rich documentation on Louis XIV and his court: the commentaries of courtiers and foreign envoys; records of conversations; reports; not only Louis XIV's *Mémoires*, rich in anecdote and revelatory of Louis's intentions, but also those of Madame de Lafayette and Madame de Motteville, among others. The "signifying relief" that Rossellini gives to events, the degree of presence that he creates in the succession of scenes that constitute the film, and the dialogue that he puts into the mouths of his characters are justified by documentation, even if he sometimes plays a bit freely with his sources in the process of representing them filmically.

Rossellini's major source of historical information (but not the only one) is historian Philippe Erlanger's *Louis XIV* (Erlanger appears as historical advisor in the film's credits). Erlanger's text is the kind of biographical history that must have appealed to Rossellini: it tells its story following the linear development of the king's life, it avoids excessive discursive commentary, and it presents historical moments with a great richness of anecdotal detail. Moreover, Erlanger's account of situations and events is enriched with psychological analysis: he foregrounds the historical characters' intentions, closely intertwining the political and the personal. In the following passage, for example, the historian explains how conceit, self-deception, and fatal underestimation of the personality of the young Louis would lead Surintendant Fouquet to his ruin:

> The most brilliant, the most intelligent of the ministers, Nicolas Fouquet, was totally mistaken. Didn't Anne of Austria say to him with a shrug of the shoulders: "He [the young Louis] wants to look like he's in charge (*Il veut faire le capable*)?" The Surintendant was convinced that this ardor for work would quickly dissolve under the charm of pleasures, since he, Fouquet, was resolved to spare no effort in allowing His Majesty to drown in them. This corrupter would become the dupe of his own system in believing he could debauch the King. The young man had had a rather morose youth under the thumb of a stingy authority. The Surintendant would give him every fulfillment, would "spoil" him in the proper sense of the word, and quite naturally unburden him of the responsibilities of affairs of state.[70]

The passage adopts a position of narration that is close to classical fiction. The signs of the narrator's presence—the discourse's marks of enunciation—are largely effaced in order to give the narrative an autonomous character. Events seem to emerge of their own accord. In this passage, the historian/narrator intervenes directly only twice in order to impose the ironic judgment of history: Fouquet was mistaken, and little did he know that he would become the dupe of his own system. Elsewhere in the passage, the historian relies on indirect discourse, rendering in the third person the internal thought processes of Fouquet's character. We "hear" the voice of the historical character who appears to narrate on his own behalf. Indeed, Erlanger's narration often gives us the signs of subjectivity that Käte Hamburger identifies as essential to fiction: "Epic fiction [the novel] is the only epistemological instance in which the I-origo (or subjectivity) of a character can be evoked in the third person."[71] By contrast, Rossellini's film is more externally focalized, restricting itself to representing the characters' words and actions as opposed to giving us direct access to their thoughts and feelings.

If one compares the film's narrative to Erlanger's text, it becomes clear how Rossellini reshaped material in the process of transposition. There is of course the necessary work of selection and reduction: the one-hundred-minute film could not have recounted, using the resources of cinematic representation, all the events and all aspects of events that Erlanger's verbal narrative accomplishes at great length. Rossellini is obliged to construct a simpler narrative by cutting a thinner slice of history. Some events that, in Erlanger's account, are crucial to motivating Louis's actions are not represented at all. For example, the sumptuous fête Surintendant Fouquet offers Louis at his château de Vaux-le-Vicomte—a prefiguration of Versailles—which the king experienced as a humiliation, is not represented at all, perhaps due to Rossellini's limited production budget. Other events are represented *en creux* (i.e., receive comparatively minimal treatment). For example, the formulation of economic and social reforms in the early regime is represented by a single short sequence in which Colbert explains to the rapt attention of his king the vision he has for a modernized France. The work of condensation that takes the place of an ample discussion of the revolutionary policies is transparent. On the other hand, the events Rossellini represents as "significant" receive a scenic treatment that gives what Ann Rigney calls the sense of presence: the lengthy and detailed representation of specific actions that the narrative thus pushes into the foreground.

Through his tendency to evoke as scenes specific historical moments, Erlanger provided Rossellini with the sort of concrete representations that could be transposed through cinematic mise en scène. In most cases, Rossellini scrupulously follows the documented interchanges between characters. He quite accurately represents, for example, Erlanger's account of the last meeting between the dying Mazarin and the young king, including the documented dialogue, even if he quotes the doubtless apocryphal statement attributed to Mazarin: "Sire, je crois m'acquitter de tout en vous laissant Colbert" ("Your majesty, I believe I have fully done my duty by leaving you Colbert").[72] As Erlanger puts it, if the phrase is not authentic, "it reflects the essential," and one cannot really quibble with Rossellini's decision to include it. Moreover, he uses much of the anecdotal information the text provides in terms of details of behavior, action, or setting, representing through visualization the historical circumstance that Erlanger explicates. The queen's chamber maid, Pierrette Dufour, sleeps in the royal apartment, and Rossellini closely follows the historian's account of how she communicates the news of Mazarin's death to the king: "When at daybreak Pierrette Dufour heard the King stir, she approached and silently made the agreed-upon gesture. Mazarin had died between two and three in the morning."[73] However, in passages where Erlanger *tells* rather than *shows*, transpositions are not so simple or direct.

Rossellini's narrative strategy is to adopt an exclusively *mimetic* mode of representation in which the narrator pretends to give up his power of narration to allow the characters to speak for themselves. The filmmaker thus eschews any discursive intervention in the form of intertitles or voice-over—mediations that would belie his assertion that historical action can be represented "literally" in the detached, observational manner of his earlier films that focused on contemporary reality. This modal constraint leads Rossellini at certain moments to compromise the historical "literalness" of his mise en scène through recourse to theatrical subterfuge. When he wants to include historical commentary on the situation of his characters, he puts the information in the mouth of one his characters. For example, it is the Queen Mother, Anne d'Autriche, who comments on the historical weakness of the French kings, more interested in the hunt and war than in governing. If the literalness of the dialogue is in question, the information it delivers reflects the Queen Mother's attitude and is essential to understanding the element of surprise that enabled Louis to outwit and outmaneuver Fouquet. At other points, Rossellini resorts to theatrical conventions, particularly in the guise of choral-like commentary by courtiers on the meaning of actions or "facts of daily life," to explain to the spectator what might otherwise remain obscure. We learn, for example, from a dialogic interchange that the *deuil noir* (black as the color of deep mourning) that Louis imposes on the court at the death of Mazarin is usually reserved for royalty. In another instance, the theatrical aside of one anonymous courtier speaking to another tells us that the queen's gesture of clapping her hands in bed at the moment of the *lever du roi* indicates that Louis accomplished that night his nuptial duty. Although the exegesis takes the form of dialogue within the narrative world of the film, the remarks are intended to inform and are clearly addressed to the spectator.

In *The Rise to Power of Louis XIV*, the sense of the quotidian is expressed in scenes that seem to arrest narrative action and take on a didactic character. For example, the extended consultation between the several physicians attending the dying Mazarin provides an exposition of medical practices in the seventeenth century. Even moments of intense narrative development are accompanied by documentation of historic behavior: the deathly pale Mazarin prepares to receive the king by applying cosmetics, *les fards de son éminence*. These often brief notations of practices and customs are signs of historical difference: what is routine and unexamined in past societies becomes for us unfamiliar and the object of historical curiosity. Observations of historical difference also generate a "real effect" in which the unfamiliar signifies historical contingency. In Rossellinian mise en scène, the accumulation of these signs of the real serves as the immediate context of historical action, undercutting the dramatic character of classical political history. Indeed, Rossellini insists that great historical events occur in much the same manner as events of daily life: "I always try to remain impassive. What I find most surprising, extraordinary, and moving in men is precisely that great actions and great events take place in the same way and with exactly the same resonance as normal everyday occurrences."[74]

If the entrapment and arrest of Fouquet retain considerable dramatic tension, Louis's ascension to power is described in terms of quite undramatic actions and gestures. Many sequences suggest the repetitive (iterative) character of the event described. We are given to understand, for example, that the scene in which Louis consults with the royal tailors about the extravagant courtly attire that is part of his strategy to subjugate the nobility is yet another, still unsuccessful stage in the elaboration of the definitive model. The culminating scene of the film, the representation of Louis in his new state of absolute power, is spectacular in the richness of its mise en scène but quite the contrary of resolution through climactic action. Rossellini's camera focuses on the details of the king's repast in the presence of the court and adopts the languorous rhythm of its ritualized unfolding. This narrative stasis allows the moment to take on a figurative character: the agitated, yet controlled activity of the kitchen; the heightened artificiality of pose and gesture that accompany the service; the transformation of dining from a collective activity into an organized spectacle; the imposing solitude of Louis and the rapt subservience of the court—all stand for the triumph and transcendent power embodied in the king.

The Vehicle of Expression

Rossellini adopts a particular approach to the representation of historical events that reflects not only his own proclivities as a filmmaker, but also the exigencies of transposing mainly written documentation into an audiovisual discourse. The most important choice, as I attempted to show through narrative analysis, has to do with the kind of historical character Rossellini chooses to represent. In general, he avoids the representation of collective actors, establishing rather a dramatis personae consisting of protagonists capable of making individual choices (Louis XIV or Anne d'Autriche) and flat characters who perform minor actions that are typical and predictable (the anonymous courtiers or the members of the *peuple* who comment on the doctors arriving to treat Mazarin).

The narrative choice to privilege the individual is also a cinematic one. Because of its penchant for the concrete, film easily represents the individual body that performs individual actions and the concrete space and time in which such actions evolve. Similarly, Rossellini's use of iterative sequences (a series of shots that stands for the repetition of many similar actions) is a quite cinematic transposition of verbal iterative statements in which repetition is usually expressed through abstract verbal locutions (such an event happened often, over months or years). Thus, Rossellini avoids the textual work of producing abstract entities of collective action, a major concern of other historical filmmakers. The choice of this mode of representation allows him to dispense with the obvious authorial interventions like the voice-over or intertitles; his "transparent" discourse stands in opposition to the mode of historical representation in which a dominant verbal narration marshals the film's body of visual illustrations. Rossellini maintains a constant position of enunciation: he opts for mimetic representation that allows the characters and their actions to stand on their own. This position contrasts with the shifting positions of enunciation characteristic of literary histories in which mimetic representation alternates with the discursive interventions of the historians commenting on the meaning of events.

We could say that Erlanger's *Louis XIV* (or rather, portions of that work) has the same substance of content as Rossellini's *Rise to Power*. However, the filmic substance of expression requires a transposition from one signifying system to another. As Metz and Gaudreault point out, written language is an arbitrary system with relatively weak descriptive capabilities, whereas cinema's visual track consists of images that are *motivated* signs with strong denotative power. Descriptive words produce images in the mind, whereas images in film come from the outside and flood the spectator with rich phenomenological detail. In Erlanger's text, the proper name Louis XIV produces a mental image in the spectator that is tied at best to the memory the spectator has of painterly representations of the king. Rossellini gives us a body—the image of the body of the actor embellished with reproductions of period wigs and apparel. It is this excess of mise en scène, the "body too many," as Jean-Louis Comolli put it apropos of Pierre Renoir's Louis XVI in *La Marseillaise*,[75] that disturbs historians and constitutes for the filmmaker one of the great problems of historical filmmaking. Filmmakers may adopt one of two strategies for mitigating this doubling of the actor/character and the phenomenological surfeit of mise en scène. The first consists in an obsessive work of documentation in which the filmmaker, assisted by his historical consultants, attempts to reduce to an absolute minimum the inescapable anachronism that historical representation in film entails. The second consists in developing cinematic counterparts for the abstract quality of written language and its more "versatile" powers of narration. In practice, most historical filmmakers negotiate between these two tendencies, and indeed one could argue that any historical representation in film necessarily involves some kind of fusion between the two.

In describing the long period of preparation for his historical films, Rossellini suggests that exhaustive documentation is at the base of authentic historical representation. Through his emphasis on representations of daily life and his notion that great events of history take place in the same manner as everyday events, Rossellini seeks to reduce the apparent discord between historical and cinematic representation. However, we should not accept at face value Rossellini's assertion that writing history in film consists in "simply looking," because there is nothing simple about the work of mise en scène that constructs what the camera finally "looks at." Moreover, Rossellini constantly puts in question the apparent self-sufficiency of the narration of events. At many moments, *The Rise to Power of Louis XIV* takes on a reflexive character in which a "folding over" of the text, to use Metz's formulation, allows the film to talk about its own production. The effect is profoundly ironic: the reality of the scene of history stands on the artifice of representation. In the interest of history, Rossellini reworks the classic relationship between the film and its audience. The body of "techniques" he uses prevents the spectator from an easy identification with characters and events and refocuses his attention on the meaning of dialogue and action.

There is, first, Rossellini's tendency to film his actors in a frontal fashion, creating presentational postures that tend to impose distance between spectator and characters. In many instances, the camera takes up an immobile position within a scene, and the actors turn their bodies to the camera. Short sequences—often composed of a single shot—are particularly static in this regard. For example, in the segment in which Colbert describes to Louis his vision for economic development and social reform in France, the actors face the camera, Louis at his desk and Colbert standing at his right, in a stationary medium shot. More complex sequences may include multiple shots and the play of the zoom lens, but, in these as well, Rossellini tends to avoid significant changes in the axis of the camera. With the exception of entrances and exits, he restricts the actors' movement within the frame and often maintains them in relatively rigid poses. This technique evokes the theatrical convention of the proscenium, the kind of static representation that cinema gradually abandoned in the primitive era in favor of a more cinematic expression.

Rossellini thus prevents the spectator from "penetrating" into the scene by rejecting the techniques of analytic editing: the repositioning of the camera, the variation of angle and distance that communicate narrative and psychological information and condition spectator response. The film rejects the interpolation of closer shots through editing and especially subjective shots. There is only one example of a classic point-of-view series in the film: as Louis retains Fouquet after the meeting of the council, he looks out the window (the look offscreen) to assure himself that D'Artagnan is ready to arrest the surintendant (object of the look). Moreover, the film's presentational mode is enhanced by the use of long takes and, in some instances, shot sequences. This static shooting strategy is facilitated by the Pancinor zoom, which produces a fluid movement between different focal points, shifting between longer and closer views of the scene without shot changes.

Other effects contribute to this ironic "flattening" of mise en scène. The choice of actors, particularly in the case of Jean-Marie Patte as

Louis XIV, plays on the disappointment of spectator expectations: how can this actor's body be equated with the historical body of Louis XIV? The neutrality of Patte's facial expression and his deliberately flat delivery of lines further underscore the dissonance that Rossellini develops between the mechanism of transmission and the historical reality to which it refers. Despite his pronouncements, Rossellini's mise en scène is already a critique of the possibility of revivification.

The composition of the frame often underscores this tendency to visual flatness and inertia through a conscious imitation of pictorial composition in seventeenth-century painting. Take, for example, the moment in the long sequence of the consultation between physicians in which Mazarin submits to bleeding: the cardinal slouches in a chair, his elongated body draped in white, creating a diagonal composition of mortal agony. Rossellini's imitation of painterly composition has been variously interpreted. Martin Walsh argues that Rossellini uses the technique to attenuate the "degree of 'naïve' realism"[76] that would be the result of a more "cinematic" relationship between camera and action. De la Brethèque sees in the imitation of historical iconography an inherent flaw in cinematic mise en scène: "It comes down to saying, once again, that access to the 'reality' of a period can only be obtained through representations that are already mediated in the past."[77] Both positions are based on a similar analysis, although they reach quite opposite conclusions. In response to de la Brethèque, I would argue that *mimesis praxeos*, Aristotle's term for the imitation of action in verbal narratives, is what historians do. Any form of mimesis involves mediation, and certain features of mediation in written discourse are particularly striking. Peirce insists that the words of a language—*symbols* in his classification of signs—resemble only through the "force of a law,"[78] and the great distance between the linguistic signifier and signified imposes a level of abstraction that is always a "betrayal" of the referent.

I would contend that Rossellini's film shows an acute awareness of the danger inherent in cinematic mise en scène and its referential function: the "world of the past" can be invoked in such richness of detail that the spectator can fantasize the presence of history and engage in a relationship with the actor/characters that ignores the distance between the instrument of representation and the historical person. It is plain that Rossellini's pictorial treatment of scenes has a deliberately artificial character, and, I would argue, this reflexive structure that foregrounds the mimetic act is part of a strategy that aims at exposing to the spectator the synthetic and mediated quality of historical representation. Rossellinian mise en scène turns on representational irony. He says in effect: this is and is not the figure of Louis XIV; these are and are not the acts that led to absolutism in seventeenth-century France.

3

THE HISTORICAL CHARACTER

THE PROBLEMATIC OF HISTORICAL
FILM AND THE IMAGINARY

This chapter addresses a central problematic of historical representation in the cinema: is it possible to construct a properly historical character in film?

The term *character* seems hardly appropriate since it is defined in many dictionaries as "one of the imaginary persons who figure in a work of fiction." The term *historical actor* presents a similar problem since the actor plays a role, and the theatrical notion is not applicable to history except, one assumes, as metaphor: the role played by Napoleon in "exporting" the French Revolution. In defense of the epistemological break between history and fiction, historians have resisted conceiving of history as narrative because they associate narrative with the creation of imaginary worlds. They are not given therefore to examining the nature of those narrative agents that act upon and are acted upon in the course of historical events. It is no wonder, then, that historians confronted with representations of historical figures in film are highly skeptical. They consider cinema as a spectacle irremediably tied to the imaginary, particularly because of the feature that characterizes all visual representation of historical action: doubling. There is the doubling of mise en scène, in which a set in a theater or a location in a film, so clearly part of the here-and-now of the act of representation, are intended to stand in for the real place in the past. Similarly, there is the doubling of the actor and his role: the actor belongs to the moment of performance, the role to the person or social entity that acted in the historical past.

The doubling implicit in mise en scène and the actor's performance correspond to the two moments in time that referential narratives necessarily embody: the moment of enunciation from which the historian/narrator speaks and the historical moment to which his discourse refers. But, historians would argue, fiction, particularly dramatic or filmic fiction, is characterized by excess. There is first the excessive presence of its mechanisms of representation: film needs to *show* us characters, settings, and actions in their phenomenal reality, a duplicated reality mediated by filmic processes. By contrast, history *tells* us about the past; it retreats into the discretion and distance of written discourse, where narration becomes the act of aligning verbal facts on a chain of cause and effect so that the already constituted characters and events would seem to speak for themselves. The historian does not *represent* the past—representation is too close to resurrection—he *refers* to it. Moreover, under the ethical constraints of a referential discourse, he removes all the supports that sustain the notion of character in fiction: he rejects the representation of historical scenes in descriptive detail and the use of dialogue *in extenso*; embracing truth rather than verisimilitude, he resists the anachronistic urge to psychologize the historical character using what Käte Hamburger calls "verbs of internal action"; and he refuses to reduce the collective forces of history to a configuration of protagonists and antagonists acting out their roles according to the conventional codes of narrative.

One cannot, of course, argue with the ethical constraints that govern historical discourse or defend the historical spectacle film and its fictionalized characters, which clearly belong to the realm of the imaginary. If film is capable of constructing historical characters, then it also must eschew the techniques of the imaginary and operate under the constraints that govern what can be said about the past. However, I argue in the following that history—written or filmed—*is* narrative; therefore, there is a fundamental kinship between factual and fictional storytelling. As Jean-Marie Schaeffer compellingly argues (see Chapter Two), narrative is always a mimetic activity: novels, histories, plays, and films all imitate events, and events are all representations of the actions of the actors, whether historical or not. So, we are faced with a dilemma: is it possible to acknowledge on the one hand the kinship between history and fiction as narrative and on the other hand preserve the specific identity of the historical actor?

I propose to approach the problem from the perspectives of two disciplines: narrative theory and philosophy of history. Narratology reflects on the general question of the nature and function of the character in narratives, whether written, theatrical, or filmic. I emphasize the work of Philippe Hamon in "Pour un statut sémiologique du personnage" ("For a Semiological Status of the Character") and *Le Personnel du roman: Le système des personnages dans les* Rougon-Macquart *d'Emile Zola (The Personnel of the Novel: The System of Characters in Emile Zola's* Rougon-Macquart), which offers a semiological model of the character, supported by the work of structural linguists and narratologists. Philosophy of history, on the other hand, establishes a special notion of the character, the subject/object of historical actions, which is consistent with the scale of historic discourse and in large measure serves to define the nature of historical representation. The work of Maurice Mandelbaum in *The Anatomy of Historical Knowledge* and the meditation Paul Ricoeur offers in *Time and Narrative* on Mandelbaum's notions are rich in ideas relevant to our discussion. By calling on these two domains of theory, I look first for a broader notion of character that includes the agents of history and second for the criteria according to which historiography specifies the nature of the historic character.

NARRATOLOGICAL APPROACHES TO CHARACTER

In his introduction to *Le personnel du roman*, Philippe Hamon describes the concept of the character as a "complex field of study" with three major aspects. There is first the *figurative*, which presents the character as modeled on experience and therefore contributes a *reality effect* to the narrative. The work of figuration endows the narrative actor with the apparently arbitrary features of existence: descriptive details of behavior that have no function other than to connote the real. The use of details by nineteenth-century historians, for example, provides the reader with images of individual personalities that go well beyond the functional demands of narrative: Louis Blanc represents Robespierre as the revolutionary who takes his solitary walks "accompanied by his faithful dog and, occasionally, stops to listen to the *petits savoyards* ... as they sing their songs from the mountains."[1] Indeed, what historian does not relish the documented detail, the sign of real existence, even as he describes the "anonymous" actors who perform the fundamental actions of history.

Second, the character is the *anthropomorphization* of the narrative, which attributes to the narrative agent certain capacities of the person. In his *Dictionary of Narratology*, Gerald Prince defines the character in precisely the same anthropomorphic terms: "An EXISTENT endowed with anthropomorphic traits and engaged in anthropomorphic actions; an ACTOR with anthropomorphic traits."[2] The character is, then, the entity capable of taking the position of the subject or object of an action. As I discuss, the historical character may be a human being, but may also be an abstraction or a force of nature.

Finally, the character is a *crossroads of projection*, where the desires of the author, the reader, and the critic or scholar meet and are satisfied or not.[3] As many philosophers of history acknowledge, desire, at least part of which is unconscious, is at the root of scientific curiosity and the commitment the historian makes to specific events and actors. Therefore the historian has the moral duty to talk about what he is searching for. As Henri-Irénée Marrou puts it, he must "describe his internal itinerary, for all historical research, if it is truly fecund, implies progress in the soul of its author."[4] The reader, scientific or not, also searches for satisfactions that cannot entirely be defined as intellectual. The reader of history, who seeks historical comprehension of events, all the same chooses histories of a particular kind and finds pleasure in the exploits of the protagonists, even though historic actors are often collectivities or even "impersonal" forces of nature.

Why, then, in the contemporary era, have we held to the model of the character as the psychological individual, a kind of quasi person? Hamon describes the dominant trend, beginning in the seventeenth century, that subjects the character, explicitly or implicitly, to a psychological analysis that "systematically conflates *person* and *personnage*, *experience* (the real) and *experimentation* (the textual)."[5] Hamon identifies the sources for what he calls this "overvaluation" of the individual subject: the rise of the individual in the modern period as "the juridical and philosophical essence," as "universal value," in contrast to the exemplary quality of characters in medieval literature; the increasing valorization of the novel and its aesthetics of representation since the seventeenth century; and the "influence of theories of history that continue to privilege the perspective of the human individual as the center of creation," that is, the conception of political history of personalities, dominant well into the twentieth century.

This "personalist" conception of character is supported by the attitudes adopted by readers, authors, and critics. The reader, through the process of identification reinforced by the solitary nature of reading, takes pleasure in the projective impression that characters really "come alive." The author, for his part, indulges in a fantasy about his characters' autonomous "lives": how many novelists in interviews have spoken about how their characters "take off on their own," as if liberated from the constraints of the writing process? In much critical discourse, the "living" quality of characters becomes the hallmark of good literature and overshadows consideration of the rhetoric or stylistics of the textual construction of characters.

From a semiological perspective, Hamon observes, the character cannot be a corporal entity because there is no way to localize "him." The character is "everywhere and nowhere" in the text: he is glimpsed in the textual web of dialogues in which he speaks or which speak about him, in the descriptive and narrative passages, in the themes that emerge from the telling and the reading. Like other products of narration, the character is a *semantic effect* of the accumulating text: "Manifest in the form of a discontinuous group of traits, the character is a diffuse unit of meaning, progressively *constructed* by the narrative. ... A character is then the base [*support*] on which rest the semantic constants [*préservations*] and transformations of narrative; 'he' is composed of the sum of the information provided about what he *is* and what he *does*."[6]

A semiological analysis of the notion of character argues, then, that the character is a unit of signification and not a human individual. However, the twentieth century is still under the sway of the psychological conception of the character as pseudo person and the pronouncements of Henry James and others, who see in the internal states and movements of individualized characters the wellspring of all action and meaning. Semiologists struggle, Hamon argues, to disengage literary criticism from the "psychoanalytic" perspective that tends to confuse the experience of the real individual and the construction of the textual unit that acts in the manner of a subject. In discussions of the psychological sort, still quite common in courses on literature or cinema, the critical act consists in "discovering" the key to the behavior of characters. As Hamon puts it, "We plunge into full judicial arguments, exactly as if we were speaking of *living* beings whose incoherent behavior must be justified."[7]

Major theoreticians of narrative agree with Hamon that characters in narratives are *constructed* entities. For Claude Lévi-Strauss, "the character can be compared to a word encountered in a document that cannot be found in the dictionary, or to a proper name, that is, a term stripped of its context,"[8] which only the unfolding of the narrative can provide. For Tzvetan Todorov, "the 'semantic label' of the character is not a stable 'given' that exists a priori and that the reader only needs to *recognize*, but a *construction* that takes place during the time of a reading."[9] In *Structural Semantics* A. J. Greimas takes a further step in disassociating the entities acting in narrative from the notion of the personalized character.[10] *Actants* are defined not by "who they are" but as narrative functions, a limited number of positions adopted by various actors in relation to the narrative's trajectory. The character may have one or more functions, and a function may be assumed by more than one actor according to Greimas's classification: the subject (the protagonist, the searcher) and the object (what the subject looks for); the sender (the motivator of the search) and the receiver (of the searched-for object); the helper (who/which favors the subject's action) and the opponent (who/which opposes the subject's action). Moreover, actantial functions may be fulfilled by nonhuman entities (the grail as the object of the quest or the contrary winds that impede the ship's progress as opponent) or ideas (the religious concepts that propel the subject-crusaders on their mission). This kind of functional analysis of character is just as pertinent to history as it is to fiction. Indeed, as I attempt to show in the case studies to follow, Greimas's functions have parallels with the categories historians employ in asking questions about historical events. What entities constitute the historical protagonists? What is the object of the action? What forces propel the protagonists into action? For whom or what are the actions undertaken? What elements favor or thwart the subject's goals?

Semiology, then, proposes a broader notion of the character that is not limited to mimicking the psychological individual, the privileged character in novelistic fiction, but allows us to consider fictional and historical characters as performing similar functions in narrative texts. Indeed, semiologists would argue that the analyst is unable to differentiate, in functional terms, between historical figures, individual, collective, or inanimate, as they appear in historical fiction and as they appear in legitimate historical narratives. It is much easier to distinguish between the "real" and the "fictional" characters of the same name on the basis of the work of construction that each entails.

Hamon proposes a category of actors he calls *referential characters*. These are not only historical characters, but also mythological and allegorical ones, which bring with them into the world of the fiction a set of actions, behaviors, and especially images that are part of the shared cultural baggage of the reading public. They appear, Roland Barthes observes, as "citations," ready-made figures lifted from the commonplaces of the cultural codes, to which the author refers without making any effort to "to construct—or reconstruct—the culture they give voice to."[11] Unlike other narrative actors, these referential characters do not "come alive." They make relatively short appearances in fictional texts—Napoleon in *War and Peace* or Abraham Lincoln in *The Birth of a Nation*—where they signify for the reader/spectator a place, a time, a situation, their meaning and destinies fixed in advance. Fictional protagonists, on the other hand, are semantic "blanks," unknown characters with proper names that are gradually characterized as the narrative develops. I would add a second type of ostensibly historical characters: the protagonist who adopts the name, the position, and some of the acts of the historical person—but is taken over by the fictional imagination. Thus, the historical figure is "filled out" with anecdotal details of behavior and signs of inner subjectivity that belong to the unknowable of the historical past. The cinematic costume drama, the Hollywood biopic, and other subgenres of the history film provide countless examples of such pseudohistorical characters.

We can make some initial assertions about narrative actors in history by comparing them to the types of characters that appear in fiction. In contrast to the referential character, the character in historical narrative is not a citation, an unexamined figure lifted from the already known of a culture; he, she, or it is an entity reconstructed by the labor of the historian. He is not a semantic "blank," even if the historian proposes to study a figure neglected by previous histories, since the historian's work is based on what it is possible to know about the real past of the protagonist of an action. The historical character exists, more or less latently, more or less formed, before the historian begins to research or write about his existence. In contrast to the *fabulations* of the costume drama, the historical character is constrained by the traces of his existence and all the other histories of which he has been the subject. However, he retains something of the fictional protagonist because the historical character is not prewritten: the historian assigns the historical actor to his proper place in the chain of events, charting his role in the teleology he is reconstructing.

HISTORIOGRAPHICAL APPROACHES TO CHARACTER

We pass now to the camp of the historians to consider how they describe the nature of the character in history. As Antoine Prost observes, historians are largely in agreement about the nature of the objects of their study; he demonstrates this by citing statements by many major figures of modern history. Fustel de Coulanges asserts that history is "the study of human societies." Charles Seignobos echoes him: "History, in the modern sense, is reduced to the study of men living in society." Lucien Febvre separates history from metaphysics: history is not interested in the human as universal essence, "some notion of man as abstract, eternal, at bottom immovable, perpetually identical to himself," but in a concrete notion of organized human activity, "men always captured in the framework of societies of which they are members." Marc Bloch emphasizes that the historical subject is always the group, not the individual: "Rather than the singular, favorable to abstraction, the plural, which is the grammatical mode of relativity, is suited to a science of the diverse."[12] The historical character is normally, then, a collectivity, a social group of varying proportions: the Nation, the International Community, the Arab World are large-scale historical characters; a political faction, a trade union, or a militia are smaller-scale historical characters. As for the individual human subject, he may be considered as a historical character under specific conditions:

> In order for an individual man to interest history, he must be, as we say, *representative*, that is representative of many others, or else he must have had a verifiable influence over the life and destiny of others, or finally that he brings out, by his very singularity, the norms and habits of a group in a given time.[13]

The historical individual embodies, in the manner of the synecdoche, the traits of his class, acts "alone" on the stage of history in relation to collective actors, or serves as a foil whose difference paradoxically signals the general social patterns from which he deviates.

The subjects of all historical narrative are human beings, organized in groups and living in society. The field of historical characters can only rarely be reduced to an individual or a number of identifiable individuals. Historical narrative is, then, more abstract than psychological fiction in that historical characters do not conform to the fictional model of a configuration of individual protagonists. The historical actor is a collective figure involved in collective actions. On the other hand, the historical character is not abstract in the philosophical sense of the universally human, always and everywhere the same. As Paul Veyne would say, history is a sublunary form, attached to concrete time and space.

As the privileged subject of social discourses, the collective actor can act, desire, or feel like the individual actor. In the following passage, Prost brings out the anthropomorphic qualities history attributes to abstract entities:

> *Society, France*, the *bourgeoisie*, the *working class, intellectuals, public opinion*, the *country*, the *people*: so many concepts that

have as their characteristic feature the fact that they subsume a group of concrete individuals and appear in the historian's discourses as plural singulars, collective actors. They are used as the subject of verbs of action or volition, even sometimes under the reflexive form: the bourgeoisie *wants, thinks that, feels itself secure* or *menaced,* etc., the working class is *dissatisfied,* it *revolts.* Public opinion is *anxious, divided,* it *reacts,* unless it *resigns itself.*[14]

But is it proper to assign to the collective actors of history the qualities that seem to belong to characters in novels? Historians and sociologists have long resisted this transference and have denounced as "naïve realism" the act of giving to social groups the attributes belonging to the novel's human "individuals." But faced with the common phrases that Prost offers as examples in the passage just cited, we have to yield to the fact: historians cannot help but use the language of individual intentions and psychology in representing the actions, feelings, desires, and even emotional states of historical actors. What does the use of such a vocabulary mean? If fictive and historic actors are defined by the same process of attribution, then can we conclude there is a direct relationship linking them together?

It is Paul Ricoeur who has reflected in the deepest and most subtle ways on this question. At the beginning of the first volume of *Time and Narrative,* Ricoeur observes that there is a deep split between narrative discourse in historiography and narrative in fiction, and an essential part of this split hinges on the differentiation between actors in history and actors in fiction. At the end of this same volume, Ricoeur retraces "*an indirect filiation* linking historiography to narrative intelligence" that does not deny in any way the "epistemological *break* between the historiographical entities and narrative characters." The break resides in the distance separating the *anonymous* historical entities who act "in the background of individual actions" and individual narrative agents.[15]

To respect the epistemological break, Ricoeur proposes a notion of the historical actor that maintains with the fictional actor an indirect link of kinship. He calls the societal agents of history *entities of participatory belonging.* This formulation rests on the definition of society that Maurice Mandelbaum gives in his *The Anatomy of Historical Knowledge:* "A *society,* I shall hold, consists of individuals living in an organized community that controls a particular territory; the organization of such a community is provided by institutions that serve to define the status occupied by different individuals and ascribe to them the roles they are expected to play in perpetuating the continuing existence of the community."[16] Ricoeur underscores the importance of the three aspects of the definition: the community's link to a territory; the institutional regulation of the social identity of the individual; and the community's continuity of existence.

Mandelbaum permits us therefore to envisage a single society as a quasi person located in a specific space, made up of organized groups of individuals, and acting within a duration that articulates past, present, and future. The historical character resembles, then, other narrative agents. Like the individual human agent, the historical character is capable of having desires and intentions, behaves as the subject or object of verbs of action, and accumulates attributes, as novelistic agents accumulate "character traits." Moreover, he operates within a narrative world that has spatial coherence and temporal continuity. In his definition of society, Mandelbaum insists on the collective nature of social entities while at the same time making what Ricoeur terms *oblique reference* to the individuals who make them up. Society, since it is made up of individuals, acts like a great collective individual. The relationship between the individuals and the society is based in the notion of *participatory belonging*, and the individual actors participate in collective action through their attribution as *members of*. To quote Ricoeur's summation:

> It is because each society is made up of individuals that it behaves like one great individual on the stage of history and that historians can attribute to these singular entities the initiative for certain courses of action and the historical responsibility—in Aron's sense—for certain results, even when these were not intentionally aimed at. But it is because the technique of narrative has taught us to dissociate characters from individuals that historical discourse can perform this transfer on the syntactical level.[17]

TECHNIQUES OF REPRESENTING HISTORICAL ACTORS

I would like to return to a work of theory on historical representation that proceeds inductively from the study of specific historical texts. In *The Rhetoric of Historical Representation*, Ann Rigney approaches the problem of the construction of historical actors through an analysis of three histories of the French Revolution written in the nineteenth century: Alphonse de Lamartine's *L'Histoire des Girondins*, Jules Michelet's *L'Histoire de la Révolution française*, and Louis Blanc's *L'Histoire de la Révolution française.* Her work, informed by contemporary narratology, analyzes historical writing in terms of the pragmatics of textual construction. Rigney underscores the problems the historian/ narrator faces in conceptualizing and developing a discourse on the French Revolution. What is called the revolution is in fact a vast "event-worthy" field (Veyne) that can be traversed in many ways, according to the perspective the historian adopts. The revolution is made up of events in which a multitude of characters, individual and collective, participate. For the most part, the actors of the revolution do not occupy the scene of history in continuity; subjects or objects of action, they appear and disappear at the dictate of the broad concerns of the macronarrative. Thus, the historian, unlike the novelist, cannot organize his narrative around a stable configuration of characters "whose recurrence across the narrative syntagma provides ground against which the continuities and transformations in the represented world can be measured, and whose hopes and fears provide the basis upon which any such changes can be evaluated."[18] Rather, it is the historian's task to identify and configure a shifting field of actors that embodies the collective development of the revolution and shows the way to its ultimate effect. As Rigney demonstrates, the choice to include or exclude particular figures determines how the "collective historical subject" is identified at each moment of the drama.

What is at issue in the macronarratives of the revolution is the development of a grand social entity—the Nation or France, for example—"the subject of 'History'"—which is by definition impersonal or, rather, "transpersonal." Its evolution is manifested in the actions and interactions between individuals, institutions, and groups at each moment of narrative development. Groups may be "ad hoc formations," or they may have the more stable existence of an institutionalized entity, even if the name of the group does not always refer to the "same" stable membership. The name attached to the individual or group has the advantage of reference for the reader: a name is a shorthand identification of an actor that enables the reader to "follow his progress throughout the narrative." To a certain extent, the characters of the revolution are prefigured; that is, they exist as already identified individuals or groups who play a well-known role—Robespierre and the Garde Nationale, for example—and they bring with them meanings, a semantic dimension, that preexists in the received culture of the public of readers. However, even the individual actors whose presence is obligatory in any account of the revolution are open to refiguration: the historian may modify or radically transform the received meaning of characters; he may assign them a particular place on the chain of causality or may determine the role they play (subject or victim, hero or antagonist) and their ideological character (reactionary, progressive, for example). The individual historical character may have a biographical dimension, and to the extent that his actions, words, and behavior have been documented, he can be the object of psychological analysis. How many historians have reflected on the "personality" of a Danton or a Robespierre?

However, historical characters often are not distinguished by a proper name because they are anonymous or because their "personalization" is not relevant to the narrative of events. Rigney emphasizes the conventional character of the language that refers to social entities. The group, composed of a number of unidentified individuals, presents itself as a figure named in the singular, le Peuple, for example, as the entity appears in Blanc or Michelet. When the nineteenth-century historian chose to present a character that was unknown to his reading public, he had several means of identifying him: through his actions and conduct or by his belonging to a class or category of actors—sex, profession, nationality, and so on. The historical actor is presumed to share the attributes and the symbolic or moral values by which his group is defined. As Rigney tells us, nineteenth-century historians linked moral values and physical appearance. Thus, with Lamartine only the royal family retains the moral and aesthetic qualities of humanness, evoked in lengthy descriptive passages. All the others are part of the madness of the crowd, grotesque in appearance and bereft of human motives. To the extent that the historian foregrounds a character as member of the group, he embodies in this individual the aspirations of the collectivity. The focalization on individual but previously unknown characters that Rigney calls "figures in the crowd" serves to define the group. The narrator attributes to this lone face only those traits relevant to the description of the historic situation and to the role his group will play in events, that is, the signs he manifests as *member of* his class.

In general, historical characters are defined in relation to the other actors involved in the same narrated event, and the play on resemblances and differences between characters is one of the foundations of narrative, whether fictional or historical. The historical character is also related by his diachronic links with actors who have already acted or will act in the future. As we have seen, the historian's retrospective understanding of events allows him at any given moment of his narration to position the historical character not only in relation to his past but also in relation to events that have not yet taken place.

These general considerations on the nature of the character in historical discourse are predicated on written texts, and it is certainly true that the cinematic means of expression impose specific conditions on the identification and elaboration of characters (see Chapter Two). However, nothing prevents us from applying to filmic representation the definition of the historical character, as developed in this chapter, and the textual problems of representation that Rigney analyzes in terms of written narrative.

Leger Grindon has argued (following Georg Lukacs's analysis of the historical novel) that the dramatic structure of the historical film attempts to blend the personal and the collective. The collective is the properly historical aspect of representation, with its emphasis on the group profile, common action, and public ritual. The individual, revealed in intimate scenes, is the locus of the identification through which the public experiences the psychosocial motivations that drive the individual protagonist toward historical action.[19] As we saw, skeptical historians deride this admixture of the personal and the "historical" as a mayonnaise that does not take and consider the extrapersonal elements of collective action or spectacle as nothing more than the historical alibi for what is at the heart of the film: the psychological or epic drama of imaginary protagonists. However, I argue in the following analyses that historical films indeed privilege the extrapersonal in one of two ways. Either the film works to include the individual within the social by describing the distinct personality as an aspect of the group profile and incorporating the intimate scene as part of a collective action, as if the personal and the extrapersonal were simply different scales of representation chosen at particular moments, or the film uses a rhetorical strategy in which the individual embodies a whole social position, the intimate scene condenses the collective situation, and, in the manner of the synecdoche, individual actions stand for collective destiny. The two films that are the objects of the following case studies, Jean Renoir's *La Marseillaise* and Mikhail Kalatozov's *I Am Cuba*, construct the protagonists and antagonists of the most convulsive of historical events: revolution.

CASE STUDY: A HISTORY TO SAVE THE REPUBLIC— JEAN RENOIR'S *LA MARSEILLAISE* (1938)

The narrative goal of nineteenth-century republican histories of the French Revolution, Ann Rigney suggests, was the construction of a grand subject of history, one that would embody the aspirations of the new era. A very similar intention would seem to motivate Jean

Renoir's *La Marseillaise*, a film that looks back nostalgically—but also with a certain desperation—to the founding moment of contemporary France and the metanarrative that recounts how that transpersonal, transcollective character of the Nation emerged from the ashes of the old regime. How does the historical representation of the Nation that Renoir constructs in *La Marseillaise* in 1938 fit into the tradition of republican history for which it seems a latter-day reflection?

Antoine Prost observes that "history is a social practice before being a scientific one."[20] Historians address their public—the society, or segments of society, in whose interest they pursue their research and for whom history takes on meaning. Ultimately, history is not erudition for its own sake but a discourse that functions to connect the members of a society to their historical past. In the wake of the turbulent events of nineteenth-century France, the Third Republic (1870–1940) understood that it was in the national interest to establish universal education for all social classes and to make the study of history—republican history—an essential part of the curriculum. In the period between 1880 and 1882, left-leaning majorities in the Chamber of Deputies and the Senate laid the foundations for the modern French system of instruction by making education secular, free, and obligatory. The close relationship between a political vision of the French nation and the teaching of history emerged as a strategy for mediating social divisions, especially through the fusional figure of the Nation.

Thus, through a process of exclusion/inclusion, French historians retrospectively realigned the significant events of the French nation. The republican view imposed order and meaning on the complex and sometimes inchoate developments of French history and rendered a valuable service to the state. The anachronistic survival of this so-called *école méthodique* in a scholarly context that called for objectivity in the historical sciences was largely due to the useful social function it performed in educating young French students for civic life.

> While doing this [elucidating the historical causes of contemporary situations], [historians] explain to the French their divisions, give them meaning, which allows the French to accept them and to live them in the political and civilized mode rather than in the violent mode of civil war. History's mediation has permitted, by means of a reflexive detour, to assimilate, to integrate the revolutionary event and to rearrange the national past in relation to it. French society gives itself representations of itself through history, it understands itself, thinks itself through

history. In this sense, it is profoundly true that history is the foundation of the national identity.[21]

Because of the social power of republican history, a truly analytic, critical history made a tardy entrance into the historical institutions in France. Indeed, Pierre Nora dates the final demise of this last predominant form of history/memory with the collapse of the Third Republic, that is, in the cataclysmic events that ended in an occupied France in World War II. Until then, it sustained a tradition of memory based in the notion of the Nation: "Throughout this period, history, memory, and the nation enjoyed an unusually intimate communion, a symbiotic complementarity at every level—scientific and pedagogical, theoretical and practical."[22] In the course of the 1930s, Nora argues, a movement of desanctification emerged among historians that put into question the couple Nation-State and substituted for it the couple Society-State. While the concept of the Nation embodied ultimately the reconciliation of differences in the interest of national solidarity, the concept of Society acknowledged social conflicts and contradictions that might be irreconcilable and threaten the notion of an overriding unity. Thus, the new historian, in his theoretical and pedagogical roles, rejected the function of the standard-bearer of a tradition, the messenger who transmits values. He was no longer "part priest, part soldier," as Nora puts it, but a critical instrument that "sows doubt; it runs the blade of a knife between the heartwood of memory and the bark of history."[23]

Doubt was, however, politically dangerous in the France of 1938. The notion of the Nation, so recently desanctified by professional historians, needed to be resanctified and revitalized as the ideological center of history under the Third Republic. The choice to situate the origins of the modern French world in the events that follow on 1789 is significant. The grand historical narrative of late nineteenth- and early twentieth-century France is republican in character, and the curriculum in history begins with the assumption that contemporary France is heir to the tradition of the revolution, and that its identity is grounded in the affirmation of this historical continuity. Skirting the embarrassing problem of the Terror, the Third Republic erects a bridge across the Empire, the Restoration, and the Second Empire to reestablish its historic roots in the ideals of the French constitution.

Historian Guy Bourdé observes that the educational policy of the Third Republic—formed by highly placed members of the state administration and forces within the university—developed according to specific goals: "to educate the new generation in the love of the Republic in order to consolidate the social base of the regime; to subdue clerical obscurantism by removing from the Catholic Church control over the human mind; to prepare for revenge against the hereditary enemy, the German Reich."[24] This militant program, at odds with the reevaluation of historiography that was taking place within the university, found its pedagogical expression in the textbooks in history, geography, and civics historians wrote for children. Bourdé notes that *Le Petit Lavisse*, the famous and consecrated *manuel d'histoire* targeted at children from seven to twelve years old, was already in its seventy-fifth edition in 1895.[25] With a young readership in mind, E. Lavisse's language was simple and lacking in nuance and the political points openly promulgated. For the last edition in 1912, E. Lavisse, doubtless with an eye on the historical crisis then developing between France and Germany, made the political goals of his textbook explicit:

> If the schoolchild does not take away with him the living memory of our national glories, if he does not know that his ancestors fought on a thousand battlefields for noble causes; if he has not learned what it cost in blood and effort to unify our fatherland and to disentangle, from the chaos of our obsolete institutions, the laws which have made us free; if he does not become a citizen infused with his duties and a soldier who loves his rifle, the schoolteacher has wasted his time.[26]

It is ironic to think of Renoir associating himself with this kind of rhetoric. Antipathetic to received ideas, Renoir had always been the filmmaker of the social differences and class antagonisms that splinter the French body politic into incompatible divisions. In this regard, his social vision is much more in tune with the emergence in the 1930s of a new history that saw France as a divided society, not a cohesive nation. Moreover, Renoir the realist was not given to conventional representations or the ideological abstraction of allegorical figures. Yet in *La Marseillaise* Renoir reshapes the old figure of the Nation, which, despite its maintenance at the symbolic center of the national curriculum, was becoming increasingly dated; the pedagogical history fostered by the Third Republic, with its tendentiousness and militancy, was out of synch with scientific developments in twentieth-century historiography.

It is not difficult to understand, however, in the chaotic world of France in 1938 the social forces that motivated Renoir. It was the role of historical memory, invoked by the Popular Front, to revivify the founding moment of the revolution and its defense against foreign attack and offer it as the model of national unity to be followed in a period of crisis. In his provocative reading of the film, Leger Grindon argues in part that *La Marseillaise* operates as a sort of *film à clef*, in which certain characters or events are covert references to contemporary figures of Popular Front politics or to polemics within the left. Thus, the vacillating Louis XVI stands for the weak socialist Léon Blum, or a scene set at Valenciennes "alludes to the division in the Popular Front over the Spanish Civil War."[27] Indeed, according to Grindon, Renoir's film can be read as a history of the Popular Front: "Viewed in this context, *La Marseillaise* expresses the euphoria of the campaign, the tensions within the coalition, and the disillusionment with leadership."[28]

It strikes me as more likely, however, that Renoir, in the realization of the film, sought to take his distance from the internecine politics of the Popular Front. Paradoxically, Grindon makes this point as well, citing Renoir: "It would be impossible for us to make a film on the present political situation; this would risk provoking polemics and being disagreeable to a public which goes to the cinema simply for distraction."[29] Indeed, the film seems to avoid specific historical parallels in favor of a grand vision of the revolutionary tradition of the alliance of classes—the Nation of republican history—that is intended to bolster the general social program of the Popular Front.

As Renoir's remark indicates, *La Marseillaise* was intended for the broad French public in whom the film aimed to revive the ethos of nationalism. It is precisely his project to evoke a political kinship between two historical situations, even though the militant initiatives of the revolutionary forces in the period of 1789 to 1792 hardly resemble the demoralized inertia of French society and the faltering, factional left of 1938. The Nation is a kind of "mystical union," here portrayed as the abiding historical force that will come to succor the internally and externally besieged France on the brink of war. In response to internal crises and the threat of the German war machine, Renoir's film reworks an ideology that is not based in class conflict but in national harmony and unification against France's traditional enemy. The kind of cross-national sympathy expressed in the French and German aristocratic or working-class characters in Renoir's *La Grande Illusion*, produced only a year before, is unthinkable in *La Marseillaise*, in which such bonds take the form of treacherous cross-national allegiances between French royalists and their German counterparts against the emerging French nation.

In *La Marseillaise*, Renoir's strategy for representing historical characters binds together two apparently disparate representational tendencies: to construct the character as a figure of participatory belonging, an abstraction of the attributes of his class, and to anchor the character in the concreteness of the individual (most notably in the photograph-able body) and the specific details of mise en scène. As I attempt to show, the tension between the abstract and the concrete underpins the major aspects of the film's approach to its material: the narrative roles the film assigns to its characters; the description of the social group-ings as members of (or outlanders to) the Nation; the representation of difference and the effacing of difference among the members of the Nation; and the filmic strategies that modulate and combine the abstract and the real.

The Nation is an abstract large-scale entity that seems to bear few of the anthropomorphic traits that distinguish the character in nar-ratives. It is very far from any "personalist" conception of the actor. It is not modeled on direct experience; it produces no *real effect* because it lacks material existence. In semiological terms, the Nation does not belong to the realm of denotation because no body or group of bod-ies can directly represent it; indeed, it is characterized by its physical absence. In *La Marseillaise*, it belongs to the intangible realm of the symbolic: it cannot be represented, it can only be *signified*. More like a projection than a normal character, the Nation is quite literally "every-where and nowhere" in the text: it never speaks, it is spoken about; it does not act in its own name but operates at a remove through the intermediary of more concrete characters. Its existence is signaled nonetheless by a name. The "Nation" is frequently on the lips of the films' protagonists, and its identity is progressively constructed as the film unfolds. It is a semantic effect, the ultimate signified of the posi-tive human actions the film represents.

Indeed, one can see the film as the narrativization of the virtues of the Nation. *La Marseillaise* is therefore less an action plot than a work of figuration in which, by example or counter example, every actor and every action serves to fill the abstract Nation with meaning. The Nation is patriotically French (the artisan, clerk, priest), not allied with foreign powers (as are the royals, particularly Marie Antoinette); it is impas-sioned and vital like the orators at a political meeting in Marseille, not nostalgic and moribund like the aristocrats in exile at Coblentz; it is popular and democratic (the citizen, the foot soldier), not elitist and hierarchical (civil authorities, generals, and the cavalry).

The process of figuration in *La Marseillaise* is very close to the trope of synecdoche: the concrete actors and actions stand as partial (and incommensurate) embodiments of the abstract concept of the Nation. It is therefore not surprising that Renoir's film does not cor-respond to the narrative model in film. In classical cinema, attention is focalized on a few individualized protagonists who are the privileged instruments of the action (and of meaning), and the action itself is organized into a tight chain of cause and effect, forming the dynamically structured plot. *La Marseillaise* proposes, by contrast, a multiplicity of characters, who are conceived less as individual protagonists than as members of their class and whose acts are therefore not personal feats but the exemplification of collective action. Moreover, the film is episodic in structure: we move from place to place, from one event to another, not because one action is the immediate cause of the next but because Renoir wants to illustrate the general spheres of revolutionary and counterrevolutionary action.

Given these deviations from classical structure, how can we describe the film's characters and their positions within the narrative? I would argue that the actantial model, briefly described in the section on narratological approaches, offers an effective instrument not only for the analysis of characters in films like *La Marseillaise* but also in historical narratives in general. A. J. Greimas makes a productive distinction between *actant* and *actor* thus providing a more flexible conception of narrative agencies, one more appropriate to historical discourse. The actant is a basic role in a narrative that can be carried by multiple actors; actors are characters who are so many concrete embodiments of the actant in the narrative. The actant is therefore more general and more abstract than the individualized actor and corresponds more adequately to the conception of the collective entity that often acts in historical narratives. It is not tied to the notion of the character as a pseudoperson or to the stable configuration of protagonists and antagonists, which assumes that narrative is the product of interpersonal conflicts. The actantial model is therefore able to comprehend the shifting field of actors who appear and disappear at the dictate of historical narration and account for a large-scale actant like the Nation. Such changes in the dramatis personae do not disrupt narrative continuity because historical action is not necessarily tied to the continuous acts of specific actors.

An actantial analysis of *La Marseillaise* makes Renoir's project quite clear. The *subject* can be identified as the Marseillais, the revolutionary army that ventures north in the defense of the revolution, but also le Peuple, the French body politic exclusive of its political masters (the royals, the aristocrats, civil authorities, generals, etc.). That is, the subject is all those actors who act in the interest of the Nation. The defense of the revolution is then the *object* the subject seeks. However, there is a second object of the quest, a necessary corollary of the first, the formation of the Nation, an ideological construct that the actors illustrate through their commitment to action. National fusion also emerges through a process of identification in which the different social actors, suppressing all social division, merge their interests with those of the Nation. One becomes part of the Nation through a process of initiation, best exemplified by the character Bomier, who at first rejects as pompous and foreign, then gradually masters the revolutionary hymn, "La Marseillaise." To learn "La Marseillaise" is to adhere to the Nation. During the march toward Paris, an unidentified soldier speaks with a second soldier, perhaps a courier, about to depart, charging him with two commissions: giving twenty francs to his nephew and teaching him "La Marseillaise." The Nation-seekers' actions all target a single object, the fusion—represented in the film as the literal coming together in revolutionary Paris—of the patriotic social classes from all regions of France. At the end of the film, the Nation, invested with the actions of its adherents, becomes the collective entity that Renoir proposes as the subject that will defend France against foreign attacks (in the wake of 1789 or in response to the German threat in 1938).

The *sender*, who transmits values to the subject and motivates him in his quest, is embodied in several characters: progressive priest le Père Paget, who calls on the young to join the revolution; the patriot Moissant, who urges the citizens of Marseille to take the city's four forts; Louise Vauclair, Parisian fishmonger, who insists the Marseillais volunteers go to Paris to take care of the traitors—the king, the queen, the members of the National Assembly who fear le Peuple de Paris— before attacking the Austrian army; and the shadow puppet performance in Paris, which represents the King and the Nation separated by the abyss of the Brunswick Manifesto, issued by the German army invading to safeguard the monarchy.

The *opponents* of the quest are the royals and the aristocracy, whose allegiances are to their foreign brethren and who unleash the Austrian army on their fellow Frenchmen; the higher echelons of the army who are aristocratic and defeatist; and the Swiss guards, foreign mercenaries whose fealty is to their employers. The *helper* is manifest in Bomier's mother, who allows him to sell the family vineyard to pay off his debts so he can join the march to Paris with the Marseillais volunteers, and the priest who brings sustenance to the troops as they move north in the valley of the Rhône. As an actantial analysis of the film suggests, the narrative of *La Marseillaise* is reflexive: the subject, the Marseillais and le Peuple, in the process of defending the revolution, stands as an exemplar of the object, the Nation, and it is therefore not surprising that the *receiver* of the object is the selfsame Nation in all the diversity that its actors represent.

The narrative project of the film already announces itself in the *distribution* of characters in the opening credits, which divides French society at the time of the revolution into social categories: the Court of Louis XVI, Civil and Military Authorities, the Aristocrats, the Marseillais, le Peuple. These abstract social groups will, of course, be transformed by the techniques of cinematic representation: the incarnation of essential characteristics in the bodies of actors and expressive features of mise en scène. The antagonism between social categories is quickly established as the succession of exemplary tableaux that constitute the film unfolds. In the film's second sequence, the peasant Anatole Roux is brought to trial by the local lord for killing a pigeon, a crime against aristocratic privilege. Physical and moral traits distinguish the plebian from his titled persecutor. Roux is unkempt in appearance and natural in his demeanor, witty and wily, integrated into the society that witnesses the trial and engineers his escape; the aristocrat, by contrast, is formal in appearance, stiff and haughty in demeanor, humorless, and ineffectual against the wiles and humor of the crowd.

In the third and fourth major episodes of the film, we find a similar delineation by contrast. The title, "Marseille October 1790," introduces us to a political meeting in which the Marseillais patriots accuse reactionaries in business, political office, and the army of compromising the revolution. Citizen Moissant summarizes, in his impassioned, declamatory style, the situation for the ebullient crowd and calls for taking the forts of Marseille where rebel officers support the reactionaries. The citizens subsequently take possession of the last fort not by violence but through a ruse: the Trojan horse of a cask of wine offered by the city to the fort's occupants conceals a patriot who succeeds in opening the gate for his comrades, who surprise and defeat the reactionary officers without bloodshed. The fourth episode is located at the Hotel Stadt Coblentz, in April 1792, where exiled French aristocrats have sought asylum. Their sorry state is proclaimed by a notice: "Our gentlemen guests are kindly requested to pay the week in advance." A melancholic air sung by a bewigged woman in court attire evokes the aristocratic regrets for the France of the old regime; in the atmosphere of trifling activities, the insightful Monsieur de Saint Laurent and the militant Monsieur de Fauguerolles argue about the advantages and dangers of an alliance with the Prussians (even among the doomed class there are sages); a foppish aristocrat attempts to lead the assembled in a gavotte but has forgotten the movements. The Marseillais and the aristocrats serve as foils for each other and bring into relief the contrasting class cultures that characterize them as historical antagonists:

the fervor and bonhomie of the rising classes, the lifeless narcissism of the nobility. Moreover, the groups are defined by their allegiances: the Marseillais are partisans of the Nation; the *aristos* ally themselves with their Prussian and Austrian class brothers.

Among the partisans of the Nation, Renoir is careful to represent the heterogeneity of the group—differences in social position and occupation that are effaced in the overriding camaraderie of the revolutionary movement. These representations conform to a basic typology. Le Roux, the cunning peasant who escaped from the tyranny of aristocratic law, joins a group around a fire in the backcountry that includes Arnaud, an educated clerk, who is the voice of reason and possesses a certain dignity of class; Bomier, a mason who displays the fervent naiveté of his popular Marsaillais origins; and Paget, the poor, good-hearted priest who is to be distinguished from his aristocratic and debauched bishop. Humorously contrasted, the characters function as signifiers of diversity. The differences they represent dissolve into the solidarity they adopt against the enemies of the Nation. The depiction of regional difference is equally benevolent. With his commitment to social realism, Renoir delineates and contrasts the linguistic and gestural specificity of his characters. As the battalion of the ebullient Marseillais arrives in the northern capital, where banners on a tribune proclaim "strength and union," it encounters the Breton battalion and is immediately integrated into the solidarity of regional forces come there to defend the revolution. The encounter between the Marseillais and le Peuple de Paris is equally felicitous: Bomier the mason falls in love with la Petite Louison, and overcoming regional difference becomes as easy as the Marseillais learning to eat the exotic potato.

There is no need to multiply the examples, which are obvious in their intent. Renoir's film ceaselessly works on the social and cultural categories: those that are irredeemably oppositional and those that are capable of assimilation. We are dealing here with a representation of historical actors that emerges from the nationalist school of history that belonged to the Third Republic: a history that sacrifices social and cultural differences to its political project. In his analysis of the *manuels scolaires* published between 1884 and 1914, Guy Bourdé shows how French history is written in terms of the forces that lead to the ultimate victory of the Republic and those that constitute obstacles to this final realization of "eternal France":

> The inhabitants of this beautiful country belong to a collectivity that progressively becomes national. Nothing really

distinguishes them from each other: regional characteristics are effaced; social inequalities are blurred. The "others," the different individuals, are identified with foreigners, enemies, aggressors. The long march toward the formation of the Nation-State unfolds like a succession of exceptional events in which virtuous heroes distinguish themselves.[30]

In certain passages, *La Marseillaise*'s depiction of exceptional events seems to imitate the "picture gallery" format of the *manuels scolaires,* the *Petit Lavisse* and its imitators: a rhetorical strategy that reduces complex historical situations to conventional imagery. The film's episodic quality reinforces this impression by separating the narrative into isolated moments. The major narrative segments are chronologically ordered and frequently dated, but they often lack the kind of narrative continuity between sequences typical of the fiction film. Each episode takes on an emblematic character: the actions represented and the characters, with their "typical" physiognomies and gestures, stand for the contending forces of the revolution. In the film's first sequence, for example, the Duc de la Rochefoucauld-Liancourt announces the fall of the Bastille to Louis XVI, who receives the news reclining in bed, a chicken leg raised to his mouth. This is the image, bristling with irony and humor, of the inept and distracted king focused on his own pleasures. Renoir's Louis XVI is perhaps well-meaning, sentimentally attached to his people, but he cannot master events and will be led to betrayal by the pressure of a heartless and malevolent queen—that Austrian and enemy of France who will browbeat the king into signing the repressive measures of the Brunswick Manifesto. The film reprises from nineteenth-century historians certain telling gestures and words that seem to confirm Renoir's depiction of the king's personality and his destiny. Louis's wig is askew as he reviews the Garde Nationale just before the insurgents attack the Tuileries, and as the royal family crosses the Tuileries gardens on their way to the National Assembly to seek asylum from the insurrection, Louis remarks that the leaves have begun to fall early this year.

In his effort to give figurative representation (in the sense the term has in painting) to the forces that become the Nation, Renoir relies on specific filmic strategies. As I argue in Chapter Four, devoted to the problems of historical rhetoric in film, filmmakers who seek to recount collective actions performed by collective actors are obliged to develop techniques of representation that countervail the tendency of the filmic image toward the specific and concrete. Master of the telling detail, Renoir's constant concern is to negotiate between the particular (the actor's individual physiognomy, the concrete and circumscribed locations, the depiction of singular actions) and the general (the anonymous group, the broad historical space of events, and the collective nature of historical action). In *La Marseillaise*, the particular is the individual, endowed with a proper name, who appears and reappears in the development of the narrative and whose personal destiny becomes a matter of concern to the spectator. The general exists in the representation of the mass, which cannot be identified by a proper name or a personal history; the crowd's identity is specified, rather, by signifiers of class and social position, regional characteristics, and political allegiance. For Renoir, the particular is essential in presenting the human face of the historical actant and in soliciting the spectator's identification with the collectivity. The general provides the historical dimension of events and the historical impact of individual action. This alternating evocation of the specific and the general resembles the rhetorical figure of the *zeugma*, the "grammatical coordination of two words that possess opposed semantic features," often the abstract and the concrete.[31]

Articulating the specific with the general and the concrete with the abstract is a central preoccupation of Renoir's films of the 1930s and is particularly visible in his use of the moving camera and deep-focus cinematography allied with the long take. In *La Marseillaise*, this strategy is one of the underpinnings of Renoir's historic vision. One of the clearest examples—and the most virtuosic—is the scene of the departure of the Marseillais volunteers, which is made up of a single shot and exploits the linking function of the moving camera and deep-focus mise en scène. The shot begins in the treetops—the dappled sunlight on the bark of plane trees that signifies Provence, where a banner floats, proclaiming: "Volunteers of Marseille—to Paris to save (to indicate that the rest of banner's message is not visible)." A young boy straddles a limb watching the events unfold in the square. The assembled intone "La Marseillaise." The camera begins a fluid movement at a high angle above the crowd, tracking into closer views of the smiling and singing crowd. The camera lingers a moment on the face of a young girl in her white bonnet, a man in his *chapeau bicorne* kissing women goodbye, the song leader singing the next verse—all briefly focalized by a slowing movement of the camera. Bomier the mason comes into view with his mother behind him: she falls to her knees and Bomier stoops to comfort her. A circle of distraught women takes up the emotion of Bomier's mother, grouped around a bright spot of light and dappled shade.

The camera swings around and approaches Bomier and his comrade Cugulière, who initiates a snatch of dialogue: "Tu chantes?" ("You're singing?"). Bomier, still hiding his love of the anthem of the revolution, replies, "Je chante pour faire comme tout le monde" ("I sing to be like everyone else")—words that epitomize the film's project. Bomier takes his leave, and the camera remains static as Arnaud and other volunteers pass by and kiss Bomier's mother. Thus, the figurative strategy that individualizes the actors and links them in a chain of solidarity is embodied in the unity of the long take with its "democratic" moving camera and the deep focus that contextualizes every action and gesture.

In the representation of the march on Paris, Renoir juxtaposes two types of representation to achieve a similar integration between the general and the particular. The first is the depiction of the mass—the straggling line of soldiers seen in long and very long shots; the second is the depiction of individual actions, captured in brief scenes made up of several shots. Thus, for example, we watch Bomier attempting to master the "Marseillaise" and Javel fuming about reactionary priests, while Arnaud reminds him of the positive role priests play in the revolution (an example of the film's reconciliation of contradictions). The scene is a moment of continuous development, but even while Renoir seems to center our interest on a particular action and particular characters he insists on contextualizing the focalization. For example, after an interchange between volunteers about the best way to stuff their boots, the camera becomes distracted by an "anonymous" soldier passing through the frame and shifts to follow him. It is important for Renoir to show that Bomier, Arnaud, and their comrades are not exceptional heroes, and that the crowd generates such individuals constantly, as if the camera needs only tarry a bit in one part or another of the immense field of history for such individuals to emerge. The principle of the historical individual is that he is representative and therefore replicable.

Another type of reconciliation between the particular and the general occurs within a single shot through the artifice of deep-focus mise en scène. In the massacre of the invaders of the Tuileries by the Swiss Guard, Arnaud is hit and Bomier mortally wounded. We witness Bomier, pulled into the courtyard of a building, dying in his sweetheart's arms, but the personal suffering of that moment is already contextualized: beyond the pietà composed of Louison and Bomier and through the carriage gate, we continue to witness in deep focus the vicissitudes of the battle as the insurgents first retreat and then return victorious. We soon learn that the palace has been taken, the Swiss executed, and the king deposed.

The film ends at the front where the Marseillais defend their freedom against the foreign invader, and here the historical past and the crisis of 1938 occupy the same scene of representation. A title announces the French victory against the Prussian army at Valmy and cites Goethe, who was present: "In this place and on this day began a new period in the history of the world." While *La Marseillaise* conjures the defeat of Prussia in 1792, the smoke of war is barely lifting, as if this great moment of closure opens onto a new period of danger for the republic. As the German armies mass on the borders of France in 1938, *La Marseillaise* calls on all French citizens, in memory of the revolution, to forget their differences of class and culture and to rally to the collective defense of the Nation.

CASE STUDY: STANDING FOR THE REVOLUTION—
MIKHAIL KALATOZOV'S *I AM CUBA* (1964)

Russian filmmaker Mikhail Kalatozov began work in 1962 on the Soviet-Cuban production (Mosfilm and ICAIC) that would become *Soy Cuba*. It would be based on a text by poet Yevgeny Yevtushenko and Cuban writer Enrique Barnet. Kalatozov was to work with cinematographer Sergei Urusevsky; their collaboration on *The Cranes Are Flying* (1957) and *The Letter Never Sent* (1960) had already shown an extraordinary combination of vision and technique. Kalatozov (born in 1908) was inspired by the example of Sergei Eisenstein in his ambition to create an epic film of the Cuban revolution based on an innovative cinematic "language." Preproduction took more than a year, during which the director, his cinematographer, and the two writers researched the film in Cuba, carefully structured the script, and planned the visual effects. Actual work began a year after the Bay of Pigs debacle and shortly after the Cuban missile crisis had awakened the world to the reality of the nuclear threat.

The press packet for *I Am Cuba* describes the film as a "wildly schizophrenic celebration of Communist kitsch, mixing Slavic solemnity with Latin sensuality."[32] This characterization seems fashioned to cover the embarrassing gap between its initial release, at a moment when Castro's Cuba still represented for many a socially progressive regime, and its American distribution some thirty years later when the collapse of the Soviet Union and revelations about how Castro's revolution had become another brand of Stalinism served to undercut its historical relevance and relegate it to the realm of dated propaganda. The film's release under the patronage of American auteurists Francis Ford Coppola and Martin Scorsese signaled *I Am Cuba* as an aesthetic event, which indeed it was, and critics considered the film significant, not for its representation of the Cuban revolution, but for its spectacular cinematic and formal qualities ("Visually Staggering," "ecstatic," "delirious"). Could one see in *I Am Cuba* simply a recent example of that process described by Gérard Genette in which the pragmatic urgency—the "relevance"—of a text is eroded by time and the work survives on its aesthetic merits?

I don't think so. I argue that *I Am Cuba* is a superb example of historical representation in cinema. In the following analysis, I consider how the film organizes the event-worthy field of the Cuban revolution and, in particular, how it constructs characters that are both historiographically and cinematically coherent.

I Am Cuba is divided into a prologue and four parts. The prologue evokes the beauty of pre-Columbian Cuba, rendering the island through a telescoping of scales: grandiose helicopter shots over the island are almost geographical in scope; as the helicopter descends, the palm trees can be distinguished, shot with infrared film stock that gives them a ghostly look; then, the constantly moving camera descends to skim the earth from a skiff that gives us views of villagers engaged in daily activities. The text speaks of Christopher Columbus, the happiness of Cubans at the time of his landing, and the tears shed as Cuban sugar is opened to colonial exploitation.

Each of the four parts of the narrative focuses on a particular location, a particular social group, and a particular moment in the development of the revolutionary struggle. The first section evokes the city of Havana in the 1950s as a colonial playground where rich businessmen pursue Cuban women, victims of the island's poverty who are forced to submit to degradation and self-denial. The film focuses on a particular victim, Maria (also known as Betty), who represents not only colonialism's degraded women in Havana's pleasure industry, but, through metonymic extension, the plight of the urban poor who inhabit the same Havana shantytown.

The second section moves to rural Cuba, where the film recounts the ruination of an old peasant named Pedro, who stands for his social class in the manner of the allegorical figure. Unknowingly, he relinquishes the rights to the land he cultivates with a thumbprint on a document the landowner persuades him to "sign." The landowner, a powerful armed figure on horseback, sells the land to United Fruit, and the disenfranchised Pedro torches his house and fields rather than allow his work to be appropriated by foreign interests.

The third section recounts the revolutionary student movement in Havana and centers on the character Enrique, who represents the students' revolutionary commitment to support Castro's insurgency and bring down the Batista government. He also embodies the ideological conflicts of the movement: is it morally or tactically correct for Enrique to assassinate a sadistic police officer responsible for the death of his comrades? As he becomes the symbolic center of a demonstration, Enrique marches to his own death at the hands of the same police officer.

The fourth section describes the insurgency in the Sierra Maestre. A poor peasant, Mariano, stands for the emerging revolutionary consciousness of his class. In the first sequence, Mariano invites an exhausted insurgent to eat with him, but when Mariano sees the soldier's rifle, he asks him to leave his home because, he says, he wants to live in peace. In the second sequence, Mariano's house is demolished in a bomb raid by Batista forces, and one of Mariano's children is killed. Radicalized by events, Mariano decides to join the insurgency. In the third sequence, Mariano finds Castro's troops and meets again the rebel soldier he threw out of his house. The soldier tells him, "I knew you would come." Mariano captures a gun in battle. The film ends in a propagandistic flourish: the guerrillas march triumphantly toward revolutionary victory. (A fifth segment of the original screenplay on "the struggle on the plains" was never shot.)

This brief synopsis of the action reveals several important aspects of the film's narrative design and the way it organizes the historical events.

First, it is helpful to recall Ann Rigney's analysis of the narrative operation in history as a process of inclusion and exclusion or Paul Veyne's notion of an itinerary the historian constructs across an event-worthy field. The historian includes certain actions and certain actors while he relegates others to the background or simply excludes them. Such narrative choices construct a reading of historical events and simultaneously position the reader/spectator in relation to them.

This essential historiographical operation is at work in *I Am Cuba*. The prologue sets up the long historical view: pre-Columbian Cuba is a paradise lost in which a harmonious relationship between a land and its people prevails. Disrupted by the Columbian discovery, Cuba is opened to the West and to a history of exploitation and suffering. The brutal transition from the idyllic landscapes of the prologue to the raucous rock-and-roll trio and the vulgar beauty pageant on the terrace of a Havana high-rise indicates that the film will take up Cuban history after Batista's coup d'état of 1952. The first two parts of *I Am Cuba* describe Cuba under the sway of American investments: the American mafia's transformation of Havana into a playground for Western businessmen and American corporations' exploitation of Cuban agriculture. Thus, through a work of condensation, the economic and human exploitation represented in parts 1 and 2, held in place, as we see in part 3, by a repressive state apparatus, stands for the revolutionary imperative.

The structure of causality in *I Am Cuba* is then quite simple: the historic circumstances that constitute the prerevolutionary situation described in parts 1 and 2 provoke the revolutionary actions undertaken in parts 3 and 4: the student movement engages in militant action, disseminates propaganda, and battles Bastista's repressive police force; a peasant exposed to the violence of military repression is radicalized and joins the insurgency in the Sierra Maestra that will lead to revolutionary victory. Moreover, the four parts of the film are organized around a geographical alternation between the city and the countryside: the two spheres of oppression and revolutionary action. The scenario of *I Am Cuba* is the result of what Robert Rosenstone has called the work of *condensation* and *compression*, in which large-scale historical situations and events are synthesized or represented symbolically. As I have suggested, this work of symbolization is often founded on the figure of the synecdoche, in which the part stands for the whole, the particular for the general.

Second, each of the four parts of *I Am Cuba* is a distinct narrative development that shows no immediate relationship to the others. There is no stable configuration of characters: with one minor exception, the protagonists act within the context of one of the four sections of the film and do not recur. They do not, in the manner of fiction, carry the action forward as the agents of continuity. Characters appear and disappear from the scene of representation according to the historical logic the film imposes. In terms of plot, there is no specific chain of cause and effect that links, in the manner of fiction, one part to the next. This episodic structure stems from the ambition of Kalatozov and his collaborators to construct collective, not individual, characters. The writers' intention was not "to elevate any one individual ... , but to show the 'historic necessity of the people's break from Bastista's American-backed government.'"[33]

Third, despite the episodic nature of characters and actions, *I Am Cuba* is a coherent narrative. That coherence does not exist at the level of the actors, conceived as individual protagonists occurring on the surface of the narrative; it depends, rather, on the deep structural organization of narrative functions, like the one I suggested for *La Marseillaise*. Using the categories of the actantial model, I propose the following simple analysis of *I Am Cuba*: (a) The subject of the narrative is the revolutionary actor, embodied in student militants Enrique, Alberto, and others; the peasant Mariano after his radicalization; and the insurgent army. (b) The object sought by the subject is the end of neocolonial exploitation and the revolutionary transformation of Cuban society. (c) The senders (the motivators of the action) are the figures of the oppressed embodied in the film's passive or defeated characters, particularly Maria/Betty, the unwilling prostitute, and her neighbors, other shantytown dwellers; Gloria, who is aggressed upon by American sailors and protected by student militant Enrique; and Pedro the exploited peasant. (d) The opponents who act to thwart the pursuit of the object are the instruments of oppression or repression: pleasure-seeking businessmen, United Fruit and big landowners, the sadistic policeman who shoots students, Batista, the government's military forces, and so forth. (e) The helpers include René, the fruit salesman in love with Maria; the street singer whose voice dissuades Enrique from killing the police officer; Gloria, who calls out to Enrique during the fatal demonstration; and the rebel soldier, who represents for Mariano the necessity of armed struggle. (f) The receivers of the object (fruits of revolution) are the exploited and oppressed masses represented in the film by the victimized women, the urban poor, the exploited peasants, the cigar factory workers, among others.

What allows us to move immediately from the actorial to the functional levels of the narrative is the fact that the characters in *I Am Cuba* are all *entities of participatory belonging*, to use Paul Ricoeur's formulation. Each character is not simply an individual actor but embodies the characteristics of the social group to which he belong; each action takes place simultaneously in the circumscribed space of the scene and on the more abstract stage of history. I propose to analyze one such historical character: Maria/Betty, the unwilling prostitute of part 1.

In Chapter Two, I cited Francis Vanoye's analysis of the differences between written and filmic discourses. If the *substance of the content* (actors, events, ideas, and so on) are common to both mediums, the *forms of expression* are radically different. Thus, when I describe a character like Maria/Betty in narrative or symbolic terms, as I did in the previous paragraphs, I am talking about a content that could take cinematic or written form. In analyzing *I Am Cuba,* it is important to grasp how the film expresses this character, how it establishes her relationship to her social category, and how it constructs her symbolic position.

I begin with the observation that the film is not discursive in the usual sense: the voice-over is quite discreet and does not constantly intrude to organize events or to comment on the characters and their actions. In the part we are considering, it intervenes only at the very end of the last sequence and speaks its mind directly to the fleeing pleasure-seeker, Jim, who is nothing more than a dot on the shot's horizon. The events that take place in part 1 are apparently singulative rather than iterative (single occurrences rather than repeated ones), and as representations of individual actions, they all have great "signifying relief." History in *I Am Cuba* is expressed scenically, that is, through filmic sequences we take to be quite continuous in time and space. Ann Rigney observes that such moments of textual expansion in written history (compared with moments that are presented more generally or more elliptically) are "the locus of the heaviest symbolic and rhetorical investment on the part of the historian."[34] Historical representation in *I Am Cuba* operates in exactly that manner: while the continuous sequences seem to give us depictions of specific places, characters, and actions, the film invests these depictions with symbolic and rhetorical significance.

Thus, *I Am Cuba* cannot be read according to the well defined codes of cinematic representation; indeed, the film is highly experimental and constantly breaks from the norms of film practice in commercial cinema. It is this deviation that accounts for the film's rhetorical power. The most obvious areas of innovation include Mikhail Kalatozov's expressionistic mise en scène, abetted by Cuban painter René Portocarrero; the dazzling effects of Sergei Urushevsky's mobile camera and long takes; and the radical experimentation on the relation between sound and image, including the poetic dual-language voice-over and the "unrealistic" synchronization of sound.

Part 1 of *I Am Cuba*, which features Maria/Betty, is made up of four segments. In segment 1, the central protagonist, Maria/Betty, does not appear. It opens instead with a black singer caught in the expressionistic mise en scène of a Havana nightclub: we see him from a very high angle, framed by bamboo curtains and lit with dramatic source lighting. The sense of composition is strong: unsettling diagonal lines and the dark masking of portions of the image suggest the projection of an inner vision. The singer is dwarfed by a "primitive" statue, which, along with other elements of the decor, introduces the theme of exoticism. Exoticism, which in its most positive sense can be the experience of difference, loses here all authenticity. Exoticism is the mise en scène of the "native," the Western projection onto the Other of all the attributes of the "savage" (Gauguin expressed his desire to escape from Western bourgeois culture and morality as, "I want to go live among the savages."). The native takes on the traits the Westerner denies in himself: primeval appetites, the reign of the instinctual over the rational or the moral.

As the camera follows him in a very long take, the singer (played by the former falsetto lead of the Platters) sings, strangely out of synch, a

song about "Loco Amor": unbridled love, the eroticism that is inseparable from the experience of the exotic and that can be indulged
precisely because of the native object's presumed primitivism. As he
moves away from the camera, we see that a white mask is affixed to the
back of his tuxedo. The racial theme (the reference is to Franz Fanon's
Black Skin, White Mask) is allied to the theme of exhibitionism: I
exhibit (and betray) myself as the mask of the exotic Other the cus-
tomer desires. The camera continues to track the singer as he moves
behind a bar, his white mask striking in profile; in the foreground, we
are given medium shots of beautiful women of color in evening gowns
seated at the bar: the feminine Other offers up her body as a spectacle
of difference, a commodity to be consumed.

The camera climbs again to a high angle and searches out a table
of three white businessmen, framed as before in emphatic fashion by
a bamboo curtain and the play of light and shadow. A waiter stands
ready to take their order. The camera moves to a medium close shot
of one of the businessmen in sunglasses, who looks offscreen and says,
referring to a woman seated at the bar, "I'll take that tasty morsel."
A second businessman approaches him from behind and says lubri-
ciously: "And I'll take that dish." The singer finishes his act kneeling on
the floor. Are his contorted gestures signs of mad love or of agonizing
self-denial? (His performance anticipates Betty's dance in segment 3.)
The camera tilts up to reveal the group of businessmen and the women
they have chosen. One of them says, "Nothing is indecent in Cuba if
you've got the dough." The sequence ends with a dance that combines
themes of exoticism, eroticism, and the duplicity of the masked face. A
line of women dancers in "primitive" costumes that leave their bodies
nearly naked surround the businessmen, and as they exit the frame,
each removes her mask to briefly reveal her face to the camera.

What is striking about the first nightclub sequence is the figurative quality of its mise en scène: the setting, the characters, and their
actions are intended to be read symbolically. The nightclub is not so
much a credible space as a vision of a colonial netherworld where the
characters take their place in a symbolic drama of exploitation. The
American businessmen are near caricatures whose vulgarity and
insensitivity are signifiers of the heartlessness of colonial exploitation.
The Cubans—performers for hire—play the parts assigned to them by
Western exoticism, their self-denial the price of their "participation"
in a colonial economy. The symbolic relationship in which a specific
aspect of setting or specific characters and their actions represent
larger historical situations and events is well expressed in Ricoeur's

notion of *standing for.* The three remaining segments continue to play on the figurative possibilities of mise en scène.

In the second segment, everything about the mise en scène is antithetical to the first segment: the location is exterior, not interior; the lighting is dazzling in its brightness, not dramatic and low key; the vistas are open, not claustrophobic. These qualities are immediately perceived as the symbolic matrix within which we see Maria for the first time. Identified with light and openness, she bears the name of womanly purity. However, the light/dark antithesis evident in the contrasting mise en scène of the first and second segments is recalled by Maria's costume: she wears a white scarf that contrasts with her dark dress, suggesting the paradox of her dual identity (Maria/Betty). The long takes persist, but as the camera shows us Maria and her fiancé, René the fruit seller, it moves horizontally and gives us eye-level views of the couple, suggesting the normalcy of their relationship. René, the honest worker whose vendor's song contrasts with the nightclub singer's, is connected to the revolution; he is a helper and conceals papers (leaflets?) in his fruit cart for student militants. As the camera focuses on René, it tilts up so that he is dominated by the white cathedral, from which we hear a passage of organ music. René sings to Maria—once again the voice strangely out of synch with the image of the singer—and tells her they will be married there, and that she will wear a white dress. He moves around his cart and chooses a single piece of fruit, a tangerine, whose significance is emphasized by an extended close-up, and gives it to Maria. Maria slips out of frame, in a movement that suggests her discomfort. We are left with a view of René, set against the cathedral's façade, as he says: "I love you. Maria! Maria! Maria!"

A fourth call to Maria is heard over the first image of segment 3: a close-up of Maria, framed by a bamboo curtain in the low-key lighting we recognize from the nightclub of segment 1. She is now dressed in black evening clothes appropriate to the milieu; the only discordant note is the shining crucifix she wears. She moves behind the already-familiar bar; a woman calls her name, "Betty!" (the generic moniker for the Latin American female) and ushers her into the company of the American businessmen we met in the first segment. The impact is startling because we already know this particular hell and because the chromatic (and symbolic) contrasts with the previous sequence condense into an instant our recognition of the story of this fallen woman. She carries into the scene two symbolic objects: the first is the tangerine, the gift of love, which she puts into her purse as one man jokes about it; the second is the crucifix, a sign of purity and resistance, which draws the attention of Jim, the least coarse of the three businessmen.

The game of seduction continues. By lot, Jim draws Betty as his dancing partner. The dance itself stages Betty's emotional experience of her fall: she resists Jim, but as the dance becomes frenetic, she loses control and is thrown from one partner to the next. Betty's torment is emphasized by a series of frenzied movements toward the camera, which catches her momentarily in close-up. Then, somehow Betty is extricated from her partners' aggression; the swing music is muted, and we hear instead the rhythm of bongo drums. She dances alone as if carried away by some primitive instinct, her face revealing her torment. Close-ups of Betty's frenzied dance alternate with tracking shots of the grotesque onlookers egging her on. She dances around the "primitive" statue from segment 1 as the crowd chants, "Betty, Betty, Betty!" We cut to the entrance of the nightclub, where the Americans are leaving with their women. Jim tells Betty it would be "interesting" to see her place.

Maria/Betty is a symbolic entity: she both suffers and resists and thus stands for the collectivity of exploited women—most immediately, the category of women who line the bar in the nightclub scenes. The symbolic function of the character does not, however, suppress the character's other functions. It is also the filmmakers' intention to represent in Maria/Betty the experience of oppression from "inside," that is, the (historically real) struggles and suffering of women defeated by the overpowering effects of poverty. These sequences do what cinema does very well: they call on us to identify with the subjectivity of a character, whose plight gives us access to the emotional cost of exploitation. Can such empathy be considered historical? I would argue that the representations of Maria/Betty's psychological state are part of what philosopher R. G. Collingwood calls the *a priori imagination*. We observe the existence of the top of a table, and we imagine the necessary existence of its underside. As Collingwood suggests, "We cannot but imagine what cannot but be there."[35] In the same manner, we know through the factual record that women in Havana were exploited in the sexual trades. We are therefore authorized to *imagine* the necessary historical reality of their suffering.

In segment 4, a taxi ride during which Betty demurs from Jim's advances serves as a transition between the place of exotic spectacle and the "real" social space of Betty's ghetto existence. Paradoxically, the shantytown, which one might think would be treated in a realist manner, is rendered in an expressionist mise en scène that is as distorted as that of the nightclub. The enormous American taxi comes to a stop in the middle of an immense puddle, the car's length exaggerated by a wide-angle lens. Jim's initiation to the underside of colonialism is fraught with discomfiture. He and Betty make their way into this new symbolic space by stepping from stone to stone across a flooded landscape. The deliberately artificial lighting design, which resembles something out of a Murnau film, allows the couple's image to be reflected in the water and justifies the kind of self-conscious framing and masking we saw in the segments in the nightclub. The set design is also theatrical in character: the shanties, far from being realistically rendered, are constructed as images; their most salient feature is the tangle of power poles that give the impression of disjointed crosses—another example of symbolic mise en scène. Inside Betty's shack, seduction and resistance center on the crucifix that Jim admires. Betty removes it; Jim tries to replace it around her neck, but she throws it on the floor and gives vent to her anguish by beating on the wall. She turns back to Jim and slips her dress off her shoulders. Jim turns off the light.

In the second sequence, we see in daylight a chair on which Betty has placed objects from the night before: her handbag, the pearls that decorated her hair, and two keys to the symbolic drama, the crucifix and the partially eaten tangerine. Jim's hand enters the frame and picks up a piece of the tangerine, and the panning camera follows the movement from hand to mouth. With nonchalance, Jim goes about the usual rituals of the morning after: he combs his hair, leaves money on the pillow of the sleeping Betty, returns to the chair, and picks up another piece of tangerine and the crucifix. He says to her, "I would like to buy this." When she refuses, he simply adds more bills to those already on the pillow and pockets the crucifix. We hear the voice-off of René's vendor's song. A striking deep-focus composition condenses all the tension of the moment of discovery: Betty in the foreground covers her nakedness with a sheet, Jim is in the middle ground adjusting his suit jacket, and René is framed in the brightly lit doorway in the background. René approaches Betty and faces down Jim in a close shot, which through a rack focus effect emphasizes Jim's uneasiness. René turns back to Betty, and we see Jim in depth waving from the doorway: "Goodbye, Betty." René exclaims, "Betty?" and then moves toward the door. The camera tracks in to a prolonged close-up of the distraught Betty. The filmmaker's choice to represent Maria/Betty's fall in Christian and specifically Latin terms of purity and sin serves to intensify woman's experience of colonial oppression because her own culture cannot forgive the fall, even when it is imposed by the conditions of neocolonialism.

If Betty's drama has ended, Jim's is about to begin, and it is at this moment that the film generalizes the symbolic references to the effects of neocolonialism on urban life in Cuba. What happens when colonial insouciance is forced to face the human costs of indifference? The sequence begins with a close-up of Jim, who unwraps a candy and puts it in his mouth, oblivious to his surroundings. The beginning of a nervous jazz piece challenges his composure. Jim is suddenly thrown into an expressionist nightmare: he is caught in the labyrinthine ghetto, hemmed in by a narrow passageway and threatening darkness. When he reemerges into the light he is pursued by a boy and stumbles about in a warren of cactuses and shanties. In long shot, we see him surrounded by begging children: "Money, Mister!" The tracking camera follows the frantic Jim looking for an exit, but endowed with sensitivity, as it passes ghetto residents, the camera's attention is drawn to them: an anguished mother with her child, an old man with a cigar, children staring out of what appears to be a cage, a woman and her child washing bottles in a bucket. The hysterical Jim finds himself face to face with an old man. At this moment, the camera rises in a crane shot higher and higher above the rooftops, where old tires hold down tar paper, until we have an extreme high-angle shot of Jim's escape toward the horizon, his route marked by ghetto figures who gaze after him. The voice-over returns: "I am Cuba. Why are you running away? ... Don't avert your eyes. Look! I am Cuba. For you, I am the casino, the bar, hotels and brothels. But the hands of these children and old people are also me. I am Cuba."

4

REFIGURING HISTORY IN FILM

In this section of the study, I raise two sets of questions. The first concerns the nature of historical representation: What is the relationship between a historical narrative and the reality in the past to which it refers? What models have philosophers and historians proposed for refiguring the past? The second set addresses the rhetoric of historical representation in film: How do films refigure the historical past? What differences are there between rhetorical strategies in filmic, as opposed to written, histories? Can both historical documentaries and historical films of mise en scène be considered legitimate forms of historic discourse?

THE REALITY OF THE PAST AND HISTORICAL NARRATION

In his philosophical investigation of historical narration, Paul Ricoeur begins with the question that underlies all the others: "What does the term 'real' mean when it is applied to the historical past?"[1] As Ricoeur observes, it is an embarrassing question because answering it embroils the historian in a discussion of the problems of knowledge: the documents on which the reality of the past is predicated are fragmentary, selective, and conserved in the interest of particular social forces and political initiatives. Despite what the historical science brings in terms of rigor and method, the historian can only narrate what the historical record, with its biases, allows him to know or infer about the past.

133

Moreover, he can only attempt to avoid the pitfalls of subjectivity, the unspoken affinities and predilections that underpin the questions he asks about the past; he can only attempt to counterbalance the weight of the present moment that can distort or displace his point of view. And yet, the recourse to documents and the reliance on method are the historian's refuge, the inescapable condition that founds history's difference from fiction. The historian does not invent his narrative; he *reconstructs* it, and he does so under the ethical imperative of fidelity: "Through documents and their critical examination of documents, historians are subject to what once was. They owe a debt to the past, a debt of recognition to the dead, that makes them insolvent debtors."[2]

From this ethical position stems the special character of historical representation. In written fiction, to represent means to produce mental images of things—settings, characters, actions—that are absent but imagined as present. Historical narratives do not attempt to evoke an illusory presence since history's aim is to preserve the pastness of events. Indeed, the debt the historian owes to the past excludes such free imaginative activity, and the reader of history, for his part, is called on to curb the projective activity of identification with character and action and to respect the *having-been-there* of the past. Historical knowledge passes through the concrete vestiges of the events that mediate all reference to history. It is worth reviewing here Ricoeur's notion of the trace. On the one hand, the trace marks the moment of the past to which it bears witness—concrete testimony that shows that "a man, an animal passed by here." On the other hand, like all signs, the trace is perceptible in the here-and-now and invites the historian to move back in time to find the activity (the cause) that left this vestige (its effect). The trace is therefore a *sign effect*, and the historian's task is to make it speak in his discourse. The past is conceived as a "vis-à-vis" in relationship to which the historian constructs his narrative. In history, to represent means to *stand for* and the notion of standing for distinguishes history from all other modes of representation.

THREE MODES FOR UNDERSTANDING
HISTORICAL MIMESIS

Ricoeur argues, however, that the concept of standing for does not resolve the enigma of the relationship between the discursive and the real. Through what process, on the basis of what model, does discourse construct its representations? Ricoeur proposes rethinking that relationship in terms of the "great genres" advanced by Plato in *The Sophist*: the Same, the Other, and the Analogous, each of which corresponds to one of the positions that the philosophy of history has developed to understand the ontological status of historic discourse.[3]

Under the Sign of the Same

Under the sign of the Same, philosophical thought proposes reducing the temporal distance between the moment in which the historian writes and the moment of the historical past he is attempting to represent. In this model of knowledge, the historian's activity results in a *de-distanciation* such that it produces an "*identification with what once was.*" British philosopher R. G. Collingwood's *The Idea of History* is, for Ricoeur, the exemplary text that defines how historians may conceive sameness as the principle of historical representation. Collingwood contends that the historian's goal is to detect the *thought* that underlies historical action. Historians, he argues, deal with both the *inside* and the *outside* of events. The outside is the behavioral—"everything belonging to it which can be described in terms of bodies and their movements."[4] The inside is that "which can only be described in terms of thought," and thought includes the full range of human intentions and motivations. The historian's work is to negotiate between the outside and inside of events until he reaches an understanding of their cause, which is always expressed in terms of thought. Collingwood describes the process in the following way:

> The historian of philosophy, reading Plato, is trying to know what Plato thought when he expressed himself in certain words. The only way in which he can do this is by thinking it for himself. This, in fact, is what we mean when we speak of "understanding" the words. So the historian of politics or warfare, presented with an account of certain actions done by Julius Caesar, tries to understand those actions, that is, to discover what thoughts in Caesar's mind determined him to do them. . . . The history of thought, and therefore all history, is the re-enactment of past thought in the historian's mind.[5]

Reenacting thought can come only through a complex process in which critical method, historical knowledge, and intuition reconstruct the mind of the historical other. But reduplication bears with it a certain danger because it tends to erase the temporal distance between the historian's mind and the mind of the other: "Historical knowledge is the knowledge of what mind has done in the past, and at the same time it is the redoing of this, the perpetuation of past acts in the present."[6] If the past is perpetuated in the present, then what remains of its pastness? Ricoeur argues that there is a final "decisive step" to be made in order to bridge the gap between the historian's mental reenactment and the inside of historical events. The thought the historian constructs must be posited as "numerically identical" with the thought underlying historical action in order to abolish the distance that separates them. If historical knowledge is essentially knowledge of the thought of the past and if the historian is capable of replicating that thought in his own mind, then there is, in Collingwood's words, a "sense, and one very important to the historian, in which they are not in time at all."[7]

Thus, by positing his reconstruction of thought as the *same as* the thought underlying historical reality, the historian sabotages his own enterprise by obliterating the essential quality of historical events—their pastness. In such a conception, the standing for that characterizes historic discourse's relationship to events disappears because the two terms of the relationship have become identical. For Ricoeur, Collingwood's model breaks apart because of "the impossibility of passing from thought about the past as my thought to thought about the past as other than my own."[8] Historical representation is incapable of reducing historical events to an essential *inside* that exists as if out of time.

Under the Sign of the Other

Under the sign of the Other, philosophers of history espouse a position that runs directly counter to Collingwood's. In a radical critique of historical narrative as replication of the past, they reestablish *difference*—temporal *distance*—as the essential relationship between the historian's discourse and the reality of the past. Emphasizing the strangeness of the past rather than its familiarity, the historiography of difference combats the tendency of Western historians to manipulate historical material to make it fit into their own predetermined models. The past, the partisans of difference argue, cannot be made to speak with the voice of the present. Ricoeur characterizes this conception of historic otherness as the "negative ontology of the past."[9]

Michel de Certeau offers the most radical conception of difference. He argues that the "historiographical operation" is largely determined by the social "site" of production from which the historian speaks, that is, the *institution of knowledge*,[10] housed within the university, that determines the profession's methods and practices. The historian's first gesture begins the process of misrepresentation. He takes possession of the archival material of history and redistributes it differently. This new cultural distribution "consists in *producing* such documents, through the act of recopying, transcribing or photographing these objects by changing both their place and their status."[11] For Certeau, the historian's discourse dominates the fragmentary citations of the language of the historic other, forcing them to fit within the structure of meaning it imposes. Thus, the historian's voice of knowledge speaks for the other who cannot speak for himself. It "grants itself the power to speak what the other signifies without knowing it. Through 'quotations,' citations, notes and the entire apparatus of permanent references to a first language ... , [the historian's discourse] establishes itself as *knowledge of the other.*"[12] Everything works to substantiate the historian's authority: documents certify the "factual" basis of the historian's narrative, while the fragmented and incoherent body of documentation submits to the power of the organizing discourse. "The language cited [the historical traces] thus has the function of certifying the discourse as referential, it introduces into it a real effect, and because of its fragmentation, it refers us back discreetly to a position of authority [the historian's model]."[13]

However, a discourse that "quotes" the other runs a certain risk: its strangeness may well overwhelm the apparent explanatory power of the master discourse. The "other," through the very strangeness the historian seeks to suppress, may return to unmask the historian's model. In Certeau's view, a more authentic history would involve not the construction of models, but the observation of the *gaps* between models and the materials they attempt to master. Contemporary history, then, is written on the margins since the historian's practice is incapable of explaining the meaning of past experience.

In his critique of Certeau's model of difference, Ricoeur points out that the notion of the gap is no less atemporal and no more apt at "signifying the *having-been-there* of the past" than the notion of the Same. The gap provides only a negative image of the past, "divested of its properly temporal intention."[14] Certeau's work is valuable, Ricoeur argues, as a necessary "cleaning operation" that sweeps away the pretensions of mastery on the part of historical discourse and exposes the precarious nature of an enterprise that seeks to resurrect the past by reduplicating it in the present. But, Ricoeur adds, Certeau's critique serves only as a preliminary operation. It has nothing positive to say about the survival of the past within the present, one of the central questions that historians address. How can difference occupy the role of standing for in relation to a past that "once was real and alive"? Instead of representing the past, it evokes the fleeting shadows of events, which cannot be coerced into discursive or narrative structures.

Since historical reality is unknowable, the contemporary world is cut off from any meaningful experience of the past.

Under the Sign of the Analogous

As Ricoeur argues, neither the positivism of Collingwood nor the negativism of Certeau is without merit, and both can perhaps be salvaged under the sign of the Analogous. The Analogous has the virtue of combining notions of the Same and the Other on the basis of "a resemblance between relationships rather than between terms per se."[15] We are no longer in the domain of the Same because the historian does not attempt to reduplicate past events through mental representations. Nor are we in the domain of Difference since the notion of the analogical proposes a positive relationship between discourse and the reality of the past. Under the sign of the Analogous, the historian posits a relationship of *resemblance* between the reality of the past and his discourse about it without compromising the autonomy of either. This relationship is expressed by the term *standing for*, which suggests neither identification with the past nor alienation from it, but something that lies in between.

For Ricoeur, Hayden White is the key figure in developing a theory of the Analogous. In *Metahistory* and *Tropics of Discourse*, White hypothesizes that historical representation is a poetic operation based in analogy: the narrative the historian emplots stands in a relationship of analogy to the events that really took place; the historical character is an analogue of the men and women to whose real existence the trace bears witness. As Ricoeur observes, the structure of historical narrative is complex compared to the basic structure of fiction. In writing history, the historian constructs a "model," an "icon" that is capable of standing in for past reality. The relationship between the discursive and the real is based in *likeness*, which both separates the discursive from the real—the terms of comparison maintain their identities—and connects them—the terms are nonetheless homologous. This is the same mimetic-homological model that Jean-Marie Schaeffer proposes for nonfiction, in which discourse maintains "local structural equivalencies" with the realities to which it refers (see Chapter 2).

THE RHETORIC OF PREFIGURATION

White's theory of historical rhetoric concerns the initial stage in the development of a historical narrative when the historian draws the fundamental contours of his work. He adopts the word *prefiguration* for this moment of the genesis of discourse. To represent "what really took place," the historian must first prefigure the field of historical events. White sees in prefiguration the work of *tropes* by means of which it is possible to give a first form to the objects of historical knowledge, and this form will have a determining role in the elaboration of a historical narrative. To speak about tropology, White calls on the tradition of rhetoric since Aristotle, the art of eloquence and persuasion and the techniques this art puts in practice. He proposes as fundamental poetic structures the four basic tropes of classical rhetoric: metaphor, metonymy, synecdoche, and irony. He is not speaking here, of course, of ornaments of discourse—individual metaphors or metonymies—but of metaphoric, metonymic *operations* that govern the relationship between a discursive representation and the historical reality to which it refers. Metaphor is the central figure and its vocation is *representative* since it functions to establish a relationship of resemblance between the terms of comparison: "Properly understood, histories ought never to be read as unambiguous signs of the events they report, but rather as symbolic structures, extended metaphors, that 'liken' the events reported in them to some form with which we have already become familiar in our literary culture."[16]

White suggests that the basic tropes offer structures of meaning, "models of the direction that thought itself might take in its effort to provide meaning to areas of experience not already regarded as being cognitively secured by either common sense, tradition, or science."[17] The four major tropes provide discrete modes of comprehension. The metaphoric operation is a "search for similitudes" between two phenomena that appear at first quite different from each other. Metonymy offers a "mechanistic" idea of the links between phenomena that configures the discursive field as a "complex of part-part relationships," as in the relation of cause to effect. Synecdoche is the figure of integration that understands specific, concrete phenomena as belonging to an encompassing whole and posits the possibility that any one phenomenon can stand for the totality. Irony is the figure of ambivalence and skepticism, the critic of perceived similarities and differences, offered by "all forms of metaphorical identification, reduction, or integration of phenomena."[18] For White, each type of figuration favors a specific plot genre. Metaphor is linked to romance, metonymy to tragedy, synecdoche to comedy, and irony to satire. However, such a neat correspondence between figures and genres leads to a system of classification that undercuts the depth of White's insight and limits the power of rhetorical analysis. If metaphor is the basic figure, Ricoeur suggests that metonymy, synecdoche, and irony serve to correct the naiveté of metaphor: "The prerogative of the four basic tropes of classical rhetoric is that they offer a variety of figures of discourse for this work of pre-figuration and hence preserve the richness of the historical object both by the equivocity proper to each trope and by the multiplicity of figures available."[19] There are, of course, many taxonomies of rhetorical figures, some, like White's, fourfold, others more inclusive, and one could quibble with the way he understands individual figures. However, what is crucial to retain is White's insight that the figurative operation underlies the historian's organization of the historical field; it is the motor that drives narrative understanding.

Ricoeur draws an emphatic conclusion from his analysis of White's theory of tropes: "Rhetoric governs the description of the historical field just as logic governs argument that has an explanatory value."[20] The statement is categorical, but Ricoeur imposes conditions. First, the principle of the Analogous cannot be detached from the work of the Same and the Other, which are essential to accounting for the temporality of history—the having-been-there:

> The past is indeed what, in the first place, has to be reenacted in the mode of identity, but it is no less true, for all that, that it is also what is absent from all our constructions. The Analogous, precisely, is what retains in itself the force of reenactment and of taking a distance, to the extent that being-as is both to be and not to be."[21]

Second, Ricoeur emphasizes the danger involved in holding that the moment of prefiguration in historical narration is a poetic operation like any other in the literary sphere. White's theory of tropes runs the risk of flattening the distinction between the fictional and the historical by suggesting that history and fiction are both products of the rhetorical imagination. If the specificity of historical consciousness is not to be lost, the historian must hold to the principle of fidelity to the real past that underlies all historical representation. Again, Ricoeur conceptualizes this fidelity as a *debt* the historian owes to the past:

> And their [the historians'] relationship to the past is first of all that of someone with an unpaid debt, in which they represent each of us who are the readers of their work. This idea of a debt, which may appear strange at first sight, seems to me to stand out against the background of an expression common both to painters and historians: They all seek to "render" something, a landscape or a course of events. In this term "to render," I see the desire to "render its due" to what is and to what once was.[22]

PREFIGURATION IN THE HISTORICAL FILM

If we accept then the formative role of rhetoric in the genesis of historical narratives, is it possible to discern in historical *films* the same process of prefiguration? I believe it is, but I argue that prefiguration in film must take into account two major problems. First, as I attempted to show in Chapter Two, literary and filmic texts operate very differently, particularly because of the difference of their signifiers. To prefigure historical narratives, film has recourse to specific textual strategies that are at least partially determined by film as a medium of communication, its specific capacities as a "language," and the historical development of its discourses. Second, I argue that the historical voice is not easily conveyed in film and emerges by means of a *deviation* from what I term the normative complex of cinematic codes, that is, the set of basic structures that underpin the classic fiction film. If classic films can be defined by their adherence to a system of codes they use in constructing a text, historical narration is an agency that comes from outside this system and therefore manifests itself as a conspicuous *work* of textual construction. These two problems form an apparent paradox. On the one hand, historical film must take account of the specificity of film "language"; on the other, it departs from the norms of that language as a condition of historical narration and constructs itself as discourse.

My argument that historical films are discursive in character finds support in the critique of literalism, best expressed in the work of Natalie Zemon Davis and Robert Rosenstone. Literalism is an extreme case of the rhetoric of the Same. Because film is the medium most rich in signs representing our experience of the spatial and temporal realities of the world, the temptation is to call for a work of imitation that is both endless and ultimately inconceivable: the replication of the historical past in all its phenomenological detail. Even with the advice of historians and access to written, visual, and auditory archives of all sorts, film can only hope to reduce the gap between its representations and the literal realities of historical experience. To identify the mission of historical film with the obsession for the absolute fidelity of image and sound is enough to plunge the filmmaker/historian into a vertigo of representation. Considering film's mimetic function in this literalist way has led skeptical historians to the easy accusation of anachronism: film's very excess of representation is perforce a betrayal of historical truth. Moreover, as we saw, literary theorists—Gérard Genette and Käte Hamburger, among them—also see in the surfeit of concrete detail a telling sign of fictionalization, one that triggers the skeptic's question: how do you know?

Natalie Zemon Davis suggests that it is quite legitimate for the history film to disrupt conventional realism in order to convey doubt, diversity of interpretation, or more abstract historical truths. She critiques the presumed credibility of historical films that use "period props, paintings, location and local people" as marks of authenticity. Such references take on historical meaning, she argues, only if the filmmaker places them in the context of their use and value in a historical period, and such contexts cannot be represented without recourse to more "abstract" modes of communication. "This means," Davis tells us, "that there is no automatic privileging of the 'realistic' or naturalistic film as the mode for representing the past. The symbolic or evidently constructed mode—Bazin's image film—has its role to play, too, and even a few advantages for showing how past societies work."[23]

Rosenstone begins with an incisive paradox: "On the screen, history must be fictional in order to be true!" The key to the paradox is that cinematic literalism is unthinkable in the historical film: "Yes, film may show us the world, or the surface of part of the world, but it can never provide a literal rendition of events that took place in the past. Can never be an exact replica of what happened."[24] Rosenstone makes the point that fictionalization—the creation of characters or events that never existed—does not necessarily vitiate the filmmaker's historical intentions and may indeed be an instrument for getting at historical truths. However, the more general term he proposes is *invention*, which covers a multitude of discursive strategies films may use to refer to the historical world. To be historical, a discourse of images must learn to approximate the abstractions of written history: "Film, with its need for a specific image, cannot make general statements about revolution or progress. Instead, film must summarize, synthesize, generalize, symbolize—in images."[25]

Rosenstone suggests several "fictional moves" as techniques of historical representation: *Compression, Condensation, Alteration,* and *Metaphor. Compression* is the dramatic technique of representing a relatively large historical event through relatively short scenes that compact or epitomize it or of representing social groups through specific "fictional" characters (a technique close to what Ann Rigney calls "figures in the crowd"). *Condensation* is a similar figure that applies to written or filmic history: the selection of specific facts from all the archived evidence available to represent the collective experience of large social groups. Both compression and condensation can be characterized as figurative operations on the order of the synecdoche: a part stands for the whole. *Alteration*—when it operates historically—refers to changes the filmmaker/historian makes to documented historical realities in order to make a larger historical point: lack of fidelity on the literal level leads to discursive truth. Rosenstone's concept of *metaphor* is less clear but seems to refer to techniques of symbolization in which a specific image or series of images is meant to stand for more abstract statements.

Before looking at strategies of prefiguration in two films, one a documentary, the other a "fiction" film, I propose examining some of the ways that the historical voice intervenes in the two historical genres.

We can in fact distinguish two fundamental types of historical films that have quite distinct discursive strategies. The first is the historical documentary, whose defining feature is its reliance on documents—archival images, filmed or recorded testimony, readings of historical texts, contemporary shots of historical settings, interviews with historical witnesses or historians. The second type is the historical film in which the filmmaker reconstructs historical events for the camera using all the resources of mise en scène—actors, settings or sets, costumes—and thus creates a "fictional" doubling in which representation often lacks the most obvious manifestation of the historical trace, audiovisual documents. Let's first take the case of the historical documentary and the forms of address it uses. If these forms are departures from the language of classic cinema, they have become nonetheless highly codified and routine in the mass of documentary production.

In compilation documentaries in which the filmmaker uses archival footage or filmed and auditory documents, the historical voice often intervenes in the form of the voice-over commentary or intertitles that perform the same commentative function. This kind of discourse, prevalent in the classic documentary film, has the advantage of exploiting all the resources of verbal language. Written or aural, the voice is able to place documents in a causal sequence of events, generalize from the specific documented case, explicate apparently incongruous or puzzling features of facts or actions, multiply interpretative perspectives, and set up a rhetorical verbal structure that narrates the action and determines how events are to be understood. Frank Capra's *Why We Fight* series about World War II serves as a characteristic example of how the spoken voice-over may act as the ventriloquist of history, to use André Bazin's metaphor. In such films, the extradiegetic commentary serves to organize the discourse, producing narrative coherence out of the fragmentary documents, and in the case of the *Why We Fight* series, *creating* historical events through a montage of shots that bends history to the demands of propaganda.

The ubiquitous voice-over commentary characteristic of the classic documentary strikes us as dated in the wake of the transformation of documentary methods known as direct cinema. However, it is surprisingly alive today in run-of-the-mill historical documentaries, as tuning into the History Channel quickly demonstrates. However, such documentaries also use an alternative to the voice-over: the filmed interview with historians, most often in the absence of the interviewer. Such narrations often alternate with the voice-over. Filmed historians do not stand outside the film; in their role as secondary narrators, they form in fact part of its diegesis. However, posited as historical authorities and often shot in their studies surrounded by books, they assume the same authority as the "voice-of-God" commentary and indeed become at moments disembodied voices that float above and explicate the flow of visual documents. Instead of being continuously guided by the voice positioned somewhere "above" the visual documents, the spectator assumes the task of piecing together the discontinuous commentaries into a network of historical interpretation.

Some historical documentaries rely as much on editing as on verbal commentary. This was particularly true in the silent period in the Soviet Union and elsewhere, when theories of montage were based on a comparison between the ordering of shots and sequencing in language. Films such as Eisenstein's *October* attempted to use montage as an intellectual or conceptual operation, as if film were capable of reproducing the paradigmatic and syntagmatic aspects of verbal language. It seems clearer to us now that this kind of montage is not a linguistic but a rhetorical act. In terms of the compilation documentary, placing archival documents in sequence—especially when they are not tied together as simple, linear narrative—is a figurative operation that reveals the organizing presence of the historical narrator. This kind of editing of historical materials tends to deviate from classic narrative structures—for example, through the choice of conceptual editing patterns—or is self-consciously expressive in the way it juxtaposes filmed or recorded documents. Esther Shub's *Fall of the Romanov Dynasty*, which I discuss shortly, is the prototype of this form of historical narration.

We need to make a distinction between compilation documentaries that rely on historical documents and documentaries that center on the testimony of still-living historical participants or witnesses to historical events. The latter documentaries have a strong autobiographical character, even when they include, as they often do, archival documents. Human memory is open to distortions due to forgetfulness, imaginative reinvention, or simple mendacity. The task of the historical filmmaker is to organize and evaluate the voices of memory, and, as the viewing of examples of "memory" films shows, there are many strategies for doing this. The filmmaker may adopt the critical voice of the historian and express his views in the give-and-take of the interview situation. In the case of the mendacious witness, the filmmaker may confront the witness's testimony with other testimony that contradicts it or may interpolate historical documents that perform that function. Similarly, the filmmaker may use the commentative power of cinematic devices such as framing or the emphasis of a significant detail. Of course, the filmmaker/historian is often interested in exploring the historical significance of testimony and the relevance of the recounted events to the contemporary world. He often uses the resources of editing to create relationships among the witness's verbal testimony, archival documents, and realities of the present moment. Marcel Ophuls's and Claude Lanzmann's investigative documentaries centered on the perpetrators and survivors of Nazi crimes are perhaps the best known of this historical genre.

When we turn from documentary to the historical film of mise en scène, we seem to leave behind the constraints of the archival document and embrace dramatic structures that tend to silence the historian's voice. Indeed, historical films make infrequent use of the voice-over commentary, the testimony of historians or witnesses, or conceptual montage. They seem to espouse a kind of narration that is more "self-sufficient," as in the fiction film, which gradually weaned itself from the conspicuous forms of narration typical of the so-called primitive period. Filmmakers and spectators have come to share the perception that staged scenes and voice-over commentary belong to two quite different forms of discourse. However, since I have argued that there is no historical film in the absence of the historiographic voice, how does the historian/narrator make himself heard in the textual play of his film?

Robert Rosenstone recognizes the histiographic voice in films with deviant structures, what he calls "history as experiment." The experimental film addresses us in ways very different from the so-called realist film and constructs a very different historical world: "Rather than opening a window directly onto the past, it opens a window onto a different way of thinking about the past."[26] Mainstream products embrace an unproblematic and morally uplifting narrative, foreground the individual protagonist at the expense of the social group, emotionalize and dramatize events, and render the idea of pastness as the fetishistic attention to "period style" emptied of its historical meaning. Experimental film, by contrast, contests the conventions of classic filmmaking, giving us "works that are analytic, unemotional, distanced, multicausal; historical worlds that are expressionist, surrealist, disjunctive, postmodern; histories that don't just show the past but also talk about how and what it means to the filmmaker (or to us) today."[27] In experimental films, we see the signs of the historian/filmmaker's interventions—in the construction of collective characters, the anachronistic "interpenetration of past and present," dissolves of "competing voices and images," Brechtian distancing of the spectator, or the patent artificiality of mise en scène.

As Rosenstone suggests, the experimental filmmaker works on the signifying structures of film. This work is rhetorical in nature, and its figures can be seen as standing against the seeming "transparency" of mainstream cinematic representations. Let us look at some typical strategies.

In certain historical films, the voice of history is diegeticized, that is, it appears in the form of dialogue spoken by characters. This type of intervention is less "disruptive" because the spectator is less aware of the shift between "dramatic" and discursive modes. The subterfuge is successful only if the character successfully balances between his diegetic and exegetic functions: he does not offend the audience's sense of verisimilitude while acting as a stand-in for the historical voice. The character may be an incidental presence whose function is to explicate obscure actions or behaviors or a central protagonist who takes pains to explain situations that are unfamiliar to the spectator but would be tacitly understood by the historical characters. As we saw, Rossellini's historical films employ these types of diegeticized commentary. In a strategy that is the opposite of this game of concealment, the character may look into the camera and engage in direct address of the audience. Breaking the closed space of the diegesis, the character seems to step forward to meet our look, as if the past were capable of discoursing directly with the present. This paradoxical shift in spectator address is an instance of textual "folding over" that allows the film to emerge as narration and signals the presence of the historiographic voice.

However, the historiographic voice is most often manifest as the rhetorical operation that organizes the represented world. We have already encountered strategies of prefiguration in the films analyzed in the foregoing chapters. Rossellini's *The Rise to Power of Louis XIV* is an example of a rhetorical structure I have called ironic mise en scène. Irony is the figure in which the meaning of a statement is at least partially refuted by a second, unstated meaning. In ironic mise en scène, the filmmaker stages a representation of historical characters and events while purposefully thwarting the spectator's ability to believe in them fully. The spectator feels at a distance from such representations because they openly display the inadequacy of the signifiers—actors, costumes, sets—to produce the impression of presence. Ironic mise en scène is an "anti-illusionist" strategy that can take many forms. In the Rossellini example, the actor Jean-Marie Patte's physiognomy does not correspond to the image of the historical Louis XIV in the public mind, and aspects of his performance deliberately thwart the spectator's desire to conflate actor and historical character. Another ironic strategy is to choose anachronistic locations or costumes or stage actions in ways that violate the public's sense of cinematic realism. As we saw in Renoir's *La Marseillaise*, the rhetorical work of the historical film can also be based in the notion of the "figure in the crowd"—nearly the definition of one type of synecdoche—in which the individual protagonist embodies the attributes and aspirations of his class. In Renoir's film, there is a balance between the emblematic and realistic qualities in the construction of characters: on the one hand, they are represented as credible beings accomplishing specific actions; on the other hand, they are invested with iconic qualities that place them in a kind of absolute moral sphere. Renoir resists the static figure out of respect for the cinematic realism that favors the concrete detail. The representational tendency tempers the symbolic one.

The creation of symbolic representations is a general characteristic of historical discourse in film because these representations offer to a medium defined by its strength as denotation a way of speaking about events in more general or abstract ways. I take symbol in its broadest sense: "a kind of figurative language in which what is shown (normally referring to something material) means, by virtue of some sort of resemblance, suggestion, or association, something *more* or something else (normally immaterial)."[28] In the following analyses of Esther Shub's *The Fall of the Romanov Dynasty* and Theo Angelopoulos's *The Traveling Players*, I attempt to show two distinct strategies for constructing such a "figurative language" in film.

CASE STUDY: WEAPONS OF IRONY IN ESTHER SHUB'S *THE FALL OF THE ROMANOV DYNASTY* (1927)

As film historians recognize, Shub produced in *The Fall of the Romanov Dynasty* (1927) the first feature-length compilation film made for the most part from preexisting archival footage. The film is a documentary because it makes use of filmed documents, but it is a historical film by dint of its subject and its intentions. Like other historians of the Soviet state, Shub researched her subject in the official and private archives that became available to her after the October Revolution. As historian Jacques Le Goff has observed, archives are always *monuments*: records of the past that are intended to perpetuate the memory of persons and events and always for specific purposes. Archives are most often selective remembrances, organized in the interest of justifying a specific tradition and, in the case of official archives, preserving for the future a heritage of power. Faced with the bias of the historical record, the historian is called on to critique documents in order to reveal the intentions of the archivists, the broader context of the events documented, and the materials and points of view that have been excluded. The historian's task is not to repeat the assertions of the documentary record but to make the documents speak of the past in ways that were not intended. We can imagine Shub, fervent supporter of the revolution, faced with the official archives that glorify the regime of the czar and private archives that extol the life of the ruling classes. Her problem was to construct a revolutionary vision of history based exclusively on archival material that was largely dedicated to the preservation of the reactionary regime and its privileged elite. The question, then, is how does Shub prefigure these materials in a film intended to evoke, in Marxist terms, the historic necessity of the October Revolution?

I propose the following response. In *The Fall of the Romanov Dynasty*, Shub prefigures her narrative by choosing two basic figurative operations: antithesis and irony. This is not to say that other figures are not discernible in this text that has a distinct rhetorical character, notably synecdoche, which is one of the inescapable structures of historical representation in film. It is easy to understand why antithesis is essential to the development of the deep structure of the film. Roland Barthes's description of the figure is particularly relevant here: "the battle between two plenitudes set ritually face to face like two fully armed warriors."[29] The metaphor Barthes chooses is quite apt because Shub's film concerns the class struggle that opposes two implacable entities: the Romanov regime and the social classes and institutions that are in solidarity with it versus the exploited masses—the peasantry, the proletariat, the army. Beginning with the macrolevel of the narrative, it is obvious that the figure of antithesis plays a central role in the construction of the film's scenario. The entire preparation for the "final struggle," which takes up more than half the film's length, positions the combatants in opposition to each other, very often through a simple structure of alternating sequences in which Shub juxtaposes the conditions of oppressor and oppressed. The same structure of antithesis operates *within* many sequences constructed according to the ideological opposition inherent in parallel editing. Shub opposes, on the basis of contrasting motifs, representatives of the old regime and the social classes subjected to its rule.

Antithesis operates, then, as the basic figure of the film's dramatic construction. The long sequences of exposition establish the oppositional posture of the combatants; the miseries of war then awaken the revolutionary masses to their situation; and their new class consciousness explodes in the revolutionary violence of October. However, there is a second rhetorical figure that plays an essential role in the textuality of the film. As we have seen, irony is the ambivalent figure that simultaneously asserts and denies. Shub the revolutionary historian finds herself in a parodoxical relationship with the archives she intends to exploit. They are what exists in terms of filmic testimony on the nature of the Romanov regime—there were no revolutionary documentarists before the revolution offering alternative visions of social classes in Russia. Shub must use the archival material even though it seems, on the face of it, antagonistic to her aims. She engages therefore in a critique of documents intended to force the lying image to speak the truth. Irony is the arm of criticism since it allows the images to assert themselves while subverting the message they were intended to communicate.

First, irony pierces in the film's intertitles. Through the tone they adopt and the sarcasm of quotation marks, Shub attacks the obtuseness of the images and makes them reveal what they prefer to hide. Let's take the example of a shot representing, toward the end of the Russian involvement in the Great War, frontline soldiers in their trenches receiving the visit of a procession of priests who sprinkle them with holy water as they pass. The bite of the intertitle that follows strips the image of its innocence: "The 'holy fathers' tried to prop up the troops' fighting ability with 'the word of Christ.'" Irony also surfaces in numerous passages in which Shub uses the intertitle to point out the false consciousness of the exploited masses. In these cases, the image presents the worker, the peasant, the soldier engaged in activities whose meaning they misapprehend, preceded by the discursive intertitle that glosses the image in advance. The following example of paired images and commentary, taken from the long sequences representing preparations for war, is typical in this regard:

Intertitle: "Those who will be led to the carnage"

Image: Shot showing workers in a factory

Intertitle: "The hands of the workers prepare the death of their brothers."

Image: Shot showing proletarians working in a munitions factory.

In this example, as elsewhere, intertitles have an exegetic function and produce a combined linguistic/visual statement that is ironic in nature. However, Shub's discursive intervention is not always so heavy and pointed. As one of the great editors of the Soviet silent period, she seems to prefer, when possible, to make the image speak by means of the ordering of shots. Editing is her chosen instrument of critique. The following extract from the film shows clearly how irony functions at the level of the organization of the image track. This is an example of a parallel sequence based on the ideological opposition of oppressor/oppressed. We reencounter here, of course, the familiar figure of antithesis.

1. Intertitle: "The czarist governors ruled over the countryside."

2. Intertitle: "The peace and tranquility of provincial cities."

3. Images: Three shots representing the ease and richness of life for the privileged. (Motif A)

4. Intertitle: "The lands of the great property owners covered enormous spaces."

5. Image: Very long pan (right to left) showing the wealth and extent of the domain. (Motif A)

6. Intertitle: "And next to them, villages bereft of land and plunged into poverty."

7. Image: Very long pan (left to right) showing a village and women drawing water from the communal well. (Motif B)

8. Intertitle: "The landowners. The governor of Kaluga."

9. Images: Three shots representing the governor and his wife, accompanied by their dog, descending the monumental staircase of their mansion; a pond full of ducks and swans ornamented by the play of a fountain; a spacious terrain into which the couple penetrates. (Motif A)

10. Intertitle: "The peasants work under the yoke of the owners' land."

11. Image: A shot of peasant women harvesting wheat. (Motif B)

12. Images: Three shots showing the governor and his wife tak-
               ing coffee in the garden; a vast landscape with a herd
               of cattle; the couple rising and leaving the garden
               and the domestics arriving to clear the table. (Motif
               A, although Motif B returns within the third shot in
               the contrast between master and servant.)

13. Image: Shot of harvest time and peasant labor. (Motif B)

After the long sequence at the beginning of the film in which Shub
inventories the groups that make up the old regime in Moscow—nobility, big landowners, bourgeois, priests—she refers us to the countryside, second place of oppression. The irony of the look—and of the
voice—is already established. As in most parallel sequences, there are
two series of motifs, identified above as motif A and motif B. Motif A
refers to all the shots or groups of shots that represent the richness of
the land and the ease of life in the countryside where the governors
rule: 3, 5, 9, and 12. Motif B refers to the shots that represent the corre-
sponding misery of the peasantry: 7, 11, and 13. The fourth visual shot
of the sequence (number 5 above) illustrates the intertitle that precedes
it: the enormous spaces of the land controlled by the governor that we
discover in the sweep of the panning camera. In response to the shot of
land wealth, there is a second sweeping pan, but this time of a village
"bereft of land and plunged in poverty." However, the shot appears to
have a strong aesthetic character, suggesting not so much the misery of
village life but its picturesqueness, a reading that Shub seeks to undermine by the parallel she constructs between the shots. The false likeness is already established in the juxtaposition of the motifs (space of
the rich versus space of the poor) that the camera movements, parallel
but juxtaposed, underscore: right to left in the first, left to right in the
second. The intertitle provides the metonymic shock, "Next to them,
the villages bereft of land and plunged into poverty": these two contradictory spaces are in fact contiguous.

Shub focuses then on a specific great landowner, the governor of
Kaluga. The first group of shots (motif A, number 9 above) shows the
governor and his wife making the rounds of their property: the couple,
accompanied by their dog, descends the monumental staircase in front
of their mansion; ducks and swans swim about in a pond ornamented
by the play of a fountain; the couple emerges into a descriptive shot
representing the richness of their land. There are so many images of
the wealth of the governor, signifiers of his social position and power.
A single shot (motif B, number 11) shows us peasant women harvesting

wheat. The second group of shots (motif A, number 12) shows us the governor and his wife taking their coffee in the garden. A second shot of a landscape with a large herd of cattle evokes their excessive wealth. In the third, we rediscover the couple getting up from the table and disappearing offscreen as their servants come to clear the table. The motif of domestic labor, which was to signify again the wealth of the governor, is linked, through an ironic reading, to motif B, which asserts itself in the final image of the sequence representing the harsh productive labor of the peasantry.

The rhetorical work that is everywhere visible in *The Fall of the Romanov Dynasty* stems from the relationship between Shub the historian and the archival material she exploits. Shub's voice ceaselessly intervenes through, either verbal language or the "language" of editing, to correct what the visual record has left as vestiges of the old regime. From her superior position of historical distance and enlightened class consciousness, she imposes the revolutionary vision of the present and realigns the images of the past in terms of the culminating event that makes sense of it all. *The Fall of the Romanov Dynasty* is certainly more heavily rhetorical than most historical films, and the marks of enunciation that signal the presence of revolutionary consciousness, the voice that undercuts and restructures, emerge from the fundamental irony of its historical position.

In analyzing Theo Angelopoulos's *The Traveling Players*, we deal with the kind of historical film generally recognized as such by the public and film scholars. Unlike Shub's *The Fall of the Romanov Dynasty*, *Traveling Players* does not make use of preexisting visual documents. It relies, rather, on the imitation of events by means of mise en scène. The filmmaker selects a location or constructs a set, brings the actors before the camera, rehearses their actions, dresses the set and the actors, chooses the lighting, and so forth. He also establishes camera angle, distance, and camera movement—what André Gaudreault calls the *mise en cadre*, all the work of organizing the visual field within the frame to achieve particular effects. The organization of materials through mise en scène also leads to much greater control at the stage of editing the images and sounds. The filmmaker is not limited to preexisting footage, which can only be cut or intercut, never amended or reshaped. Rather, he has chosen the materials he shoots and fashioned the shots in terms of their eventual montage.

It is this sense of mastery and overt manipulation that seems to distress historians. It's one thing, a historian recently told me, to talk about the compilation film that uses documentary footage, although this is in itself no guarantee of a film's historical character. It's quite another to consider a film historical that includes no archival material at all and mimics historical events using the techniques of the fiction film. This commonsense position considers the indexical character of the cinematic sign—its real relation to what it represents, as Pierce describes the index—as the guarantor, in the manner of the barometer or the weathervane, of the authenticity of the documentary image. As Martine Joly observes, "If we admit that the strength of the image is linked to its historically dominant character as index, we can understand that we expect from it the strength and the authenticity of the real from which it is taken."[30] The indexical property of the cinematic sign lends it a factual character, but in films of mise en scène, this factuality, Marc Ferro argues in *Cinema and History*,[31] applies to the image only insofar as it bears witness to the film's production: the persons and objects brought before the camera, the locations or sets where they are filmed, and so on. When a historical film is staged, where is one to locate historical facts, those intractable givens of any historic discourse? Referential constraints seem to all but disappear as the filmmaker imagines a concrete diegetic world that he paradoxically asserts really existed. For the historian, the being-there of the imagined diegetic world—the very realism of its presence—overwhelms the more elusive and intangible having-been-there of the past.

Now it is important not to succumb to the temptation to reduce the cinematic sign to its indexical aspect, what historians consider its "documentary" value. As in all films, the indexical sign in historical films establishes an existential relationship between the cinematic image and its immediate referent—the materials that the camera films. However, the rhetorical work that proposes a relationship of analogy between the film's audiovisual discourse and the reality of the past necessarily involves an *iconic* activity of reference. I use icon in the Piercean sense of a sign that refers to a denoted object through analogy: "Finally, the icon is that which exhibits the same quality, or the same configuration of qualities, that the denoted object exhibits."[32] Fiction films produce the iconic representation of imaginary worlds that exist in the mind of the spectator and nowhere else. Historical films also construct iconic representations in the mind of the spectator, but the spectator takes these representations as references to a world of the past. In the iconic sign, the denoted object is not the materials that the film records but the historical past to which the film refers. As Oswald Ducrot and Tzvetan Todorov describe it, the icon does not establish a simple relationship of resemblance (here, between the audiovisual materials and the reality of the past). The film cannot represent the past by substituting for it a savant imitation. In rhetorical terms, Ducrot and Todorov tell us, "the icon is a synecdoche rather than a metaphor";[33] it is the part substituted for the whole. The historical film creates a reductive and partial representation that stands for the broad field of events to which it refers.

Denotation in the historical film operates, then, at two distinct levels. The spectator "reads" the images indexically as representations of the "realities" that the film records in the process of shooting. This reading is a process of "recognition" that appears "automatic" and immediate: we recognize persons, objects, movement, spatial depth, and so forth. The second level of denotation is iconic in nature and is constructed on the first. Here, the process of recognition is not automatic or immediate but requires an intellectual reading. Having recognized the audiovisual field the film literally represents, the spectator is asked to interpret the relationship between the first level of denotation and the ultimate referent of the film: the past that it can represent only indirectly and through a process of intellection. We now examine in some detail how this process of iconic figuration takes place in a specific historical film of mise en scène.

CASE STUDY: THE DEGRADATION OF TRAGEDY IN THEO ANGELOPOULOS'S *THE TRAVELING PLAYERS* (1974-1975)

The Traveling Players belongs to a trilogy of films (with *Days of '36* and *The Hunters*) that Angelopoulos made on the history of Greece from the Metaxas dictatorship to the end of the dictatorship of the colonels (1936-74). This series of history films is among the most important and innovative in cinema.

Angelopoulos refers to "The Traveling Players" as "a voyage in time and space" intended to document the period between 1939 and 1952, during which Greece endured a "series of occupations."[34] As the film opens, we see the proscenium curtain of a theater. An old actor emerges and addresses the spectators (of the play, of the film) in the following words: "The Play you are about to see in five acts is Spyridon Peresiades's immortal idyll 'Golfo the Shepherdess.'" The spectator soon becomes aware of the irony of this speech. We will never see the five acts of "Golfo," whose performance is repeatedly interrupted by historical events, but we will witness the five acts of a historical drama as refracted through the backstage existence of a troupe of ambulant thespians.

Although the film does not organize events into acts, it does treat the following moments of Greek history. (a) The Metaxas dictatorship flirts with fascism in the late 1930s, before Greece, dependent on

Britain financially, enters into World War II on the side of the Allies. (b) The Germans occupy Greece beginning in 1940 and are met by the forces of resistance led by the Communist Party (the National Liberation Front) and its military arm, the People's Liberation Army. (c) As liberation approaches in 1944, all parties agree to a Government of National Unity, which was to include the National Liberation Front. However, British General Scobie, head of the occupying forces, orders the People's Liberation Army disarmed. Protests result in bloodshed and the two month Battle of Athens. The Varkiza agreement ends the conflict with promises of amnesty and representation for the resistance, promises that are not kept. Many members of the National Liberation Front return to the hills to regroup as a guerrilla army. The British force the "disgraceful parody" of an election that legalizes a "monarcho-fascist" regime (1946). (d) The Civil War begins in 1946 pitting the army of occupation and the Greek right wing against the nationalist guerrilla army. In 1947, at the British request, President Truman agrees to participate in the Greek occupation. The People's Army ultimately acknowledges defeat in 1949. (e) Anticommunist fighter Marshall Papagos is elected president in 1952. American influence in Greece is consolidated as the Cold War begins.

In the general lines of the film's scenario, *The Traveling Players* takes up these periods in their linear progression. However, the film is well known for the disconcerting freedom with which it treats historical chronology. Even more disturbing is the way it violates what we presume to be the temporal continuity of shots, so that an apparently continuous sequence of shots may represent two historical periods separated in time. Angelopoulos describes this strategy as a dialectical exchange between "two historical times," a comparative structure that leads to "historical conclusions." He is not interested in replicating events in a simple chain of cause and effect; rather, his representation of events is intended as an analytic interpretation of history. Therefore, he disengages events from their linear sequence to resituate them in the present of discourse: "Those links [between historical times] do not level events but bypass the notions of past/present and instead provide a linear developmental interpretation which exists only in the present."[35] The asequential ordering Angelopoulos chooses at these moments seems in part rooted in his analysis of the circularity of this period in Greek history: the repetitive cycles of occupation from which Greece seems unable to extricate itself.

Let's take the example of the film's first three sequences in which we are introduced to the troupe of actors in relationship to whom the situations and events of Greek history are presented. The first sequence is made up of a single long take and gives us a distant view of the traveling players, aligned across the screen with their luggage, moving slowly from the train station in the background toward the camera as one of the actors' offscreen voice comments: "In the fall of 1952 we returned to Aegion. We were tired and hadn't slept for two days." In the next sequence, we see the troupe approaching the camera in a street hung with banners proclaiming the candidacy for president of Marshall Paragos, the anticommunist fighter. A voice from a loudspeaker, which emanates, we soon become aware, from a primitive sound truck, broadcasts Paragos's political slogans. As we learn only retrospectively, we have entered the film's narrative at what is to be its final moment. In the third sequence, we are again in a street in Aegios approaching a square that will become a familiar place of historical action in the film. The troupe leader emerges into the frame from behind the tracking camera, followed by the other players. The visual cues seem to establish the temporal continuity and the spatial contiguity between this take and the previous two, although a closer examination of the figures reveals that the composition of the troupe has changed: its leader is not the same, a young boy has appeared, and the players carry different burdens. An offscreen voice, soon to be identified as that of a man walking his bicycle into the town square, marks the historical shift: "Tomorrow afternoon the Minister of Propaganda of the Third Reich, Goebbels, accompanied by Ioanis Metaxas, our National Leader, will pass through our town on his way to ancient Olympus." We find ourselves at the chronological beginning of the film's fabula, 1939.

This particular emplotment of events calls for several observations. First, narratologists call this kind of sequencing a *prolepsis* or anticipation of events because the order of the telling does not correspond to the order of the events in their linear progression. We leap forward in time while the film has not yet made reference to chronologically earlier actions. Such movements in time are quite common in historical narratives, and it is not unusual for the historian to begin with the narrative's final moment (the effect to be elucidated) in order to link it with the situations in which it takes root. Angelopoulos, who is not constrained by the methods of written history, does not immediately make clear the meaning of the juxtaposition of two historical moments. However, the sequence of the telling suggests a retrospective, synoptic vision (Mink) of historical events in which the actions that are still to be narrated are already invested with their narrative finality. Indeed, the Greek audiences who flocked to see *The Traveling Players* as it was released after the fall of the dictatorship of the colonels certainly had the impression of already *having followed* the story and were doubtless sensitive to the irony of this deliberate confusion of chronology. In this sense, we can call Angelopoulos's historical view fatalistic: the sequence of historical actions loses the sense of contingency; the end exists, quite literally, already in the beginning.

At several other moments in the film, Angelopoulos suggests the circularity of events in this period through the interpolation of unmotivated flash-forwards or flashbacks in the progression of events. As the troupe's leader in 1940 prepares to depart to battle the advancing Italian army, we return briefly and without transition to the election of 1952 and the recognizable motifs of the second sequence: the sound truck and the scattering leaflets. The interpolation is not gratuitous but suggests the irony of this period of Greek history: the tragic failure of initiatives of national defense and liberation that all end in events like the rigged election of 1952. The final ironic reversal of chronology occurs in the last shot sequence of the film: we return to the train station of the film's first sequence, to the players and their luggage aligned in long shot, and we hear the offscreen commentary voiced by one of the actors. The traveling players, tired and sleep deprived, return to Aegion, but this time the date is 1939. As *The Traveling Players* opens with the fabula's concluding moment, the film closes with the event that is its chronological beginning.

Returning to the first three sequences of the film that I described in narrative terms, let's examine the rhetorical operations those sequences involve. The visual signs of continuity suggest that sequence three is elliptically related to sequence two through an apparent match on movement: a 180-degree shift in angle represents by ellipsis (a brief jump in time) a second view of the trajectory of the players through the streets of Aegion. These visual clues of continuity are shortly contradicted by the voice that stipulates in effect, "This is not 1952, this is 1939." However, the authority of the voice is partially undermined by its mise en scène: How can this ostensible public proclamation emanate from a man idly pushing his bicycle across a deserted square? And where is the public to whom the voice is addressed? This lack of verisimilitude already suggests, as it does elsewhere in the film, that we are dealing with a space that is as rhetorical as it is real. It is this space of the town square that will be the locus of many of the film's representations of collective historical action. In the next sequence, for example, it will be the site for the drill by Greek fascist militia.

I would suggest that Angelopoulos's figurative strategy consists in the following. The realistic representation of place and the apparent continuity of action serve as the ground (in the rhetorical lexicon, the *tertium comparationis*) against which the terms of the figure are cut. Here, we are not dealing with the classical trope or ornaments of discourse; we are dealing with rhetorical operations. The two terms to be compared—the fascist-leaning Metaxis dictatorship and the regime of anticommunist Marshal Papagos at the beginning of the Cold War—meet on the chain of discourse, and their presence together is justified by the codes of cinematic representation that anchor them in the "same" space and time, even if we acknowledge retrospectively that the codes have led us astray. The emerging awareness of the disparity of the historical moments bring the realization that we cannot "understand" the sequence in terms of the "literal" continuity the film seems to construct. Instead, we are led to search out the features of comparison that will reveal the underlying meaning that cannot be determined in terms of narrative logic (the sequence is not in fact sequential) or the spectator's experience (different moments in time cannot normally be conflated in this way). One might at first assume that the figure that binds the elements together is a metonymy: the two historical moments can substitute for each other, can be compared and "equated," because of their physical proximity to each other in the space of the scene. However, the two historical moments do not coexist in a referential space; as Angelopoulos clearly indicates, they are brought together only on the chain of discourse. We are therefore dealing with a metaphor, or more properly a metaphoric operation, that establishes an unanticipated resemblance between the two apparently disparate elements.

A similar rhetorical strategy can be seen in the film's telescoping of narrative action in which successive historical events are represented as occurring within a single long take. The work of extreme condensation, this paradoxical mode of representation, reveals "a basic doubleness of meaning between what is meant and what is said (the tenor and the vehicle)."[36] Thus, the long takes suggest the continuous development of the *scene*, in which screen time and story time are taken to be the same (the vehicle, what is said), whereas the spectator understands the long take as an elliptical representation of a much longer duration (the tenor, what is meant).

Let's take the example of the dance hall sequence, which follows a reference to the "disgraceful parody" of elections that legitimate a "monarcho-fascist regime" (March 1946). Elektra, stalwart sister of partisan soldier Orestes, enters the dance hall. We learn from a banner stretched across the wall above the band that it is New Year's Eve 1946. The customers are divided between the anticommunist thugs and the sympathizers of the People's Army. A song duel ensues between the groups in which the fascists mock the flight of the People's Army and call for the return of the king, while the rebels sing of their lack of fear for the Scobie regime and their belief in the power of the people. After the confrontation, the fascists, all males, triumphant but isolated, dance with each other. Elektra crosses the dance hall and remains standing to the side of the band. She then exits through a back door and is joined by the troupe's old accordionist, whom we have seen as part of the dance hall band. Elektra says to the old actor: "Orestes has turned in his arms. The war is over." But 1946 is just the beginning of the civil war that will end in 1949. This heavily condensed representation of the civil war is symbolic in character. If the combative groups in the dance hall stand for the ideological battles of the period, Elektra is the emblematic figure of the tragic denouement; her demeanor from the beginning of the sequence suggests the defeat of 1949.

The next shot sequence appears to take place in the early morning hours as the drunken anticommunists, having left the dance hall, stagger down the street singing right-wing songs (preceded by a tracking camera). Again, the continuity of the duration of action is contradicted by the development of the thugs' actions. The group of men twice crosses the street. With each shift in position, the group becomes more organized until the thugs form a militia marching in lockstep. They emerge onto the square, where a loudspeaker disseminates a political speech, and as the camera pans to show us the speaker and his party aligned on a balcony, we realize that time has shifted once again to the Papagos election in 1952. The shot sequence has condensed the period 1949 to 1952, representing the growing ascendancy of the monarcho-fascists after the civil war, through a synecdoche, the figure in which a part stands for the whole.

Angelopoulos is one of the great poets of modern cinema, known for his unusual use of imagery. Cinema is the medium richest in signifiers of the real, and the cinematic image can be characterized by the ease with which it denotes real experience. Imagery, however, suggests more than pure denotation; it has special resonance because of the way in which the work, cinematic or literary, calls attention to it. An image can become imagery because of its repetition or, in cinema, because of the way it is emphasized through framing, lighting, or color or the way it detaches itself from other denoted objects in a film. Imagery is the effect, then, of another "doubleness" in which the denotative meaning is invested with meaning at another, symbolic level. In Angelopoulos's work, imagery appears to emerge from the "real" world he represents, but some aspect of its representation, its mise en scène, associates it with the world of the uncanny.

We see in his imagery the hand of the artist who pushes the image into the foreground of our awareness. Many striking examples in others of Angelopoulos's films come to mind: the giant sculpted hand suspended over the sea by a helicopter in *Landscape in the Mist*, or in *Eternity and a Day* the image of men in iridescent yellow slickers riding bicycles through a dark, rain-drenched landscape, or the refugees hung like ciphers on the wire fence at the border protecting Greece from the poorer Balkan states. Such images have a figurative dimension because they appear not so much as visual observation, but as part of a *vision* that must be accounted for in symbolic terms. The tension of Angelopoulos's imagery derives from the fact that its symbolic meaning often seems elusive and escapes immediate understanding. *The Traveling Players* is full of strong imagery, but while it retains considerable ambiguity, its symbolic intent is clear: to characterize, especially in political terms, the meaning of large historical events.

Let's look at an example. Angelopoulos chooses to represent the Varkiya agreement (crafted by the British occupiers and the Greek right wing) through a series of striking images. The power of the occupying forces is rendered as a pompous architectural structure, open in the center and guarded by armed soldiers of the state, its forbidding character suggested by imposing long shots. A voice from a loudspeaker (a metaphoric representation of a distant, disembodied authority) announces the end of the civil war and asserts the benevolent British concern for the future of Greece. A symmetrical 180-degree change of angle reasserts the setting's crushing institutional structure. The loudspeaker announces the articles of protocol: the free expression of political convictions, the abolition of repressive laws, the disbanding of the People's Army, and the conditions of amnesty for the rebel forces. In startling contrast, we see the arrival on horseback of a long line of bedraggled soldiers from the People's Army, who one by one depose their arms in the center of this symbolic space. Their vulnerability and humanness stand in rhetorical opposition to the power that debases them.

I would like to consider one last aspect of the rhetoric of reference that *The Traveling Players* uses: the troupe of actors. Dressed in dark clothing, the players appear at first as an undifferentiated group, at the train station, for example, where the long shot avoids any individuation. Moving in unison through the streets, they seem visually separate from the events that seem to overwhelm them. However, distinctions do emerge based on the positions that the central characters adopt in relation to historical developments. Certain actors leave to fight in the theaters of war and become subjects of historical action. The father and troupe leader, a national patriot, enlists in the Greek army and leaves for the front and the antifascist fight. In his absence, his wife consorts openly with her lover, and the father is eventually betrayed by the adulterous couple. Orestes, his son, is a member of a Marxist formation, and the film devotes three sequences to presenting the group's political ideology and its analysis of revolutionary conditions. Orestes, like his father, leaves the troupe to join the People's Army in the resistance and then in the Civil War. Orestes's two sisters, Elektra and Chrysothaeme, are foils to each other. Elektra is the implacable representative of political consciousness and personal fidelity. She stands for her father and for Orestes amid the passivity and opportunism of the other actors. She keeps company with the rebel forces, protects her brother and his Marxist comrades, speaks directly into the camera about the British betrayal of Greece, and participates with other militants in the Battle of Athens. Chrysothaeme is a "survivor": she compromises her Greekness, plays the exhibitionist for a masturbator who rewards her with a bottle of oil, consorts with the British occupiers, and marries an American soldier.

The film never follows the protagonists of action into the fields of battle. We remain, rather, with the troupe itself as it wanders from place to place, from performance to performance, staging and restaging its irrelevant pastoral tragedy. Objects rather than subjects of action, the traveling players are inconsequential victims of history. As the civil war is represented in the village of Aegion as a stylized skirmish between opposing forces, the troupe moves surreptitiously through the streets, avoiding an encounter with either army. Always off center, on the periphery of meaningful events, the actors do a "command performance" of *Golfo* on a beach for members of the British occupying force until they are interrupted by guerrilla gunfire.

As several characters' names suggest, Angelopoulos has quite literally emplotted the film on the model of the Oresteia. Why this choice? In an interview, Angelopoulos gave the following explanation: "Greek people have grown up caressing dead stones. I've tried to bring mythology down from the heights and directly to the people."[37] However, *The Traveling Players* is something more than the transposition of Greek tragedy into a narrative about relatively recent Greek history. The film works on a trope, to use Hayden White's language: the Oresteia prefigures the field of history the film seeks to represent. Although the reworking of modern Greek history in terms of a mythological story is an audacious mixture of the fictional and the historical, the seriousness of intent in *The Traveling Players* is not in the slightest undermined.

On the contrary, Angelopoulos establishes a deep structural relationship between mythological and historical events. The spectator—the Greek spectator in particular—becomes involved in a comparative reading. There is first the overlay of the dramatis personnae. As the characters' names and the course of the action make clear, the internal drama of the troupe replicates, models itself on the Oresteian tragedy. As the father (the Agamemnon figure) leaves for war, his wife (the Clytemnestra figure) mocks his patriotism and moves in with her lover (the Aesgisthus figure), a fascist sympathizer, who usurps the leadership role in the troupe. Although the father is betrayed but not murdered by the adulterous couple, Orestes, encouraged and abetted by Elektra, kills his mother and her lover while they are performing on stage in *Golfo*. As in Greek legend, the crime of Clytemnestra and Aesgisthus is on the one hand personal—the sexual betrayal of Agamemnon; on the other, the crime is one of "lèse majesty" against the authority of the father while he is away waging a patriotic war. Indeed, it is the cringing opportunism of the Aesgisthus figure that defines his treacherous character: he is not ennobled by patriotic feeling; rather, he is drawn to fascism as a rising force, fingers the "Englishman" the troupe is hiding, and attempts to save himself from the Nazis who arrest the players ("Me, comrade," he pleads in pidgin German).

The constellation of characters mirrors that of the Oresteia, but it is, of course, a distorting mirror. In *The Traveling Players*, the royal family of murderous intent and bloody revenge is reset in the marginal world of ambulant actors. Aegisthus consorts with Clytemnestra in the seedy room of an inn. Agamemnon leaves for the patriotic war as a humble volunteer. Even Orestes's murder of his mother and her lover takes place within the proscenium arch of a shoddy theater. *The Traveling Players* has therefore something of the classical genre the French call the *burlesque*, in which noble characters are played as rabble. Indeed, the mixture of high and low permeates the film's representation of serious events and establishes an ambivalent rhetoric based on metaphor (Angelopoulos's characters and their actions are *likened* to these mythological figures and actions) and irony (how *unlike* are the stations and the deeds of these characters in relation to their mythological counterparts). Similarly, Angelopoulos sets up a disparity between the seriousness of the historical actions to which he refers and the way he represents them. This rhetorical dissonance is infused with irony and sets us at a distance from the events the film references. Thus, the political positions of the combatants in the Civil War are represented in terms of a song duel in a cabaret; the misery of the Greek population during the fascist occupation is evoked by the troupe's comic pursuit of a chicken across a field of snow; the nearly farcical celebration of Elektra's sister's marriage to an American soldier on a beach stands for American domination of Greek culture in the early 1950s.

However, the film is not so much playful as it is bitterly ironic: this degradation of tragedy does not eliminate the peril experienced by the characters or the real consequences of historical action for the Greek world of the period. Indeed, the momentous events of history continue to reach the scene of representation even if they are "defused" by comic distancing, subjected to a heavily rhetorical mise en scène, or relayed through the account of a secondary narrator, as are the offstage scenes of horrific events in tragic theater. The People's Army soldier (the Pylades figure) who recounts the torture of political prisoners under the government of "reconciliation" does not speak within the frame of a closed narrative world (the single long take shows us no interlocutor); rather, he directly addresses the spectator. This direct address demolishes verisimilitude—the scene does not conform to expectations of "realism"—and establishes a dialogic link between the (Greek) spectator in the present and the representation of his immediate historical past. The overwhelming response to the film (made under the dictatorship but released during the transition to democracy) demonstrates to what extent the Greek public recognized through Angelopoulos's strategies of representation the events that shaped their contemporary reality.

5

FILM

A Place of Memory

FILM AS AN INSTRUMENT OF PUBLIC MEMORY

This section of my study takes up the question of the role of historical films in managing collective memory. Film—and other "nonprofessional" forms of social remembrance in television, journalism, and the popular press—have not been welcomed by the ranks of academic historians, who have often complained about the media's lack of method and training and their tendency to sacrifice truth to drama and emotion. However, the importance of cinema in this social endeavor is undeniable. Indeed, historians acknowledge that filmic representation has such power that it overwhelms other forms of recollection by imposing indelible images of the past on the public imagination. They are at a loss in their efforts to combat and correct what they consider erroneous but compelling representations. Historical "fictions," they argue, tend to replace the real documents of events in the public imagination. Marc Ferro laments in an article from 1987: "Are not the images of the Revolution of 1905 which dominate our memory those from Eisenstein's work [in *The Battleship Potemkin*]?"[1]

In the domain of the historical documentary, the situation is different, but similar concerns remain. Documentary footage taken of historical events is necessarily fragmentary. The filmmaker has chosen—or circumstances have obliged him—to film only certain events, from certain angles and for certain durations, for reasons that are technical, logistical, or ideological; editing, whether by filmmaker, producer, or sponsor, further reduces and shapes the material destined for public consumption. Yet these fractional and often tendentious representations tend to impose a set of images that is, in the public mind, the essential imagery of events. This is particularly true of the broadcast media, which can operate to the detriment of public memory. Film and television often undermine the collective task of remembering by ceaselessly repeating fetish images of past events: what the media have "captured" on film or video tends to overshadow and replace all other recollection. Anton Kaes contends that "the mass media have become the most effective (and least acknowledged) institutional vehicles for shaping historical consciousness."[2]

The danger is very real and concerns the general tendency in the era of simulation to offer the public packaged substitutes for the act of reminiscence. The Vietnam War, for example, subjected to intense coverage by the media, particularly television, survives in the public imagination in the form of highly selective and distilled images that, once "captured," are manipulated and repeated. Kaes makes a similar analysis of the "memory" of the Third Reich:

> It is a memory consisting largely of images that have by now become so conventionalized that they determine what is a "correct" representation of the period and what is not. Images of Hitler or of the war have engraved themselves so indelibly on the public consciousness that new images are hard to imagine. Thus history films increasingly replace not only historical experience but also historical imagination.[3]

However, Kaes points out that the New German Cinema produced history films whose aim was not only to reconstruct the past but also to "jog the memory of the living": "They provide alternative ways of seeing with their self-reflexive narrative and visual style, their refusal for the most part to recycle endlessly repeated and clichéd images of the Third Reich."[4]

It would be a mistake to overemphasize the negative impact of the media. If media-packaged events tend to undermine the human responsibility to remember, the media are also, potentially and in reality, capable of stimulating enormous public discussion of collective concerns. In the sphere of history, we could cite the many films or television programs that have served as catalysts to remembering and have brought about a public reflection on the realities of the past and their meaning. One need only think of the social impact of historical documentaries like Alain Resnais's *Night and Fog* or Marcel Ophuls's *Le Chagrin et la Pitié* or "fictions" like Fassbinder's ambitious filmic retelling of the history of Germany in the twentieth century. And one can even quote Ferro himself to contradict his negative assessment of historical fiction. In an article that appeared just two years after the one just cited, Ferro seems mystified by what he calls the "Potemkin paradox": "How is it possible that this film, better than any historical work, erudite or critical, succeeds in evoking admirably a revolutionary situation, whereas the greater part of the facts that the film evokes, as D. J. Wenden has shown, are purely and simply invented by Eisenstein?"[5] Here, the historian comes close to admitting what elsewhere he found clearly inadmissible. *Potemkin* brings together the dramatization of historic events that did not take place (at least in the manner Eisenstein represents them) a carefully constructed mise en scène, a self-conscious aesthetic of composition, and editing—all rudiments of fictional and artistic practice that lead, "paradoxically," and in the absence of documented facts, to the truthful representation of a historical situation. Moreover, the film was conceived to serve the interest of the new Soviet state—indeed, its propagandistic force was powerfully felt in the West and beyond—and one cannot discount the fact that Eisenstein's motivation for making the film was in part the desire for "narcissistic prestige." So many flaws that turn out not to be fatal.

The paradox is less startling if one examines the elements that seem to justify *Potemkin* as a significant historical film. The first is the seriousness with which Eisenstein undertakes to commemorate a period of revolutionary history for the largely illiterate Russian public, an act of remembrance tied to the survival of the new social order. Eisenstein establishes a meaningful relationship between past and present, one of the primary tasks of the historian. Second, if we look beyond the historian's concern with the immediate "verifiability" of what the film represents to us, we are struck by the extraordinary structure of representation that Eisenstein invents. He emplots the film's actions in terms of the social forces that bring them about, and he constructs characters who act in the interest of the antagonistic social classes to which they belong. It is out of this structure of representation that Eisenstein creates his historic model of the revolutionary situation in Russia in 1905.

Eisenstein's film, exceptional in many ways, is not exceptional as an example of films that fulfill the social need to remember.

DEFINING COLLECTIVE MEMORY

What do we mean when we say that a film, or a history, or a television series has a memorial function? What is meant by "historical memory," a term that is widely used but little understood? The term seems to derive its meaning from a kind of metaphor in which memory, the individual faculty for reviving images of things past, is extended to an abstract collectivity existing in historical time. Is individual remembrance the foundation of all conceptions of memory? What does it mean to extend the faculty of remembering to a social group? What is the relationship between social memory and the historian's discourse?

In *Memory, History, Forgetting*, Paul Ricoeur addresses these questions through an examination of the "models" of private and collective memory proposed by the history of philosophy. It is worthwhile summarizing, in admittedly reductive terms, the broad outlines of Ricoeur's analysis as he charts our way through philosophical concepts. What is particularly interesting for the purposes of this study is the distinctions Ricoeur is able to draw between the private memory represented in the mind of the individual, collective memory that is shared by members of a social group, and historical memory that seems to abandon the phenomenon of presence to the consciousness of mind. Perhaps more important, he considers the possible *transitions* between individual and collective reminiscence and the distant, alienated world of historical representation.

Private memory is housed in the individual mind and manifests itself for Plato as "the present representation of an absent thing." The presence of the image in the absence of perception evoked great astonishment in Saint Augustine: how is it that people are not surprised that "when I was speaking of all these things, I was not seeing them with my eyes."[6] Augustine is struck by the "infinite profundity" of human memory, which, although part of the mind, the mind cannot fully understand or control: "Some memories pour out to crowd the mind and, when one is searching and asking for something quite different, leap forward into the center as if saying 'Surely we are what you want?' With the hand of my heart I chase them away from the face of my memory until what I want is freed of mist and emerges from its hiding place."[7] Memory refers in fact to two distinct concepts: memory as the (passive) presence of the image to the mind, and memory as the intentional activity of recollection.

Moreover, for Augustine memory is inseparable from the human experience of time. Past time belongs to the individual consciousness (and not to another's); it is "my time" that I possess in the continuity of my own existence. Memory as the activity of individual recollection constitutes the past in the present of the mind. It is a reflexive activity. In ordinary language, Ricoeur observes, the reflexive verb of remembering (*se souvenir* in French) suggests that the subject acts on himself as much as on the object of memory: "In remembering (*se souvenant de quelque chose*), one remembers oneself (*on se souvient de soi*)."[8] In this conception, then, memory is "radically singular" and exists as the link between the mind and its past. Through remembrance, the individual is able to move back in time to the earliest childhood recollections, which memory evokes and organizes into a linear narrative. In his *Confessions*, Augustine offers the metaphor of the "vast palaces of memory," thus ascribing to internal life a kind of space where memory exercises itself: "Memory's huge cavern, with its mysterious, secret, and indescribable nooks and crannies, receives all these perceptions, to be recalled when needed and reconsidered."[9]

In the Age of Reason, John Locke also conceived of memory as an activity of consciousness that operates within the individual mind, but he emphasized the role of the memorial function in establishing the identity of the person. Personal identity exists because the human individual, in the process of perceiving, is aware of himself as the entity that perceives. Thinking necessarily involves consciousness, and *self-consciousness* is the condition of selfhood. The self is always the same, never another, at every moment in the time of his existence. The self possesses continuity in time, and therefore the present person is the same actor who performed actions in the past that persist in memory. The continuity of the life of consciousness maintains itself despite mental distraction, lapses in memory, or any other changes in "substance." The self, consciousness, and memory are therefore inextricably bound together so that self is the same agent of action who acts now and in the past: "And as far as this consciousness can be extended backwards to any past Action or Thought, so far reaches the Identity of that *Person*; it is the same self now it was then; and 'tis by the same *self* with this present one that now reflects on it, that that Action was done."[10] Locke's notion of the self and of memory, like Augustine's, does not allow for any conception of a shared consciousness since consciousness is the very definition of the person. We now need to ask on what basis it is possible to construct a conception of collective memory.

For Ricoeur, Husserl is a key figure because he "attempts to pass from the solitary *ego* to an other susceptible of becoming in turn a we."[11] Is it possible, asks Ricoeur, that a phenomenology of the intimate consciousness of time can be extended to a phenomenology of collective memory? In the fifth of *The Cartesian Meditations*, Husserl speaks of collective subjects that he calls "intersubjective communities of a higher order" that are constituted on the basis of a process of *"social communalization."*[12] Husserl's notion of a collective consciousness is startling since his phenomenology of interior consciousness, conceived as pure flow, would seem to set up an insurmountable barrier to any conception of intersubjective memory. Husserl contends, however, that the ego "can be a world-experiencing ego only by being in communion with others like himself: a member of a community of monads, which is given orientedly, starting from himself."[13] Even if the social entity begins in an outward movement of individual consciousness, the plurality of egos "constitutes in itself an Objective world" that "realizes itself" within that world. Intersubjective communities are social entities, and nonetheless they acquire all the "prerogatives of memory": the community takes possession of memory on the model of individual mine-ness; collective memory exists as a continuity that supposes a plural consciousness; and the community experience of time is structured around the idea of past and future moments. Ricoeur insists that this process of attribution to the collective subject is based in an analogical operation:

> With this hypothesis, which makes intersubjectivity bear all the weight of the constitution of collective entities, it is important, however, not to forget that it is only by analogy, and in relation to individual consciousness and its memory, that collective memory is held to be a collection of traces left by the events that have affected the course of history of the groups concerned, and that it is accorded the power to place on stage these common memories, on the occasion of holidays, rites, and public celebrations.[14]

It is under the sign of the analogical that the collective "we" is authorized to speak about time, memory, and history.

We turn now from philosophical reflection to the domain of the social sciences, where historians and sociologists have theorized memory as the centripetal force that binds all collective experience. In *The Collective Memory*, Maurice Halbwachs questions the idea that memory has its origin solely in individual consciousness. Individual memory cannot be separated from shared memory; we are, he contends, seldom alone in remembering: "Our confidence in the accuracy of our impression increases, of course, if it can be supported by others' remembrances. It is as if the very same experience were relived by several persons instead of only one."[15] To remember, Halbwachs argues, we need "an affective community," a group with which we are closely identified and whose solidarity allows the individual memory to "take possession of itself"; the individual needs to align himself with "the viewpoint of one or several groups and one or several currents of collective thought."[16] The social context throws a bridge across the apparently irreconcilable domains of individual and collective remembrance.

We could call Halbwachs's model of memory acquisition *developmental* because it is generated and confirmed in the process of the developing social experience of the child:

> As soon as a child leaves the stage of purely sensory life and becomes interested in the meaning of images and scenes that he perceives, it can be said that he thinks in common with others, that his thought is divided between the flood of wholly personal impressions and the various currents of collective thought.[17]

Very early memories do not exist, Halbwachs argues, because the infant is not yet a social being; the process of recollection emerges at the moment when the child begins to take his place within the social "framework of the family." Moreover, the child learns to situate himself chronologically in the succession of generations. His parents carry with them the vestiges of another period, which give to the child some lived experience of the past: "My parents belonged to this period; they acquired certain habits and characteristics that became part of their personality and made an early impression upon me."[18] The "living bond of generations" extends to the grandparents, with whom the child has close and prolonged contact and who provide the child with "access to an even more distant past."[19] Finally, the bond between generations permits us to conceive a relationship between collective memory, to which we are biographically connected, and the anonymous history that must be learned in the distancing form of written language. The adult the child becomes looks back on his remembered past and learns to integrate it into the framework of contemporary history:

> The world of my childhood, as I recover it from memory, fits so naturally into the framework of recent history reconstituted by formal study because it already bears the stamp of that history. What I discover is that by attentive effort I can recover, in my remembrances of my little world, a semblance of the surrounding social milieu.[20]

For Halbwachs, this is the furthest point in time that lived experience is able to reach. Historical distance cuts the bonds of collective memory. History conceives of time as rupture and studies, at a retrospective distance, social groups as they change over time. Memory is living and continuous; history is discontinuous, cut into periods, over and done with.

In his collection of essays, *On History*, Eric Hobsbawn discusses the reasons why human societies need to remember the past. It is above all, he argues, a question of identity and identification: how does the individual subject establish his place within society? "To be a member of any human community is to situate oneself with regard to one's (its) past, if only by rejecting it."[21] The individual identifies his place within social groups at all levels of society. In the private sphere of the family, memory relies on memorabilia, personal correspondence, family narratives, and the informal legacy of the oral tradition: "We cannot help situating ourselves in the continuum of our own life, of the family, of the group to which we belong. We cannot help comparing past and present: that is what family photo albums or home movies are there for. We cannot help learning from it, for that is what *experience* means."[22] In his book on the social function of photography, Pierre Bourdieu describes acts of remembrance within families as so many rites that mark the passage of new members into the closed social circle and reaffirm the solidarity of the group: "The images of the past arranged in chronological order, 'the order of reasons' of social memory, evoke and transmit the memory of events that are worthy of being preserved because the group sees a unifying factor in the monuments of its past unity or—it comes to the same thing—because it retains from its past the confirmations of its present unity."[23]

In the public sphere, it is the task of memorialists—professional historians among them—to preserve the accumulated experience of the community in order to perpetuate the social group. André Leroi-Gourhan calls these acts of remembrance "ethnic" memory because they ensure "the reproduction of behaviors in human societies."[24] Collective remembering is, he argues, the instrument of survival common to all societies, historical or pre-historical: "Beginning with the *homo sapiens*, the constitution of an apparatus of social memory dominates all the problems of human evolution. ... Tradition is biologically as indispensable to the human species as genetic conditioning is to societies of insects."[25] As Hobsbawn observes, memory has functioned as a conservative force; we could say an ahistorical force. The act of remembering links the present moment with the past conceived as an ideal: "For the greater part of history we deal with societies and communities for which the past is essentially the pattern for the present.

Ideally each generation copies and reproduces its predecessor so far as is possible, and considers itself as falling short of it, so far as it fails in this endeavor."[26]

The desire of collective memory to preserve the past in the present leads to distortions and "misrepresentations" because memory is steeped in emotion and is often guided by the self-interest of the group. A society's look back toward the past is infused with nostalgia for the absolute harmony of social relations and the idealized model of social organization and behavior it locates there. The affective and ideological dimensions of social memory are clearly incompatible with the professional historian's ideal of the objectivity that can come only from the rigorous application of historical critique. However, as tradition, the living perpetuation of the past, has faded with the passage of preindustrial societies—a phenomenon already well advanced at the beginning of the twentieth century—history has stepped into the role of managing public memory. Hobsbawn argues:

> Historians are the memory bank of experience. In theory the past—all the past, anything and everything that has happened to date—constitutes history.... And, insofar as they compile and constitute the collective memory of the past, people in contemporary society have to rely on them.[27]

In the "historiographical age," the change in the regime of memory brings with it a radically different character in the public's experience of the past.

RECOVERING THE PSYCHOLOGICAL DIMENSION OF HISTORY

In his introductory essay to *Realms of Memory*,[28] French historian Pierre Nora assesses the relationship between history and memory that obtains in the twentieth century. He begins by observing an irreversible change in the way social groups relate to their past: history, written by professionals, has come to replace traditional memory characteristic of older, particularly agrarian societies. Deprived of the heritage of the past perpetuated as a living part of the present, contemporary societies experience a sense of loss: "What was left of experience, still lived in the warmth of tradition, in the silence of custom, in the repetition of the ancestral, has been swept away by a surge of deeply historical sensibility. Memory is constantly on our lips because it no longer exists."[29]

The social and political events that spell the end of memory can be summed up in terms like globalization, democratization, or the liberation movements that bring old cultures into the era of nationhood and history. Historical perception, reinforced by the power of the media, has triumphed over the process of remembrance that regulated the passage from the past into the future; it substitutes for the depth and intimacy of collective memory the thin skin of the reality it is possible to know through the fragmentary traces it has left. For Nora, history and memory have parted company and are opposed to each other, in absolute terms, in their phenomenological perspective on the past:

> Memory, history, far from being synonymous, are thus in many respects opposed. Memory is life, always embodied in living societies and as such in permanent evolution, subject to the dialectic of remembering and forgetting, unconscious of the distortions to which it is subject, vulnerable in various ways to appropriation and manipulation, and capable of lying dormant for long periods only to be suddenly reawakened. History, on the other hand, is the reconstruction, always problematic and incomplete, of what is no longer. Memory is always a phenomenon of the present, a bond tying us to the eternal present; history is a representation of the past. Memory, being a phenomenon of emotion and magic, accommodates only those facts that suit it. It thrives on vague, telescoping reminiscences, on hazy general impression or specific symbolic details. It is vulnerable to transferences, screen memories, censorings, and projections of all kinds. History, being an intellectual, nonreligious activity, calls for analysis and critical discourse. Memory situates remembrance in a sacred context. History ferrets it out; it turns whatever it touches into prose. Memory wells up from groups that it welds together.... By contrast, history belongs to everyone and to no one and therefore has a universal vocation. Memory is rooted in the concrete: in space, gesture, image, and object. History dwells exclusively on temporal continuities, on changes in things and in the relations among things. Memory is an absolute, while history is always relative.[30]

The past is no longer alive in the collective present of the group. Memory belongs thenceforth to the human individual, who is the only entity that remembers, and to the disciplines of psychoanalytic theory and the therapeutic practices of psychology. Once memory has been consigned to archives and historians have imposed the detached gaze that is the ideal of the profession, public experience of the past becomes contemplative rather than direct. However, as Pierre Nora suggests, because our relationship to the historical past has become irreversibly fractured and discontinuous, we engage in a paradoxical search for proximity; we "rediscover" the closeness and intimacy of the past through the burgeoning testimony of its witnesses and the concrete vestiges collected in museums obsessed with preserving artifacts. If history holds us at a distance, the materials of memory put us in touch with the palpable traces of dead reality.

Nora describes the effect as "hallucinatory re-creations of the past"[31] that are generated out of our desire to possess what has forever flown out of our grasp. "Old" history aimed at the resurrection of the past, as if we could experience, through the historian's narration, the past "as it really was"; "new" history seeks to *represent* the past through the material existence of artifacts. Such representations, fragmentary but specific, allow us to recover some of the psychological and emotional dimension of historical events embedded within them. It becomes the mission of the historian to trace itineraries through the realia of archives and construct, for the collectivity, the meaningful links between past and present. Thus, in contemporary societies deprived of an immediate relation to their own past, history exercises the memorial function crucial to the survival and maintenance of a social group. Indeed, as Jacques Le Goff reminds us, the loss of collective memory would threaten the social organism with disorder and crisis, just as aphasia and amnesia can endanger the very identity of the individual human subject.[32]

The reorientation of history toward the total life of a people over time and the opening up of new archives of all sorts correspond to a growing public taste for the direct experience of historical traces. In the 1970s, the institutions of memory began to multiply exponentially. This is the period of the emergence of oral histories, the proliferation of museums dedicated to lost traditions, the revival of folklore and festivals, the memoirs that public figures of any consequence felt compelled to write, the vogue of historical programming on television—in short, the emergence of the salvage mentality. The imperative is to save it all, even if one does not know what it is being saved for. Pierre Nora describes the effect produced by this memory mania: "We cannot know in advance what should be remembered, hence we refrain from destroying anything and put everything in archives instead. The realm of the memorable has expanded without reason: we suffer from hypertrophy of memory, which is inextricably intertwined with our sense of memory's loss and concomitant institutionalization."[33]

Memory demands representation. This is what Nora calls the "problem of incarnation." How do the proliferating vestiges of past experience take on meaning within contemporary institutions? They come to reside in specific cultural spaces, the *lieux de mémoire* (places of memory) of the work's title. As Nora puts it, memory clings to places just as history clings to events. However, not all accumulations of artifacts constitute such places of memory, which, Nora argues, must correspond to the three aspects of the meaning of the word "place": the material, the functional, and the symbolic.

The place must be material, that is, it must have a concrete existence; however, it is not necessarily topographical and may take different material forms: World War I memorials to the dead that have their place in every French village; a veteran's organization dedicated to not forgetting past heroism and sacrifice; a historical journal that serves as an inculcation of a vision of the national past. The place must be functional in the sense that the vestiges of the past it collects and displays are part of a social effort to transmit memories, an activation of the past embodied in rites of remembering: public holidays that commemorate the origins of a nation; the folkloric reenactment of traditions and events (e.g., in associations dedicated to the accurate depiction of life in and near the battlefields of the Civil War); Washington's Vietnam Memorial, Auschwitz, and other places of pilgrimage. In addition, each of these material and functional places must be endowed with a "symbolic aura" that resonates in the public imagination: a site that organizes and condenses the public's emotional and ideological experience of the past. Finally, Nora argues, a place of memory is constituted through a "will to remember," the desire to "stop time, to inhibit forgetting, to fix a state of things, to immortalize death, and to materialize the immaterial."[34] Memory in the active sense implies a collective determination to remember. Without this elemental motivation, traces of the past are simply irrelevant to public life and are relegated to the sphere of historical erudition. As far as collective remembrance is concerned, it is "memory that dictates and history that takes dictation."

Places of memory emerge rather spontaneously as their need becomes expressed. The public practice of memory is particularly self-conscious in France, where the will to remember is accompanied by calculated attempts to create an institution of memory. Not long ago, I encountered the following example of a specific place of memory in which film plays a central role. The rite of commemoration took place on October 7, 2000, in the small village of Les Mées in the rural French backcountry of the Alpes de Haute Provence (formerly known as the Basses Alpes). The historical memory evoked was the peasant insurrection that contested the coup d'état carried out by Louis Napoleon on December 2, 1851, which toppled the Second Republic and created the Second Empire. The insurgents, isolated from the cities with which communication was slow at best, displayed enormous courage in defending the Republic against the usurper, not realizing that the urban masses had accepted the advent of the Empire with general passivity. Launching their resistance from the base of the village commune—the same base of action that *communards* adopted in Paris in 1871—and led by a cadre of artisans organized in secret societies, the insurgents worked militarily and politically toward the goal of assuming power at the level of the *préfecture* of the department. They waited in vain for an uprising in Marseille that would amplify a peasant revolt into a powerful regional insurrection. Despite a few glorious victories in the Basses Alpes and in the Var, the rebellion was crushed by the military forces of the Empire, and thousands of the movement's leaders and peasant troublemakers were sent to the miseries of the French colonial prisons in Algeria.

The commemoration of the insurrection was sponsored and organized by the Friends of Les Mées, and the Association 1851–2001, a society composed of descendents of the insurrectionists, historians, schoolteachers, and citizens of republican persuasion in this traditionally "red" area of the French southeast. The events of the day included a *débat*, chaired by the president of the association, with the participation of two professional historians from nearby universities, a history teacher from a local high school, and amateur historians with roots in the communities. The *débat* was followed by a ceremony renaming the street that starts from the central fountain of Les Mées, bearing a plaque to the memory of the insurgents, and leads down to the former battlefield where the peasant forces won a brief victory against the armies of Napoleon III. The street now bears the emphatic name of the Rue de la Liberté and des Insurgés. The inauguration was presided over by the town's mayor, a man of clearly republican sympathies, and featured a chorus of young schoolchildren impersonating the spirit of the insurrection. The mayor invited the assembled crowd to participate in the *apéritif* and the *repas républicain*. The afternoon featured an exhibition of documents—letters, proclamations by revolutionary leaders, public communications from Napoleon III's counterinsurgent administration—and the projection of the film, a "historical documentary" entitled *1851: Ils se levèrent pour la République* ("They Stood Up for the Republic"). The screening was followed by a public discussion in the presence of the filmmaker, Christian Philibert, and some of his collaborators, the film's producer, and one of the historians featured in the film.

As Nora observes, "memory clings to places." The choice of the site of this day of remembrance was significant: Les Mées, the place of a victorious battle against the forces of Napoleon III, possesses prominently displayed in its central square, possesses the only public memorial to the insurrection in the department of the Alpes de Haute Provence. The objective of the day's events was not only to revivify the events of 1851, but also to establish in the village another visible marker of the insurrection to "block the work of forgetting" and "materialize the immaterial." Moreover, this most recent commemoration was linked to other historical moments when the memory of 1851 emerged from its latency to serve as a major historical reference for the present, notably in the twentieth century in the antifascist movement of 1934 and at the moment of the liberation from Nazi occupation. That there was a strong public "will to remember" was evidenced by the crowds that filled the local movie theater for the *débat* and the film. Discussions were punctuated by emotional statements by participants and the public, particularly those of the descendents of the insurgents who conserve as family treasures the letters from their ancestors writing home from prison in Algeria.

The overriding concern expressed by participants and the public was the exclusion of this important piece of republican history from the national curriculum of the public schools, which is centered, they asserted, around the kings and dominant political leaders. Positioned against "official history," the evocation of the insurrection of 1851 is an example of history from below and involves a pedagogical campaign to restore events to the regional and even national memory. The film is a crucial element in the strategy. Produced independently, *1851: They Stood Up for the Republic* was scheduled for release on regional television. However, channel FR3 broadcast the film nationally in February 2001. Subsequently, the film was offered to history teachers in regional schools as a supplement to the official curriculum, and a theatrical collective used the film as part of a traveling spectacle to be featured at local fêtes in the region.

As this example illustrates, film can be a place of memory insofar as it engages the public in a collective recollection that revivifies or creates a meaningful link between a past event and the identity of the social group in the present. Such films often call on the social group to remake its future on the basis of its reawakened knowledge of the past. In the following case studies, I describe two historical documentaries that constitute such places of memory. Ken Burns's *The Civil War* was broadcast repeatedly on public television and has been preserved on videocassette in nearly every public library in America. Rithy Panh's *S21: The Khmer Rouge Killing Machine* received the International Human Rights Award in 2004 for its interrogation of memory of the Cambodian genocide.

CASE STUDY: LOSSES OF MEMORY—
KEN BURNS'S *THE CIVIL WAR* (1990)

Ken Burns's *The Civil War* sets out to recount the historical events of the Civil War as the founding moment of the American nation-state. Writer Shelby Foote comments in the concluding moments of the series that a significant change in subject-verb agreement denotes this shift from the relatively loose federation of states to the indivisible nation: before the war the United States was a plural noun requiring a plural verb, "the United States are"; after the war, the United States became singular, "the United States is." The project of *The Civil War* is to endow this large-scale social entity, whose origins are rife with divisions that will also "long endure," with something like a collective memory. As the film's montage will make concrete, the war can be reenacted only as a structure of conflict and pain.

In the first episode of the series, Burns raises the problematic of memory in relation to historical events. How is it possible to bridge the distance between the collectivity—the American nation in 1990, embodied in the public television audience to whom the film is addressed—and the historical past, which is cut off from personal experience and perception? Can there be communication between generations at such a historical remove? Ricoeur's notion of the "triple reign of the predecessors, contemporaries, and successors" in which the dead are constantly replaced by the living, suggests that the succession of generations is both breech and continuity. The successor belongs to the new generation but maintains a biographical link with the predecessor. Moreover, heredity has a social as well as biological character: the fact of reproduction becomes a symbolic value of the highest significance.[35] Collective memory belongs then to the realm of the symbolic; that is, it is tied to ordinary language and the social fact of the oral transmission of family narratives. Halbwachs sees in the stories told by one generation to the next a "broadening of the temporal horizon," a partial bridge, an initial link to the anonymous realm of history.

In *The Civil* War, Burns presents us with filmed footage of such acts of transmission: an ancient veteran of the war recounting his experiences to the young listeners surrounding him, newsreel footage of Civil War veterans of North and South shaking hands across the murderous wall of the battle of Fredericksburg, or the Veteran's Day parade in which the last human vestiges of the war are displayed in motorcades for public commemoration. But between these archival images that record the last experiential contact with the elders and 1990, the moment of the film's broadcast, we fall into the anonymity of historical memory, the breach that can be only partially mended through writing. Alienated from our heritage, we can know the past only through mediation: "the distancing in time is thus consecrated by the distancing of writing."[36] However, as Burns's film shows, writing history is not reserved exclusively to the domain of verbal narrative but includes the filmmaker's act of montage, taken in its broadest sense, which constructs a discourse out of visual and verbal material. *The Civil War*, like written history, is the product of mediation and speaks with a discursive voice, but the film constantly meditates on this loss, we could even say, rebels against the gap that alienates us from living history.

Writing history begins with traces, which are, on the one hand, material vestiges of the past (of the *passage* of human actors, to use Ricoeur's notion), and systems of signs that refer to the past according to their specific modes of signification. The historical events known as the Civil War have left their marks in the visual and verbal documents the film organizes into a discourse. Visual documents include photographic images of events, pictorial renderings of historical scenes, maps, newspaper articles, death notices, and so forth. The verbal documents aurally transmitted include readings from letters, diaries, memoirs, public statements, and proclamations. Such material testimony is not part of a living public memory but lies dormant in archives and libraries and is awakened by the occasional focused exhibition (e.g., the Chicago Historical Society's exhibit, "A House Divided," cited in the film's credits) or commemorative activity (for example, historical reconstructions on the battlefields of the war performed by "reenacters"). Most Americans do not consciously maintain a living link to the past of the Civil War; this collective remembrance, as Nora suggests, must be artificially constructed through places of memory. In producing *The Civil War* as such a place of memory, Burns attempts to block the work of forgetting and to memorialize death: to remedy the loss of a whole period of history and to do the quite literal work of remembering the dead, whose lives have been perpetuated through the fractured testimony of archives. What are the strategies of representation the television series uses to construct a collective memory of the war?

One might have expected in a film about the Civil War a classical piece of military history, whose perspective is *from above*, and indeed the film intermittently espouses this point of view: the overarching strategies of war (described by the voice-over and symbolically rendered in maps); the major military and political figures whose character and actions determine the unfolding of military events; and the anonymous troops, who can be only represented as masses in action, reduced visually to the abstraction of arrows of movement on the map of a military campaign. However, Burns often prefers to represent the experience of the normally anonymous actors of military history: the officer, the foot soldier, the private citizen who chronicle what they see of the war and their personal reactions to it.

In the pretitle sequence that opens episode 4, for example, the film makes its multiple focal points clear. The first shot shows us a detail from a photograph representing a domestic rather than a military scene: a washtub and a pair of hands (accompanied by sounds of rubbing and splashing). The camera then pans up to the face of the soldier at the washboard. The second shot reframes the whole of the original photograph and places the figure of the soldier, previously caught in close-up, as a member of a group engaged in similar activities. The voice-over that accompanies these two shots seeks to "level" the wars' actors: "In this army, one hole in the seat of the britches indicates a captain, two holes a lieutenant, and the seat of the pants all out indicates the individual is a private" (unattributed statement). Although the members of the group remain anonymous, one at least has been individuated through the use of the panning camera. Such "small-scale" actors constitute what Ann Rigney calls "figures in the crowd," modest individuals who stand for the group through their status of participatory belonging.[37] Some minor actors of history are identified by name and raised to the status of individual historical witnesses.

Thus, the characters mandated by history—presidents and generals—are accompanied by a second string of protagonists—officers, foot soldiers, or private citizens. History from above is balanced by history from below. In the opening moments of episode 4, Burns democratizes his dramatis personae by evoking with equal attention the figures of Stonewall Jackson; Joshua Lawrence Chamberlain, college professor and officer; Robert E. Lee; Ulysses S. Grant; and Privates Sam Watson and Elisha Hunt Rhodes. Each of the small-scale historical actors, like their big-scale counterparts, is individuated by a photographic portrait in close-up. The intermittent presence of such historically "insignificant" figures across the chain of events that constitute the war places us in the realm of personal experience. Moreover, Burns does not neglect the psychological dimension of major historical actors: Robert E. Lee's compassion for the Northern troops massacred in the battle of Fredericksburg or General Burnside weeping at his men's defeat. Thus, the film constructs a counterpoint of public and private voices whose shifting harmonies are intended to evoke the complexity of historical situations. Moreover, the affective dimension of experience expressed through the observations of secondary narrators is redoubled by mise en scène. The voiceless written narratives found in archives are reincarnated by the voices of actors, which give back to the witnesses the partial illusion of their bodily existence.

We may ask why it is that this vocal theatricalism seems more acceptable in historical representation than the visual duplication of the historical character through the body of the actor. The answer lies, I think, in the reasoning implicit in the filmmaker's choices. *The Civil War*, like most serious history films, embodies the central dilemma of historical representation in film: on the one hand, there is the desire to "resurrect" the past, to bring it to life, which is a fundamental impulse of the historical filmmaker; on the other hand, there are the limits imposed by historical reference—we can only speak about what it is possible to know about the past. As sensitive spectators of historical films, we continually assess whether a historical film remains within the bounds of justifiable representations.

In the interest of accommodating the impulse to reenact, we tolerate infractions against the limits of knowability on the condition of their discretion. The actor's voice is a discreet reembodiment since the voice of the historical character, unlike his image, has not been documented. The sound of rubbing and splashing water that accompanies the still photograph of the soldier doing his laundry is an "acceptable" real effect because noise, in Western cultures, is not being itself but an attribute of being. Moreover, the sound of water on a washboard or the sound of wind blowing through the steeple at Fredericksburg or in the surrounding forests is part of the universal and unchanging soundscape that can bridge between living presence and the absence of being in the past. The same can be said for the moments in which Burns films natural phenomena in movement in the very locations where historical events took place. In a film that uses essentially static visual representations—photographic or pictorial—the moving image is a startling anomaly. However, because nature is presumably immutable, its representation in moving images constitutes an approximate "sameness" that lends to historical narrative the effect of being in time.

At their best, such passages avoid the gratuity of the real effect. For example, Burns evokes the night of horror that follows on the massacre of Union troops at Fredericksburg. A secondary narrator, the eloquent Joshua Lawrence Chamberlain, describes night sounds on the battlefield littered with the dead and dying: the "strange ventriloquism" of sounds, "weird, unearthly, terrible to hear and bear," the cries for help and for death, the "delirious voices, murmuring loved names as if the dearest were bending over them, and, underneath, all the time, the deep base note from closed lips, too hopeless or too heroic to articulate their agony."

Visually, the sequence begins with a close-up of Chamberlain's photographic portrait: the look that introduces the subjectivity of the witness's testimony. To the static portrait, the eyes unreadable but suggestive of inner life, the actor's voice will lend the attribute of real being. The succeeding shots do not depict the human presence that is the center of the narrator's description; rather, they are filmed nocturnal landscapes, tinted in red and linked by dissolves: the steeple of the Fredericksburg church, light reflecting off ripples in the river, a quarter moon in a dark sky, two shots repeating the visual motif of light on water, and, finally, the moon rising from behind a darkened house and illuminating a scene of trees and cloud-filled sky. The images' quiet movement is accompanied by the sound of wind, giving the landscapes a full diegetic effect. Here, as very often in the film, the image track and the sound track are set off by a certain disparity: the verbal narration does not find its exact object in the image. Against the last image of the rising moon, the narrator speaks of his state of mind as he lies down among the dead: "At last wearied and depressed, I moved two dead men a little and lay down between them, making a pillow of the breast of a third." The effect is one of poetic irony: the quietude of the living landscapes belies Chamberlain's agonizing account of death and dying. At the same time, the landscape's emptiness resonates as a metaphor for loss.

The photographic images, which make up the great majority of the image track of *The Civil War*, are historical traces—a million photographs were taken on the battlefields of the war. Like all historical traces, the photograph combines presence and absence: the presence of the rich signifier of being, the absence of the subjects which have fallen away into the past. This presence/absence can be expressed, following Roland Barthes, as the *having-been-there* of the image. Thus, the photograph, despite its material existence, is arrested movement; it does not evolve in time. It is the most poignant expression of loss: the phenomenological richness of the image serves to intensify the sense of absence. Indeed, loss is one of the fundamental themes of *The Civil War*. In episode 9, the narrator describes how the photographic plates, which produced the images so sought after during the war, were sold after the war as glass for greenhouses, where the sun gradually burnt away the last traces of the events the plates had documented.

Is it possible, *The Civil War* asks, to recapture some aspect of being? The desire to reanimate is palpable in many of the techniques of representation that Burns uses in his film. The sound track, for example, often juxtaposes the animation of the noise track against the arrested life of the photographic image. The photograph preexists, but the sound track belongs to the film's moment of enunciation. The fabricated noise of battle—drum rolls, rifle and cannon fire, soldiers' screams, the whinnying of horses—evolves through time, the very condition of its representation.

The film's use of the zooming and panning camera is a second technique of animation. Its purpose is to give the already-framed photographic or pictorial image, normally read as whole and as a trajectory across the work imposed by its composition, some qualities of being. Panning can reinstall a sense of discovery—the suspense that gradual revelation creates—and the enigma the moving camera promises to resolve. For example, the film very often presents the human figure through an upward pan from the feet (the point of minimum individuation) across the body (the more expressive elements of posture and hands), to the face as the ultimate locus of identification. The photograph is thus experienced through time, despite its static character. Lateral panning performs a similar function, particularly in the panoramic scenes of battles. The zoom-in on photographs with great depth of field reveals the detail that was lost in the expanse of the broader view. In a less dynamic fashion, reframing the same photograph at various distances allows for a similar exploration of the image according to the technique of analytic editing so crucial to filmic representation: isolating and relating details or contextualizing partial views in a broader shot.

It is obvious that such techniques of presence run the risk of transgressing the boundaries of historical narrative, and that is why I have emphasized the discretion with which Burns uses them. Not all historical documentaries avoid the sins of revivification. The History Channel, for example, endlessly recycles films in which historical documents are mixed with open appeals to the spectator's imaginary. Static documents such as photographs and drawings give way to romanticized tableaus, filmed historical scenes with their human actors, whose identifying features must, paradoxically, be hidden from the viewer. The bad faith of these representations is signaled by clichéd techniques of effacement: the historic actors are seen at a great distance, from behind as they retreat from us or from below where they exhibit only legs and costume, or they are suffused into unrecognizability by lenses or gauze.

The Civil War is, by contrast, serious history, and its deepest moments are a meditation on memory and loss. Moreover, the admixture of materials is rich and varied. The voice-over narration assumes several positions. It is the knowing voice of history whose retrospective viewpoint embraces the distant horizon of events: "But the biggest tests were coming that summer where the Mississippi took a sharp turn at Vicksburg and at a sleepy corner of Pennsylvania." It interprets the character of the events' major actors: "Bold action did not come naturally to Ambrose Burnside, though he had come to Fredericksburg determined to display the fighting spirit his predecessor, George McClellan, had so conspicuously lacked." It marshals the support of participants and witnesses through citation: "Some wondered why the Confederates didn't make it harder for them to cross [the Rappahannock at Vicksburg]. 'They want to get us in,' one private said. 'Getting out won't be so smart and easy.'" It reinvests the photographic image with the historic meaning it has lost. While a long shot, empty of human presence, shows us a country lane bordered by a stone wall, the voice-over endows it with the specificity of the historical event: "Four lines of riflemen waited behind a stone wall that ran along the base of the hill. General and officers assured James Longstreet, 'A chicken couldn't live in that field when we open upon it.'"

As I have observed, the voice of history often yields to the plurality of secondary narrators, who, through the actors' voices, appear to speak in their own names. The narrative function is intermittently held by individual historians, who recount events or reflect on their meaning, either directly in addressing the camera/interviewer or commenting from offscreen the succession of visual documents. The talented raconteur, Shelby Foote, allows us to savor the Confederate soldiers' legendary "rebel" yell or the display of northern lights that occurred after the battle of Fredericksburg: "But the whole heavens were lit up with streamers of fire and whatever the northern lights are. And the Confederates took it that God Almighty Himself was celebrating a Confederate victory." The colloquial and poetic quality of Foote's language, his southern accent, and the intimate quality of the close-up evoke something of the intimacy of oral history. The film's score, based in period folk music, also plays on familiarity and works to humanize the transpersonal events of the war. We have already seen Burns's telling use of photographs and drawings, the way diegetic sound quickens the image, and his meditative use of beautiful filmed landscapes.

Collective memory can never be reduced to an objective causal sequence of dated events. If collective memory is to be held in the consciousness of a social group, it must be endowed with qualities that replicate to some degree the intimate relationship that personal memory establishes between reminiscences and the mind that holds them. As *The Civil War* reminds us, collective memory is always-already a social phenomenon because it is generated out of the social practice of narrative. If history is a large-scale narrative that stands above, and aloof from, the small-scale forces that play themselves out in historical events, *The Civil War* attempts to reinvest abstract history with the innumerable minor narratives generated from the experience of human groups and individuals. The voices of the witnesses we hear in Burns's film call for the spectator's identification: we listen to their accounts of events as if we had become parties to the intimacy of a dialogic exchange. The voices imbue their photographic likenesses with the subjectivity of being. In *The Civil War*, collective memory is a construct, a discursive strategy that attempts to reconnect us with the living reality of the past. The strength of the film resides in the fact that, all the while seeking the illusion of real being, it acknowledges the impossibility of resurrection and confronts us with inescapable loss.

CASE STUDY: COMPELLING MEMORY IN RITHY PANH'S *S21—THE KHMER ROUGE KILLING MACHINE* (2003)

Rithy Panh's *S21* is a film of rare urgency: it reopens the wound of the Cambodian genocide, even today largely unacknowledged by the perpetrators of the genocidal acts and repressed in the deepest layers of consciousness of their victims. Few works in the history of cinema embody such a moral imperative to speak about historical events. Between 1975 and 1979, the Pol Pot regime, in the name of creating a classless society, pursued unconscionable policies of deportation and forced labor that led to the death of many hundreds of thousands of people from starvation and exhaustion. Moreover, it prosecuted a paranoid program of annihilation directed against the perceived enemies of Angkar, the revolutionary party of Democratic Kampuchea: the victims included the educated classes—teachers, students, professionals, intellectuals—anyone suspected of ties with the overthrown government of Prince Sihanouk or foreign agencies, or simple people who breached rules or were suspected of harboring antiparty ideas. In a period of four years, nearly two million people perished at the hands of the Khmer Rouge.

Rithy Panh is haunted by his personal memories of genocide. He was eleven years old when his family was deported from Phnom Penh to the countryside, victims of the plan to empty the city of its two-and-a-half million inhabitants in a matter of days. In the horrifying conditions imposed by the Khmer Rouge program of reeducation, he witnessed his parents and sisters dying of hunger and exhaustion. At the fall of the Pol Pot regime in 1979, he was granted refugee status in France, where he hoped to "erase everything and begin again at zero."[38] However, Panh would not be able to suppress the psychic aftermath of the experience of genocide. In Paris, he decided to study film and enrolled in the Institut des Hautes Etudes Cinématographiques (Idhec). His emigration had made possible his choice to become a professional filmmaker, but his motivation ran deeper. "Irradiated" by the horror of his experiences, Panh waited for the maturity he needed to reflect meaningfully on a past that haunted his existence. He was determined to speak about the unspeakable human experience of genocide and use the filmmaking process as an instrument of persuasion and pragmatic action:

> Without genocide, without wars, I would probably not have become a filmmaker. But life after genocide is a terrifying void. It is impossible to live in forgetfulness. You risk losing your soul. Day after day, I felt myself sucked into the void. As if keeping silent was capitulation, death. Contrary to what I at first thought, to relive is also to take back your memory and your ability to speak.[39]

In 1996, while he was making a film called *Bophana, a Cambodian Tragedy*, based on the case of a woman who was tortured and executed for sending love letters to her husband, Panh staged the extraordinary encounter between survivor and artist Vann Nath, who painted from memory scenes of abuse and victimization, and the guards responsible for holding, torturing, and executing prisoners in the death camp named S21. In an ironic twist of history, Nath, who survived S21 because the Khmer Rouge designated him as the prison's official painter, turned his art against those he was formerly forced to serve. It was this experience of delayed confrontation that led Panh to conceive the project that would become *S21: The Khmer Rouge Killing Machine*. Panh writes that Vann Nath, whom he had first met at the Paris Peace Accords in 1991, would "become the central character of my work on memory during the succeeding ten years."

The film takes place at Tuol Sleng, a former high school in Phnom Penh that the Khmer Rouge transformed into S21 (S for security, 2 for second bureau, 1 for brother number 1, Pol Pot). For Panh, S21 is the central character of the film, a place "haunted and as if impregnated with the drama that unfolded there."[40] Seventeen thousand people, rounded up on the least suspicion of resistance to party policy, were brought here, kept in barbaric conditions, tortured, and made to confess to absurd acts of treason. Once their treachery was documented (the Khmer Rouge kept meticulous records, both written and photographic), they were summarily executed. Of the 17,000 victims, seven survived. At the time of shooting S21, there remained only three.

How, Rithy Panh asks himself, does one approach the reality of lived experience when memory is "in shambles"? It was not enough for the Khmer Rouge to obliterate all the institutions of Cambodian society— they closed schools, factories, and hospitals; shut down the banking system; attacked the family; and outlawed religion. They also moved to eradicate what Leroi-Gourhan terms *ethnic memory*: the collective recollection of traditions that ensures the survival of a society.[41] To brainwash an entire people and instill in them the ideology of the Angkar, the Khmer Rouge needed to disrupt traditions, wipe out altogether the memory of shared experience, and impose a new collective life modeled on party dicta. This was the purpose of the massive displacement of populations, the infliction of forced labor, and the suppression of all modes of communication not controlled by the party.

In prisons like S21, the attack against memory was also an attack against individual consciousness. Brutal means of extortion were devised to coerce victims into "reconstructing" their lives in the form of "biographies," preferably written in their own hand. These tissues of lies were intended to extirpate personal memory and wipe out the victims' sense of themselves as human beings. Under such traumatic treatment, dehumanized individuals are no longer able to perform the essential operation of memory: to reconstitute the past of their experience in the present of the mind. Self-consciousness and memory are no longer inextricably bound. Thus, it becomes impossible for victims, who never act but are acted upon, to conceive of the continuity of the self (Locke's personhood) because they are no longer able to establish the link between the present, where action is impossible, and their actions in the past, now obliterated from memory. The victims of torture are deprived of subjectivity: unable to remember, they cannot remember themselves.

The heart of Panh's project is not therefore the reconstruction of the past in historical terms, if we mean by that objective analyses of the Cambodian genocide. Rather, he wants to deal with collective "amnesia," the "retrospective bewilderment of a people" still traumatized by genocidal events never acknowledged by the Khmer Rouge leaders, some of whom continue to hold positions of power. The victims of genocide still live with terror; and terror, the filmmaker reminds us, acts "like an anesthesia, blocking memory, favoring forgetfulness and denial." To bring repressed memories to mind, the survivors of S21 must resist their defensive instincts and subject themselves to the pain of traumatic recollection. On the side of the torturers—those among them who are driven to acknowledge their participation in the Khmer Rouge killing machine—memory is blocked by guilty defense against the reality of their acts. They are caught between the necessity to speak and the unspeakable.

Panh, as the film's guiding consciousness, is not an objective observer; he is himself a victim of genocide and therefore a subject in search of his position within the genocidal narrative. He has come to his task after a period of "maturation" of twenty years. He has brought together and trained his Cambodian production crew, who were not chosen because of their technical expertise, but because they shared the common experience of genocide. The film's crew is characterized by their participatory belonging to an affective community in the name of which they act as instruments of memory. "I needed a team," Panh explains, "who spoke the same language, who had lived through the same history. It is a force, this cohesive team, who never hesitated even at the most delicate even dangerous moments."[42] Panh chooses Vann Nath as the film's central protagonist because Nath has already taken up the position of the heroic subject who refuses to forget and pits himself against the recalcitrant opponents of memory.

Panh's method aims at unleashing memory in the most immediate sense. He is not interested in the documentary method that illustrates the past through the montage of documents organized and directed by the voice-over commentary. Such films, he believes, manufacture events, furnishing answers determined in advance. Panh prefers to remain in the interrogative mode; his documentary method consists in listening. Moreover, he remains resolutely in the present: he sets himself the task of staging the return of memories of genocide by stimulating and provoking its living witnesses. He does not intervene directly in the film, in the manner of a Claude Lanzmann or Marcel Ophuls, but one detects at every moment the signs of his rigorous mise en scène: "I deliberately chose to stage this situation, by imposing on myself a moral rigor that requires I keep the necessary distance from the witnesses and that I not let them deviate from the goal we had set."[43] Panh's approach is confrontational: he brings his witnesses back to S21, the now empty spaces that were once the scenes of their crimes or suffering; he blocks them into uncomfortable positions and pressures them with his interrogating camera; he compels them to confront the traces of their past experience. He stages the return of the repressed: the revivification of stifled memory in the minds of the individual torturer or victim. The result is what Panh calls a "look from the inside of our collective memory."

S21's staging is profoundly psychological and involves the most painful of realizations. Pahn focuses on individuals: two remaining survivors of S21 on the one hand and, on the other, a small number of guards, interrogators, the prison "doctor," the keeper of the records, a driver of the trucks of death, with particular emphasis on Him Houy, the "chef-adjoint du Santébal." "I wanted to be able to put a name to a face," Panh tells us, "I didn't want anonymous victims or torturers with masked faces."[44] Indeed, our introduction to the traumatized world of contemporary Cambodia occurs in the rice paddies and the house where Houy lives with his parents and his wife and two children. In a moment of terrible irony, Houy the mass murderer takes his newly bathed baby on his lap. How is it possible to admit that such a gesture of tenderness comes so easily to a man guilty of monstrous acts? In the warm penumbra of the house, he complains of his symptoms (headaches, lack of appetite) and denies his responsibility ("The evil is the leaders who gave the orders"), while his parents suggest how he can assuage the bad karma of so many deaths ("Tell the truth, then have a ceremony").

The scene that follows serves as a rejoinder to Houy's denial, part of the patterns of confrontation that structure the film. It begins with a close-up of Nath's hand and brush applying color to a painting in progress as he begins to tell the story of his arrest and his arrival, along with thirty others, at S21. The words he speaks are also denoted in the painting: the blindfolded and shackled prisoners are being dragged along by a rope around their necks. The victims massed in the dark foreground are indistinguishable from each other, except for the figure Nath individualizes by applying touches of light blue; the background is dominated by an ominously lit building. The scene of Nath painting is shot in a single take. The camera pans repeatedly between the painter's hand and brush, the palette, the painting, the painter's face, sometimes tracking forward on the painting to isolate elements of Nath's account (the shackled feet) or panning up to the prison's lighted windows as Nath describes his sensations as he is being pulled up the stairs of the cell block.

Memory demands representation. What could be more evocative of the process of the representation of memory in both verbal and visual forms? Nath's verbal narration of events implicates the presence of the camera and the filmmaker (instruments of communication) and the audience for whom he is bearing witness. The camera's movements create the links between Nath's face (the locus of memory), the instruments of visualization (the hand, the brush, the palette), and the painting through which memories are rendered. As if guided by the voice, the camera emphasizes the relationship between the verbal and the visual, complementary vehicles of memory.

If *S21* begins with the individual consciousness, its goal is to represent collective subjects. Nath describes and paints a scene of shared experience: the common plight of thirty prisoners. It is through remembrance that Nath the individual takes his place within a social group; in this case, it is the relationship he establishes between himself, the solitary survivor, and the collective mass of the dead on whose behalf he feels called on to bear witness. To recall Ricoeur's principle of fidelity that animates historical representations, Nath quite literally documents the horrors of S21 to exonerate his debt toward the dead. Out of the void of S21, he recreates Halbwach's affective community— the group with which he is closely identified and that allows his individual memory to "take possession of itself." Ethnic memory, to recall Leroi-Gourhan's notion, has been nearly silenced, and the danger is, Panh suggests, that Cambodian society may not survive the fracture of genocide.

As we soon learn, Nath's paintings are not only intended as part of the recovery of social memory, they are also the locus of confrontation between the society of victims and the Khmer Rouge functionaries of terror. The film's ninth sequence, to take an example, begins with a long shot: Nath stands in the background next to a painting; five former guards on his right look on, as if they were pupils taking a lesson. The painting represents a cell: inmates, seen from above, are arranged symmetrically on the floor, feet to feet, head to head, in four rows of ten, their bodies and faces cast in the same mold of suffering. A final row, asymmetrical to the others, occupies the far background. Beyond the rows of palettes stands a guard with a whip. Nath, in close-up, looks offscreen at his interlocutors while he begins not only to describe the conditions of incarceration ("Death came every day." "So we slept with corpses.") but also to individuate the apparently identical figures by pointing at them ("I was here." "This one was hanging between life and death.").

In the confrontations Panh stages between victims and torturers, the scale of the shots is important. The close-up emphasizes the subjective, calling on the spectator to identify with the thoughts or emotions of the former victim or, in the close-ups on the persecutors, to sense their psychological response to evidence of their guilt or the truthfulness of their confessions. In the close-up in the sequence cited above, our proximity to Nath as he confronts the guards intensifies our identification with him as the victim become interrogator. The medium shot, on the other hand, produces, Panh tells us, the appropriate distance between the spectator and the witness to allow for critical judgment. In response to the close-up on Nath, Panh gives us a reverse angle of two guards in medium shot, expressing their adversarial position as they listen to the painter's admonition: "How could you get used to such acts, seeing such suffering." The blocking of the shot has the two men, Prak Khân and Him Houy, staggered in depth, an artificial disposition of men in awkward poses, suggesting they have been called on the carpet. The scale of the shot allows us to read the guards' stiff body language, their defensiveness, and the desperation of their denial.

One guard justifies his acts as the result of indoctrination by the party: "We were the party's right hand. ... We couldn't hesitate in the face of the enemy." At the word *enemy*, we cut back to a close-up of the painting, the camera refuting the epithet of "enemy" by reference to the pathetic victims. The camera then pans up to a close shot of Nath, who asks, "What about the children? They were against whom?" In response, we are given a closer medium shot of the two guards. Houy, who is placed further in depth, replies: "When the Party makes an arrest, it arrests an enemy of the people," and the enemy's family is guilty by association. The sequence ends in a close-up of Nath, who listens to the guards reiterate Angkar doctrine ("The Party, S21, never made arrests by mistake.") as we read the pain and anger in his eyes.

It was this resistance on the part of the perpetrators that Pahn hoped to break down through techniques of mise en scène. How could the guards be persuaded to bear witness to actions that were unspeakable? What mechanism might trigger remembrance in those who were desperately defended against it? Panh noticed that a younger guard, who had been abducted as a child and brought to S21, where he was indoctrinated and recruited by the Khmer Rouge, could evoke his role only by shouting slogans: "His words, delivered in a hard, hammered tone, were accompanied and completed by gestures, as if another mechanism of memory had been set in motion: the automatism of gesture, the routine of crime."[45]

This insight led Panh to the technique of reenactment: he would place the guards in the cellblock in S21 where they had worked and would ask them to reenact their daily activities. The space of the scene is no longer that of Nath's paintings; the palettes and the suffering bodies are gone. The guards perform their rounds and inspect rooms that are nothing more than vast, empty spaces. Deprived of a set and props, they must describe in words and mimic in gesture their patterns of behavior. Thus, the guards become both the narrators of their actions—a position that assumes a certain distance from what is being narrated—and the actors who place themselves in the roles of their former selves. The film contains several scenes staged in this manner, the most explosive of which feature the guard recruited as a child. As he mimics a search of a cell with another guard, his voice fills with anger at the prisoners' misbehavior: "'Get up! On your feet! Hands up!' I start my search. I look, I feel." And then: "'You! Taking your shirt off? Without the guard's permission? To hang yourself by your shirt? Give me that!' I grab it and take it away."

Rithy Panh's methodical assault on the repression of memory aims at recovering not only truth but also the psychological and emotional dimension of past experience. As Pierre Nora suggests, such closeness to the past can be rediscovered only through the testimony of witnesses and the concrete vestiges of the past collected in museums and archives. S21 the museum of the Cambodian genocide and *S21* the film possess all the characteristics Nora ascribes to places of memory. S21 is a *material* place. Panh's cinematography reveals it as a series of vast, empty rooms, haunted by memories. Moreover, his assertive mise en scène transforms the museum into a place where participants bear witness to genocide and bring alive the traces left behind in the written and photographic archives the Khmer Rouge fanatically accumulated. The museum and the film are both *functional* places committed to lifting the "taboo of silence" and transmitting to the public meaningful traces of the Cambodian genocide. Panh hopes his film will become a pedagogical tool and fill out the few pages consecrated to the subject in Cambodian school textbooks. S21 has a *symbolic* aura; it resonates in the public imagination and organizes and condenses the public's experience of the past. Finally, it embodies *a will to remember*: S21, the museum and the film, operate to "stop time, to inhibit forgetting, to fix a state of things, to immortalize death, and to materialize the immaterial."[46]

However, it is one thing for the young Cambodian public—to whom Panh particularly addresses his film—to discover the vestiges of their national past in S21 the museum. It is quite another to confront the actors of the Cambodian genocide with the painful traces of their own existence. In *S21* the film, the archives, far from objective traces of events, are powerful catalysts of memory. They stir the ashes of experiences that are not entirely extinguished for either victims or perpetrators. We first meet Chum Mey, the prisoner who survived because he could repair the Khmer Rouge's busy typewriters, as he approaches the building in S21 where he was imprisoned. The encounter is traumatic, and he weeps as he says to Nath, who tries to comfort him, "My wife, my children. … I lost everything. Nath, help me." In the next sequence, Nath reads to Mey from the record of his confession and shows him the list of the names of people he denounced under torture. Mey responds, "They beat me so badly, Nath, I couldn't take it."

S21 focuses particularly on the process of confrontation involving the prison personnel and the archival evidence of their acts. In sequence 12, for example, a guard seated at a desk at some distance from the camera reads the Khmer Rouge manual entitled "Method for Writing a Document," that is, techniques ranging from political pressure to torture used to extract confessions. As the reader's voice describes the "interrogation procedures," four guards move from the far background toward the camera and put in place a torture chair. In sequence 13, the reading of the text continues over the reenactment in which two guards enter a cell and mimic taking a prisoner away, blindfolded and handcuffed, to be interrogated. Sequence 14 returns us to a close-up of the document being read and the guard's finger following the text. Torture, we learn, is divided into three levels: "mild, hot, and rabid." A document shows us the record of the rabid group's activity and at the bottom the name of the reader, Prak Khân. The camera pans over the photos of victims lying in disorder across the desk. Then Prak Khân points out the members of the rabid group in a photograph. The camera returns to panning across the victims' photos as we hear the first words of a confession Khân has prepared: "I was arrogant and had power over the enemy. I never thought of his life. I saw him as an animal." The camera returns to a shot of the reader, Khân, in close-up, as he says, "My heart never checked my brain."

Other moments involve the perpetrators in more spontaneous confrontations. In sequence 39, for example, three former guards in a vacant room unroll a huge photographic print. One of them recognizes the subject—"It's Choeung Ek base where we killed the prisoners"— and points out the landmarks: the hut where the prisoners waited execution, the already-dug pit where the executed would be buried. Houy recalls the stench that rose up from the cracked earth. Sequence 41 places the executioners in the real site of the photograph. It is night, and a few lights illuminate Houy and a second guard, near a pit filled with water. To the incongruous sound of croaking frogs, they recount in grisly detail the procedures of execution and their own indifference to death and suffering.

The absurd documents intended to demonstrate the guilt of the victims of S21 "today turn against their authors, proving in the eyes of history the implacable logic of genocidal crime." If one examines the archives with the eye of the archaeologist, Panh asserts, one can also detect the traces of human resistance: "You discover at the turn of a phrase, behind a look, the will to resist in someone who is going to be tortured and executed in the coming days or weeks."[47] If Panh has constructed his film around the acts of remembrance of individual victims and perpetrators, his intention is to reclaim from anonymity and meaninglessness the thousands who died at S21. How is it possible to negotiate between the psychological experience of victims and perpetrators and at the same time construct a history of the Cambodian genocide? Panh's response is that historical meaning must come "through the prism of individual histories placed end-to-end."

Near the end of the film, the camera shows us a wall of photographs of victims, part of the museum's exhibition: the Khmer Rouge's photographic documentation of prisoners was as complete as the records of their confessions. The camera tracks right and reveals in depth other panels of photographs displayed on other walls—still only a sampling of the collectivity of victims. The camera continues to pan across hundreds of photographs and stops in front of the images of three young women. In the center is the face of the young woman we have seen repeatedly on the desk where the victims' confessions were recorded. We know her name, Nay Nân, and that she worked in a hospital. We have listened to Prak Khân's confession (taken in close-up by the interrogating camera) in which he describes how he abused and beat her, how he prodded her into collaborating in the fabrication of fictitious acts of sabotage—defecating in the operating room in order to discredit a model hospital—and how he coaxed her into choosing between the CIA, the KGB, or the Vietnamese as the foreign agency she worked for. She is the "face in the crowd," the human individual whose identity radiates across the apparent anonymity of the victims' photographs and brings us to the realization of the enormity of their suffering.

S21 demonstrates one of Pierre Nora's most insightful formulations: "Memory is rooted in the concrete: in space, gesture, image, and object." Without the disturbing reality of S21, whose vast, dusty spaces haunt memory; without the gestures through which the guards reconnect with their past actions; without the images—painterly and photographic—that draw out the witnesses and make them speak about their past; without the objects abandoned in S21, like the button Nath discovers amid the rubble of a vacant room at the end of the film, the Cambodian genocide cannot be remembered. However, there is nothing magical or nostalgic about the memories that emerge. They are not given to the "hazy impressions" and "symbolic details" that Nora attributes to memory; they are brutally real. History and memory, *S21* seems to suggest, are not necessarily in opposition. In this film, memory is not "a vague telescoping of reminiscences," and it does not "accommodate only facts that suit it." Rithy Panh, through his implacable methods of mise en scène, makes himself into the cruel instrument of history who ferrets out the truth of memory. *S21* disavows the notion that history "belongs to everyone and to no one."

ENDNOTES

Introduction

1. See Brian Winston's *Claiming the Real* for an acerbic assessment of ethnographic practice in film.
2. *CinémAction*, no. 65.
3. *Le Monde*, November 25, 1983.
4. *CinémAction* no. 65, p. 113.
5. Ibid., p. 114.
6. Ibid., p. 117.
7. Numbers 10/11 and 12/13.
8. *Ça cinéma*, no. 10/11, p. 3.
9. *Ça cinéma*, no. 12/13, p. 9.
10. Ibid., no. 12/13, p. 16.
11. *Douze leçons sur l'histoire*, p. 62.
12. *Cinema and History*, p. 47.
13. Ibid., p. 159.
14. Ibid., pp. 218–19.
15. Ibid., p. 23.
16. Ibid., p. 28.
17. Ibid., p. 23.
18. Ibid., p. 27.
19. *Image-Music-Text*, p. 40.
20. *Cinema and History*, p. 30.
21. Ibid., pp. 30–31.
22. Ibid., pp. 139–41.
23. "History in Images/History in Words," *American Historical Review*, p. 1173.
24. Ibid., p. 1174.

25. Ibid.
26. "The Historical Film: Looking at the Past in a Postliterate Age," in *Visions of the Past*, p. 49.
27. "History in Images/History in Words," p. 1181.
28. *Visions of the Past*, p. 15.
29. Ibid., p. 173.
30. In *The American Historical Review*, vol 93, no. 5, pp. 1186–92.
31. "History in Images/Images in History," in *The American Historical Review*, vol. 93, no. 5, *History in Images/History in Words*, p. 1207.
32. Ibid., p. 1208.
33. See pp. 2–41.
34. *Image as Artifact*, p. 27.
35. Ibid., p. 28.
36. Ibid., p. 37.
37. Ibid., p. 8.
38. "I'll see it when I believe it," p. 80.
39. Ibid., p. 81.
40. *Visions of the Past*, p. 10.
41. *Between History and Literature*, p. 230.
42. See Antoine Prost, *Douze leçons sur l'histoire*, pp. 33–36.
43. *De la connaissance historique*, p. 49.
44. Antoine Prost, *Douze leçons sur l'histoire*, p. 57.
45. *On History*, p. 24.

Chapter One

1. *The Savage Mind*, p. 258.
2. Antoine Prost, *Douze leçons sur l'histoire*, p. 102.
3. Ibid., p. 79.
4. *De la connaissance historique*, p. 170–71.
5. Quoted in Antoine Prost, *Douze leçons sur l'histoire*, p. 98.
6. *De la connaissance historique*, p. 223.
7. Ibid., pp. 231–32.
8. "Historical Discourse," p. 145.
9. Ibid., p. 154.
10. *Time and Narrative*, vol. 1, p. 151.
11. *Writing History*, p. 88.
12. In *Historical Understanding*, p. 188.
13. *Time and Narrative*, vol. 1, p. 91.
14. Ibid.
15. "Vraisemblance et motivation," p. 94.
16. *Analytic Philosophy of History*, p. 168.
17. *The Confessions*, p. 129.
18. Ibid., p. 47.

19. See "History and Fiction as Modes of Comprehension" in *Historical Understanding*, pp. 42–60.
20. Ibid., p. 47.
21. Ibid., p. 50.
22. Ibid., pp. 56–57.
23. In *Historical Understanding*, pp. 182–203.
24. *Combats pour l'histoire*, cited in Henri-Irénéé Marrou, *De la connaissance historique*, p. 74.
25. *Writing History*, p. 13.
26. *De la connaissance historique*, p. 64.
27. *Time and Narrative*, vol. 3, p. 120.
28. *De la conaissance historique*, p. 65.
29. *Writing History*, p. 36.
30. *De l'histoire considérée comme science*, cited in Antoine Prost, *Douze leçons sur l'histoire*, p. 178.
31. *Introduction to the Philosophy of History*, p. 160.
32. *The Idea of History*, p. 242.
33. Ibid., p. 242.
34. Cited in Antoine Prost, *Douze leçons sur l'histoire*, p. 169.
35. Ibid., p. 170.

Chapter Two

1. *Fiction et diction*, p. 16.
2. Ibid., p. 17.
3. Ibid., p. 19.
4. *The Logic of Literature*, p. 208.
5. See "Closing Statement: Linguistics and Poetics," pp. 350–77.
6. *Meaning in the Visual Arts*, p. 10.
7. *Fiction et diction*, pp. 26–27.
8. Ibid., p. 29.
9. Ibid., pp. 29–30.
10. Ibid., pp. 65–66.
11. *The Logic of Literature*, p. 67.
12. Ibid., p. 70.
13. Ibid., p. 73.
14. Ibid., p. 70.
15. Ibid., p. 83.
16. Ibid.
17. Ibid., pp. 100–101.
18. Ibid., p. 156.
19. "The Logical Status of Fictional Discourse," p. 324.
20. Ibid., p. 326.
21. Ibid.

22. *Fiction et diction*, p. 80.
23. *Clefs pour l'imaginaire ou l'Autre Scène*, pp. 9–33.
24. Ibid., p. 161.
25. Ibid., p. 181.
26. See "The Nonfiction Film and Its Spectator," in *A Cinema of Nonfiction*.
27. *Pourquoi la fiction?* p. 153.
28. Ibid.
29. Ibid., p. 297.
30. Ibid., p. 81.
31. Ibid., p. 105.
32. Ibid., p. 90.
33. Ibid., p. 92.
34. Ibid., p. 198.
35. Ibid., p. 218.
36. Ibid., p. 109.
37. "The Logical Status of Fictional Discourse," p. 331.
38. *Fiction et diction*, p. 59.
39. Ibid., pp. 59–60.
40. Ibid., p. 67.
41. Ibid., p. 76.
42. *Figures III*, p. 227.
43. *Fiction et diction*, p. 79.
44. *The Rhetoric of Historical Representation*, p. 12.
45. Ibid., p. 65.
46. Ibid., p. 77.
47. *Visions of the Past*, p. 235.
48. *The Folklore of Consensus*, p. 108.
49. In Robert A. Rosenstone, *Rivisioning History*, p. 172.
50. *Récit écrit, récit filmique*, p. 42.
51. *Film Language*, p. 62.
52. *Quést-ceque le Cinéma*, vol. 2, p. 33.
53. *Récit écrit, récit filmique*, pp. 42–43.
54. *Du littéraire au filmique*, p. 101.
55. *Essais sur la signification au cinéma*, vol. 2, p. 54.
56. *Du littéraire au filmique*, p. 115.
57. Ibid.
58. *In and Out of Synch*, pp. 118–19.
59. *L'Enonciation impersonnelle ou le site du film*, p. 30.
60. "'Any Resemblance to Persons Living or Dead,'" p. 478.
61. Ibid., p. 479.
62. *Cahiers du cinéma*, no. 183, pp. 16–19.
63. Cited in Peter Brunette, *Roberto Rossellini*, p. 255.
64. *La Télévision comme utopie*, p. 73.

65. *Le Cinéma révélé*, p. 176–77.
66. Cited in Peter Brunette, *Roberto Rossellini*, p. 256.
67. *CinémAction*, no. 65, p. 116.
68. *Pourquoi la fiction?* p. 198.
69. *Roberto Rossellini*, p. 254.
70. *Louis XIV*, p. 209.
71. *The Logic of Literature*, p. 83.
72. *Louis XIV*, p. 198.
73. Ibid., p. 202.
74. Roberto Rossellini, *My Method*, p. 49.
75. "Historical Fiction," *Screen*, no. 19, summer 1978.
76. Cited in Peter Brunette, *Roberto Rossellini*, p. 282.
77. *CinémAction*, no. 65, p. 116.
78. Oswald Ducrot and Tzvetan Todorov, *Encyclopedic Dictionary of the Sciences of Language*, p. 86.

Chapter Three

1. Cited in Ann Rigney, *The Rhetoric of Historical Representation*, p. 151.
2. *Dictionary of Narratology*, p. 12.
3. Philippe Hamon, *Le Personnel du roman*, p. 9.
4. *De la connaissance historique*, p. 240.
5. "Pour un statut sémiologique du personage," p. 116.
6. Ibid., p. 125.
7. Ibid., p. 116.
8. Cited in "Pour un statut sémiologique du personage," pp. 125–26.
9. *S/Z*, p. 27.
10. *Structural Semantics*, pp. 197–221. See also Greimas's *On Meaning*, pp. 106–120.
11. *S/Z*, p. 27.
12. *Douze lesons sur l'histoire*, pp. 147–49.
13. Ibid., p. 148.
14. Ibid., p. 139.
15. *Time and Narrative*, vol. 1, p. 340.
16. *The Anatomy of Historical Knowledge*, p. 11.
17. *Time and Narrative*, vol. 1, p. 200.
18. *The Rhetoric of Historical Representation*, p. 103.
19. *Shadows on the Past*, p. 8.
20. *Douze leçons sur l'histoire*, p. 14.
21. Ibid., p. 25.
22. *Realms of Memory*, p. 5.
23. Ibid., p. 4.
24. Guy Bourdé, "L'école méthodique," in Guy Bourdé and Hervé Martin, *Les Ecoles historiques*, p. 200.

25. Ibid.
26. Ibid., p. 201.
27. *Shadows on the Past*, p. 40.
28. Ibid., p. 32.
29. Ibid., p. 35.
30. Guy Bourdé and Hervé Martin, Les *Ecoles historiques*, p. 202.
31. Oswald Ducrot and Tzvetan Todorov, *Encyclopedic Dictionary of the Sciences of Language*, p. 279.
32. Milestone Film and Video, "I Am Cuba."
33. Ibid.
34. *The Rhetoric of Historical Representation*, p. 77.
35. *The Idea of History*, p. 242.

Chapter Four

1. *Time and Narrative*, vol. 3, p. 142.
2. Ibid., pp. 142–43.
3. For the following analysis, refer to *Time and Narrative*, vol. 3, pp. 143–56.
4. *The Idea of History*, p. 213.
5. Ibid., p. 215.
6. Ibid., p. 218.
7. Ibid., p. 217.
8. *Time and Narrative.*, vol. 3, p. 147.
9. Ibid., pp. 147–51.
10. *L'Ecriture de l'histoire*, p. 82.
11. Ibid., p. 100.
12. Ibid., p. 130.
13. Ibid.
14. *Time and Narrative*, vol. 3, p. 151.
15. Ibid.
16. *Tropics of Discourse*, p. 91.
17. Ibid., p. 73.
18. Ibid.
19. *Time and Narrative*, vol. 3, p. 153.
20. Ibid.
21. Ibid., p. 155.
22. Ibid., p. 152.
23. "Any Resemblance to Persons Living or Dead," p. 464.
24. *Visions of the Past*, p. 70.
25. Ibid., p. 71.
26. Ibid., p. 63.
27. Ibid., p. 61.
28. T. V. F. Brogan, *The New Princeton Handbook of Poetic Terms*, p. 299.

29. *S/Z*, p. 27.
30. *L'Image et les signes*, p. 58.
31. See the introduction, pp. 5–6.
32. Oswald Ducrot and Tzvetan Todorov, *The Encyclopedic Dictionary of the Sciences of Language*, p. 86.
33. Ibid.
34. Gerald O'Grady, Museum of Modern Art publication on Theo Angelopoulos retrospective, pp. 12–13.
35. Ibid., p. 12.
36. *The New Princeton Handbook of Poetic Terms*, p. 300.
37. Gerald O'Grady, Museum of Modern Art publication, p. 9.

Chapter Five

1. *Cinema and History*, p. 159.
2. *From Hitler to Heimat*, p. 196.
3. Ibid.
4. Ibid., p. 197.
5. Does not appear in the Naomi Greene translation. See *Cinéma et histoire*, p. 211.
6. *Confessions*, p. 187.
7. Ibid., p. 185.
8. *Memory, History, Forgetting*, p. 96.
9. *Confessions*, p. 186.
10. *Essay Concerning Human Understanding*, chap. 27, paragraph 10, p. 335.
11. *Memory, History, Forgetting*, p. 117.
12. *The Cartesian Meditations*, paragraph 58, p. 132.
13. Ibid., paragraph 60, p. 139.
14. *History, Memory, Forgetting*, p. 119.
15. *The Collective Memory*, p. 22.
16. Ibid., p. 33.
17. Ibid., p. 60.
18. Ibid., p. 56.
19. Ibid., p. 63.
20. Ibid., pp. 56–57.
21. *On History*, p. 10.
22. Ibid., p. 24.
23. *Un art moyen*, p. 53.
24. *Le Geste et la parole*, p. 269.
25. Ibid., p. 24.
26. *On History*, p. 10.
27. Ibid., pp. 24–25.

28. The English translation gives an unfortunate connotation that the original French, *Lieux de mémoire* ("Places of Memory") does not have.

29. *Realms of Memory*, p. 1.

30. Ibid., p. 3.

31. Ibid., p. 12.

32. *Histoire et mémoire*, pp. 107–8.

33. *Realms of Memory*, p. 9.

34. Ibid., p. 15.

35. *Time and Narrative*, vol. 3, pp. 109–116.

36. Paul Ricoeur, *History, Memory, Forgetting*, p. 396.

37. *The Rhetoric of Historical Representation*, pp. 111–20.

38. This and the following citations of Rithy Panh are drawn from his article "Je suis un arpenteur de mémoires," *Cahiers du cinéma*, February 2004, pp. 14–17.

39. Ibid., p. 14.

40. Ibid., p. 16.

41. *Le Geste et la parole*, p. 269.

42. "Je suis un arpenteur de mémoires," p. 16.

43. Ibid.

44. Ibid.

45. Ibid., p. 17.

46. Pierre Nora, *Realms of Memory*, p. 15.

SELECT BIBLIOGRAPHY

Nota bene: The translations of quotations taken from works in a foreign language that have not been published in English are my own. All italics and capitalization in quotations are in the original.

Aron, Raymond. *Introduction to the Philosophy of History: An Essay on the Limits of Historical Objectivity.* Trans., George J. Irwin. Boston: Beacon Press, 1961.

Augustine of Hippo, Saint. *Confessions.* Oxford: Oxford University Press, 1991.

Barta, Rony, ed. *Screening the Past: Film and the Representation of History.* Westport, Connecticut: Praeger Publishers, 1998.

Barthes, Roland. "Historical Discourse." In *Structuralism: A Reader,* ed., Michael Lane. London: Jonathan Cape, 1970, pp. 145–55.

_____. *S/Z.* Trans., Richard Miller. New York: Hill and Wang, 1974.

_____. *Image-Music-Text.* New York: Hill and Wang, 1977.

Bazin, André. *Qu'est-ce que le cinéma.* Paris: Edition du Cerf, 1958.

Bourdé, Guy, and Hervé Martin. *Les Ecoles historiques.* Paris: Editions du Seuil, 1983.

Bourdieu, Pierre. *Un art moyen: Essai sur les usages sociaux de la photographie.* Paris: Les Editions de Minuit, 1965.

Braudel, Fernand. *The Mediterranean and the Mediterranean World in the Age of Philip II.* London: William Collins Sons, 1972.

Brogan, T. V. F., ed. *The New Princeton Handbook of Poetic Terms.* Princeton, New Jersey: Princeton University Press, 1994.

Brunette, Peter. *Roberto Rossellini.* Berkeley: University of California Press, 1996.

Burch, Noel. *In and Out of Synch: The Awakening of a Cine-dreamer.* Aldershot, England: Scolar Press, 1991.

Burgoyne, Robert. *Film Nation: Hollywood Looks at U.S. History.* Minneapolis: University of Minnesota Press, 1997.

Ça cinéma. Nos. 10/11 (1976), 12/13 (1977).

Cahiers du cinéma. No. 183 (March/April 1998).

Certeau, Michel de. "L'Opération historique." In *L'Ecriture de l'histoire*. Paris: Gallimard, 1975, pp. 63–120.

CinémAction, no. 65: *Cinéma et histoire autour de Marc Ferro*. (September 1992.)

Collingwood, R. G. *The Idea of History*. Oxford: Clarendon Press, 1946.

Comolli, Jean-Louis. "Historical Fiction—A Body Too Much." *Screen* 19 (Summer 1978), pp. 41–54.

Danto, Arthur. *Analytic Philosophy of History*. Cambridge: Cambridge University Press, 1965.

Davis, Natalie Zemon. "'Any Resemblance to Persons Living or Dead': Film and the Challenge of Authenticity." *Yale Review*, vol. 76, no. 4 (September 1987), pp. 457–82.

Ducrot, Oswald, and Tzvetan Todorov. *Encyclopedic Dictionary of the Sciences of Language*. Trans., Catherine Porter. Baltimore: Johns Hopkins University Press, 1979.

Erlanger, Philippe. *Louis XIV*. Paris: Fayard, 1965.

_____. *Louis XIV au jour le jour*. Paris: La Table Ronde, 1968.

Ferro, Marc. *Cinema and History*. Trans., Naomi Greene. Detroit: Wayne State University Press, 1988.

_____. *Cinéma et histoire*. Paris: Editions Gallimard, 1993.

Gaillard, Jean-Michel. *Un siècle d'école républicaine*. Paris: Editions du Seuil, 2000.

Gallie, W. B. *Philosophy and the Historical Understanding*. London: Chatto and Windus, 1964.

Gaudreault, André. *Du littéraire au filmique: Système du récit*. Paris: Méridiens Klincksieck, 1988.

Genette, Gérard. "Vraisemblance et motivation." In *Figures II*. Paris: Editions du Seuil, 1969, pp. 71–99.

_____. *Figures III*. Paris: Editions du Seuil, 1972.

_____. *Fiction et diction*. Paris: Editions du Seuil, 1991.

_____. *Narrative Discourse: An Essay in Method*. Ithaca, New York: Cornell University Press, 1980.

Gossman, Lionel. *Between History and Literature*. Cambridge, Massachusetts: Harvard University Press, 1990.

Greimas, A. J. *On Meaning*. Minneapolis: University of Minnesota Press, 1987.

_____. *Structural Semantics*. Lincoln: University of Nebraska Press, 1983.

Grindon, Leger. *Shadows on the Past: Studies in the Historical Fiction Film*. Philadelphia: Temple University Press, 1994.

Guynn, William. *A Cinema of Nonfiction*. Cranbury, New Jersey: Associated University Presses, 1990.

Halbwachs, Maurice. *The Collective Memory*. Trans., Francis J. Ditter, Jr., and Vida Yazdi Ditter. New York: Harper and Row, 1980.

Hamburger, Käte. *The Logic of Literature*. Trans., Marilynn J. Rose. Bloomington: Indiana University Press, 1993.

Hamon, Philippe. "Pour un statut sémiologique du personage." In *Poétique du récit*, pp. 115–80. Paris: Editions du Seuil, 1977.

_____. *Le Personnel du roman: Le sytème des personnages dans* Les Rougon-Macquart *d'Emile Zola*. Geneva: Droz, 1983.

Herlihy, David. "Other Reflections on Films and History." *American Historical Review*, vol. 93, no. 5 (December 1988), pp. 1186–92.

Hobsbawn, Eric. *On History*. New York: New Press, distributed by Norton, 1997.

Husserl, Edmund. *The Cartesian Meditations*. The Hague: Martinus Nijhoff, 1960.

Jakobson, Roman. "Closing Statement: Linguistics and Poetics." In *Style in Language*, ed., Thomas A. Sebeok, 2nd. edition. Cambridge, Massachusetts: MIT Press, 1964, pp. 350–77.

Joly, Martine. *L'Image et les signes*. Paris: Nathan, 1994.

Kaes, Anton. *From Hitler to Heimat: The Return of History as Film*. Cambridge, Massachusetts: Harvard University Press, 1989.

Landy, Marcia. *Fascism in Film: The Italian Commercial Cinema, 1931–1943*. Princeton, New Jersey: Princeton University Press, 1986.

_____. *The Folklore of Consensus: Theatricality in the Italian Cinema, 1930–1943*. Albany: State University of New York Press, 1998.

_____, ed. *The Historical Film: History and Memory in the Media*. New Brunswick, New Jersey: Rutgers University Press, 2001.

Le Goff, Jacques. *Histoire et mémoire*. Paris: Galimard, 1977.

Le Goff, Jacques, and Pierre Nora. *Faire de l'histoire*. Vol. 1. Paris: Gallimard, 1974.

Leroi-Gourhan. *Le Geste et la parole, II: La mémoire et les rythmes*. Paris: Albin Michel, 1964–1965.

Lévi-Strauss, Claude. *The Savage Mind*. Chicago: University of Chicago Press, 1966.

Locke, John. *Essay Concerning Human Understanding*. London: Oxford University Press, 1975.

Mandelbaum, Maurice. *The Anatomy of Historical Knowledge*. Baltimore: Johns Hopkins University Press, 1977.

Mannoni, Octave. *Clefs pour l'imaginaire ou l'Autre Scène*. Paris: Editions du Seuil, 1969.

Marrou, Henri-Irénée. *De la connaissance historique*. Paris: Editions du Seuil, 1954.

Martinet, André. *Elements of General Linguistics*. Trans., Elisabeth Palmer. Chicago: University of Chicago Press, 1960.

Mead, Margaret. "Visual Anthropology in a Discipline of Words." In *Principles of Visual Anthropology*, ed., Paul Hockings. The Hague: Mouton Publishers, 1975, pp. 3–10.

Mead, Margaret, and Gregory Bateson. *Balinese Character*. New York: New York Academy of Sciences, 1942. Reissued 1962.

Metz, Christian. *Essais sur la signification au cinema*. Vol. 2. Paris: Editions Klincksiek, 1972.

_____. *Film Language*. New York: Oxford University Press, 1974.

_____. *L'Enonciation impersonnelle ou le site du film*. Paris: Méridiens Klincksieck, 1991.

Milestone Film and Video. "I Am Cuba" press packet. Harrington Park, New Jersey, 1996.

Mink, Louis O. *Historical Understanding*. Ithaca, New York: Cornell University Press, 1987.

Nichols, Bill. "Historical Consciousness and the Viewer: *Who Killed Vincent Chin?* In *The Persistence of History*, ed., Vivian Sobchack. London: Routledge, 1996, pp. 55–68.

Nora, Pierre. *Realms of Memory: Conflict and Division*. Vol. 1. Trans., Arthur Goldhammer. New York: Columbia University Press, 1996.

O'Connor, John E. "History in Images/Images in History: Reflections on the Importance of Film and Television Study for an Understanding of the Past." *American Historical Review*, vol. 93, no. 5 (December 1988), pp. 1200–9.

_____, ed. *Image as Artifact: The Historical Analysis of Film and Television*. Malabar, Florida: Robert E. Krieger Publishing Company, 1990.

O'Grady, Gerald, ed. *Theo Angelopoulos Retrospective, February 16 to March 4, 1990*. New York: Museum of Modern Art.

Panh, Rithy. "Je suis un arpenteur de mémoires." *Cahiers du cinéma*, February 2004, pp. 14–17.

Panofsky, Irwin. *Meaning in the Visual Arts*. Garden City, New York: Doubleday Anchor Books, 1955.

Peirce, Charles Sanders. *Collected Papers*, vols. I-VIII, ed., Charles Hartshorne and Paul Weiss. Cambridge, Massachusetts: Harvard University Press, 1931.

Prince, Gerald. *Dictionary of Narratology*. Lincoln: University of Nebraska Press, 1987.

Prost, Antoine. *Douze leçons sur l'histoire*. Paris: Editions du Seuil, 1996.

Ricoeur, Paul. *Time and Narrative*. Trans., Kathleen McLaughlin and David Pellauer. 3 vols. Chicago: University of Chicago Press, 1984–1988.

_____. *Memory, History, Forgetting*. Trans., Kathleen Blamey and David Pellauer. Chicago: University of Chicago Press, 2004.

Rigney, Ann. *The Rhetoric of Historical Representation: Three Narrative Histories of the French Revolution*. Cambridge: Cambridge University Press, 1990.

Rosenstone, Robert A. "History in Images/History in Words: Reflections on the Possibility of Really Putting History onto Film." *American Historical Review*, vol. 93, no. 5 (December 1988), pp. 1173–85.

———, ed. *Revisioning History: Film and the Construction of a New Past*. Princeton, New Jersey: Princeton University Press, 1995.

———. *Visions of the Past: The Challenge of Film to Our Idea of History*. Cambridge, Massachusetts: Harvard University Press, 1995.

Rossellini, Roberto. *Le Cinéma révélé*. Ed., Alain Bergala. Paris: Flammarion, 1984.

———. *My Method: Writings and Interviews*. Ed., Adriano Aprà. New York: Marsilio Publishers, 1992.

———. *La Télévision comme utopie*. Ed., Adriano Apra. Paris: Cahiers du cinéma et Auditorium du Louvre, 2001.

Roth, Henry. *From Bondage*. New York: Picador/St. Martin's Press, 1997.

Rousseau, Jean-Jacques. *The Confessions*. Oxford: Oxford University Press, 2000.

Searle, John. "The Logical Status of Fictional Discourse." *New Literary History*, vol. 6 (1975), pp. 319–32.

Segalen, Victor. *Essai sur l'exotisme*. Paris: Fata Morgana, 1978.

Schaeffer, Jean-Marie. *Pourquoi la fiction?* Paris: Editions du Seuil, 1999.

Sobchack, Vivian, ed. *The Persistence of History: Cinema, Television and the Modern Event*. London: Routledge, 1996.

Sorlin, Pierre. *Italian National Cinema, 1896–1996*. London: Routledge, 1996.

Staiger, Janet. "Cinematic Shots: The Narration of Violence." In *The Persistence of History*, ed., Vivian Sobchack. London: Routledge, 1996, pp. 39–54.

Stendhal. *The Red and the Black*. New York: Modern Library, 2003.

Tomasulo, Frank P. "'I'll see it when I believe it: Rodney King and the Prison-house of Video." In *The Persistence of History*, ed., Vivian Sobchack. London: Routledge, 1996, pp. 69–88.

Toplin, Robert Brent. "The Filmmaker as Historian." *American Historical Review*, vol. 93, no. 5 (December 1988), pp. 1210–27.

Vanoye, Francis. *Récit écrit, récit filmique*. Paris: Nathan, 1992.

Veyne, Paul. *Writing History*. Middletown, Connecticut: Wesleyan University Press, 1984.

White, Hayden. "Historiography and Historiophoty." *American Historical Review*, vol. 93, no. 5 (December 1988), pp. 1193–99.

———. *Metahistory. The Historical Imagination in Nineteenth-Century Europe*. Baltimore: Johns Hopkins University Press, 1973.

———. *Tropics of Discourse*. Baltimore: Johns Hopkins University Press, 1978.

Walkowitz, Daniel J. "Visual History: The Craft of the Historian-Filmmaker." *The Public Historian*, vol. 7, no. 1 (Winter 1985), pp. 53–64.

Winston, Brian. *Claiming the Real*. London: British Film Institute, 1995.

INDEX

A

Aestheticism
  modern, 46–47
Aesthetics
  conditional, 47–48
Alteration
  historical film and, 143
Anachronism
  historical film and, 3, 14
Analogous, the
  sign of the, 138, 140
Angelopoulos, Theo
  analytic interpretation of history
      and, 155–57, 161–62
  Eternity and a Day, 160
  Landscape in the Mist, 160
  the Oresteia and, 161–62
  *The Traveling Players (See Traveling
      Players, The)*
  use of imagery by, 159
  use of metaphor by, 158
Angkar doctrine, 192
Antithesis
  in *Fall of the Romanov Dynasty,*
      148–49, 150–51
Aristotle

functions of language and, 46
  logic of, 48
  mimesis and, 51, 94
Aron, Raymond
  role of imagination and, 41–42
Association of 1851–2001, 177
Augustine
  City of God, 26–27
  Confessions, 169
  memory and, 168–69
Autobiographical texts, 33–34
  memory and, 35
  narration and, 34–35
  subjectivity of, 34–35, 51
  verbs in, 51

B

Barnet, Enrique, 122
Barthes, Roland, 9, 36
  being-there and, 38
  having-been-there and, 38, 183
  historical characters and, 102, 148
  historical narrative and, 27–28
  S/Z, 36
Basses Alpes
  peasant insurrection at, 176–78

211

theory of historical rhetoric and, 138
theory of tropes and, 139–40, 161
Tropics of Discourse, 138
tropology and, 139
visual media and, 68

Written discourse
  forms of expression in, 126

Y

Yevtushenko, Yevgeny, 122